Suburban Growth

Policy and Process

SAMPLE COPY

Mark Schneider
State University of New York
Stony Brook

KING'S COURT COMMUNICATIONS, INC.
BRUNSWICK, OHIO

King's Court Communications, Inc.
Brunswick, Ohio 44212

Library of Congress
Catalogue Card Number 78-78198

ISBN: 0-89139-029-4

To   J.W.
E.P.

Table of Contents

Chapter 4

Chapter 5

Chapter 6

Preface

The study of urban government and the delivery of urban services has had a big city bias in the past. Yet we know that today most urban Americans live in suburban areas, not in central cities. The 1970 Census shows this clearly to be the case, and every Census since 1920 has shown a continued growth of suburban areas, usually at a more rapid rate than central city expansion. This volume is aimed at exploring the problems of governance and the delivery of "urban-type" services in suburban areas. Often this is a question of emphasis, wherever possible the unique problems of governance and service delivery in suburban areas have been stressed while the equally important dimensions of these questions for the central cities have been left alone. However, since, by definition, cities and suburbs live in a symbiotic (if occasionally parasitic) relationship with one another, the development of certain arguments requires extensive reference to central city practices and service problems. This is especially true in the first two chapters of this book.

The organization of this volume proceeds in (what seems to the author at least) a straight-forward logical manner. Chapter 1 discusses the rapid growth of American cities during the decades following the Civil War. Much of this growth was dependent on foreign immigration and the development of certain manufacturing and transportation technologies that maximized the rewards for central city location. The chapter concludes with a discussion of the reasons why central cities in many parts of the country stopped growing in the more recent past.

Chapter 2 outlines more specifically certain characteristics evident in metropolitan development with the end of rapid central city growth. In particular, social class, racial and fiscal imbalances between cities and suburbs are discussed. Despite a still extant image of homogeneous suburban, the second half of the chapter documents the extensive heterogeneity of suburban development at present. This chapter also introduces another consideration that the reader should keep in mind. Many of the most well-known patterns of city/suburban relationships and of suburban development e.g., poor cities, rich suburbs, are often found in the largest and oldest metropolitan regions in the country and not in the smaller and newer ones. These older metropolitan regions are concentrated in the northeast and Great Lakes States although some larger western metropolitan regions, especially Los Angeles, are not totally different. Regional differences in suburban growth must, therefore, be kept in mind. But more importantly one must ask whether the patterns of growth evident in the older regions indicate the conditions which inevitably will be duplicated in the newer metropolitan regions of the country as they age and develop.

Following on our specific concern for patterns of growth, Chapter 3 discusses one of the most basic governmental tools available to suburbs to control community development: zoning and associated land use controls. The transformation of a tool designed to protect the general welfare of local communities to a device for social and fiscal exclusion is a major focus of the chapter. Recent policy changes in the courts, the federal government, the state and local governments to reform zoning practices are also discussed.

Chapter 4 details the delivery of one of the most basic and expensive services provided by governments in metropolitan areas: education. Fiscal inequalities between school districts are a matter of concern, as are racial inequalities. The role of the courts and state governments in transforming the traditional governance of schools is also a central focal point in the chapter. Chapter 5 continues the discussion of service delivery in metropolitan areas by focusing on several other important services delivered by suburban governments: public safety (police and fire services); solid waste disposal; sewering and wastewater management; and transportation policy. Questions of government fragmentation, inequalities in service levels, and general inefficiency in the production and delivery of such services are discussed. Building on our earlier, more direct interest in the processes of suburban growth, the interaction between the delivery of services and the patterns of suburban growth is discussed throughout chapters 4 and 5.

Chapter 6, the final chapter, tries to pull the previous issues and policy debates developed with regard to specific services into focus by discussing various problems of general government and potential means of government reform that have been suggested. Suggested and actual reforms ranging from the improvement of the level of cooperation between local government to the total elimination of local governments are discussed and the present direction of government evolution in metropolitan areas through "umbrella organizations" analyzed.

It is hoped that this short volume will sensitize the reader to some of the peculiar problems of government and service delivery in metropolitan areas and in particular to those problems with the greatest salience to the suburban part of the metropolis.

Finally, as in the preparation of most books, the author owes thanks to several people. Helpful suggestions and advice were offered by my colleagues Lee Koppelman, Frank Myers, Frank Munger, and Howard Scarrow. Ann Marie Reilly provided invaluable assistance in the typing of this manuscript, as did Sandra Sussman.

Michael DeGuiglio and Patrick Moran provided valuable assistance in the preparation of the index.

**Suburban
Growth**

Chapter 1

The Evolution of American Cities and the Beginning of the Suburban Era

The arrival of the suburban era in United States history was confirmed by the 1970 Census. After a long period of massive population growth in areas surrounding American cities, for the first time a *majority* of Americans who lived in metropolitan areas lived outside the central cities. Indeed, the growth of suburbs had been so rapid that a *plurality* of *all* Americans now lives in suburbia. Moreover, the rate of population growth in suburban areas was substantially higher than that in the central cities. As a result, by 1970 not only were the suburbs the most popular place of residence in the United States, but would certainly continue to be so in the foreseeable future.

These census data indicate a significant change in the residential choices of Americans. For over 100 years after 1840, Americans overwhelmingly moved into cities and, as a result, many cities in the United States grew dynamically. Between the Civil War and World War I, the United States was rapidly transformed from a rural to an urban country. By 1920, the majority of Americans lived in cities. Since then, however, and especially since 1945, Americans seem no longer to prefer city life and many Americans now choose to reside outside the older cities. As a result, the population growth of American cities has slowed. Indeed, several major cities in the United States are now actually experiencing an absolute decline in the number of people living in them.

We can conceive of this process of population movement as "deconcentration." That is, Americans no longer live in the dense, tightly packed settlements found in cities and seek more open, lower density residential space. While Americans cannot totally escape the attraction of central city wealth and employment opportunities, they can now spread themselves out over larger and larger tracts of land in metropolitan areas to reach their goal of low density settlement. This has created the rapid growth of suburbs.

The deconcentration of living places has been matched by the decentralization of working places in metropolitan areas. Following the movement of people to the suburbs, retail establishments now conduct more and more business outside the central city and in the suburbs. For example, between 1958 and 1967, the level of retail trade in the city of Baltimore increased by 5 percent. However, the Baltimore suburbs experienced a 128 percent increase in their retail trade. Similarly, the city of Dayton, Ohio, increased its retail trade by 4 percent while its suburbs increased theirs by 126 percent. In fact, of 25 large metropolitan areas surveyed in 1973,[1] not *one* central city experienced as rapid an expansion in their retail trade as did its surrounding suburbs. Even more striking was the fact that no fewer than 7 of these central cities (Boston, Buffalo, Cleveland, Miami, Newark, Providence, and St. Louis) actually lost retail trade volume while their suburbs continued to expand. This change in retail trading patterns is more than matched by the movement of manufacturing employment into the suburbs: more than half of the same 25 central cities surveyed lost manufacturing jobs to their suburbs. In recent times, cities have also begun to lose large numbers of office jobs to suburbs.

In short, a significant rearrangement of people and jobs is occurring in metropolitan America. Activities once centralized in cities are now dispersing to outlying areas. While this rearrangement was evident as early as 1920, its significance was not fully apparent until the accelerated suburban explosion following World War II. At the beginning of the postwar suburban movement, the future looked good. Large tracts of undeveloped land were available to absorb the expansion, taxes and the cost of suburban government were low, the central cities were in relatively sound financial shape, and many racial issues were not yet of great importance or salience. In this relatively benign environment, suburban growth began in earnest.

But suburban expansion soon ran up against the realities of modern society. The demands on local governments increased and their abilities to respond successfully were questioned. Perhaps most notably, the costs of public services began to rise dramatically. This was especially true with regard to local school systems, but other local government services were affected as well. With rising costs, local taxes began to skyrocket. As the costs of government and taxes went up, the differences between local communities in the level of services available and the tax rates necessary to support them became an increasingly important issue in metropolitan areas. Related to this was the growing salience of racial and class segregation between cities and suburbs, and between suburbs themselves. Finally, the demands on the environment resulting from suburban growth were opposed by an interest in environmental conservation. The end product of these dynamic forces was that government in metropolitan areas and suburban governments, in particular, fell under frequent and usually critical examination.

The new suburban era has associated with it a whole host of suburban problems. In the pages that follow, we investigate some of the most important problems facing suburbs and some of the responses and policies that exist or are being formulated to meet the issues of suburban growth and government.

While our concern will always be on suburbs rather than the central cities, it is obvious that the two areas, by definition, live in close relationship to one another. These close ties will become apparent as we look in the next two chapters at the historical evolution of American suburbs and see that this evolution begins with the process of central city growth.

The Process of City Growth

The rate at which cities grow or fail to grow is the product of many social, economic, and political forces. In trying to capture the relationship between general environmental factors and the city growth process, Edward Banfield has argued that we should examine three "imperatives." Banfield indicates that he has consciously chosen the term "imperative" to emphasize the inexorable forces to which the nature of growth in cities must respond. To Banfield, these forces can be categorized into three dimensions:

> The first is demographic: if the population of a city increases, the city must expand in one direction or another — up, down, or from the center outward. The second is technological: if it is feasible to transport large numbers of people outward (by train, bus, and automobile) but not upward or downward (by elevator), the city must expand outward. The third is economic: if the distribution of wealth and income is such that some can afford new housing and the time and money to commute considerable distances to work while others cannot, the expanding periphery of the city must be occupied by the first group (the "well-off") while the older, inner parts of the city, where most of the jobs for the unskilled are, must be occupied by the second group (the "not well-off").[2]

This categorization into demographic, technological, and economic forces provides a convenient organization by which to investigate the factors conditioning the growth of cities in the United States. But it is important to note that Banfield nowhere mentions a specific "political imperative" in his discussion of the forces conditioning growth. The absence of such an entry is telling in its recognition of the rather limited *direct* role played by government in the United States in shaping city growth and deserves some comment.

As implied in Banfield's analysis, the United States government, and indeed the individual governments of the 50 American states, do not at present actively intervene into the city growth process. In contrast to this American restriction of the "political imperative," most Western European countries tend to maintain active control over the population movements and economic developments that affect the growth of cities. James L. Sundquist, who has done the major comparative work investigating the differences between the United States and Western Europe, finds that Britain, France, Italy, the Netherlands, and Sweden have all adopted "comprehensive and ambitious programs to influence population distribution on a national scale," and in specific, to regulate the rates of urban growth.[3] Compared to the ambitious and fairly successful program found in each of these countries, the contrast with the United States is, to use Sundquist's term, "stark." According to Sundquist, "the United States has no policy of active intervention in regard to population distribution . . ."[4] It is no wonder Banfield found no political imperative where none exists.

But the reason for the differences between the U.S. and Europe are important in their own right and throw light on the possible range of relationships between government and the process of city growth. Sundquist in his explanation of these cross-national differences relies heavily on what he sees as the failure of the American bureaucratic system effectively to implement an urban growth policy. This failure results from the nature of the institutional arrangements of the American policy process:

> Because the institutional structure of policy-making in the United States is so complex and pluralized — more so than in any of the other democracies of the world — because the policy-making circle is broader, public participation more intense, and the points of potential veto of policy innovation more numerous, a higher degree of national consensus, and a more intense commitment of political leadership, are necessary before new departures are approved.[5]

According to Sundquist, these necessary conditions have been absent in the U.S. and hence, government intervention minimal.

But another related explanation is also plausible and is of interest. The differences between the European growth experience and that of the United States revolve at least in part around the historical timing of urban growth. In particular, the foundations of most major European cities were laid considerably earlier than those of American cities. While the United States experienced its most rapid and intense period of urbanization in the mid-1800s and American cities were created from "scratch" in a relatively short time, most major European cities were already well established by the 1800s and, in fact, had already experienced considerable growth during the past century. The difference in timing of growth had major consequences since the prevailing attitudes toward the relationship between the state and the city growth process had undergone considerable change during the late 1700s and early 1800s. In 17th and 18th century Europe, there existed an intense interaction between the ruling aristocracy (the "Court") and the development of cities. Consider Louis Mumford's description of the Baroque city of 17th- and 18th-century Europe.

According to Mumford, growth in the Baroque city was planned and regulated to conform to the needs and desires of the ruling aristocracy. Governmental intervention was direct and was used to further the perceived purposes of the state. Military engineers working for the aristocracy executed city plans and construction, and the city was designed and built on a "stately" scale. Grand boulevards, large ornate buildings, fountains, squares, etc., were values held by the court and were values incorporated into city planning and construction. Indeed, Mumford argues that the need of the state and royalty to maintain its presence in the city was so great that "when royal finances were inadequate to perform sufficiently grandiose feats of building in marble, the appearance would be counterfeited in paint and plaster, or a monumental facade would pretentiously mask an insignificant building behind it."[6] The city was conceived of as a monument to the grandeur of the state, and explicit political intervention in city planning and construction was at a high point.

But the Baroque style did not last and by the 1800s, the position of the aristocracy severely eroded, losing its dominance to a new and competing class. This new elite was based on industrial and commercial activity. Capitalism and the profit motive were supreme and governmental intervention was viewed negatively. The emphasis on profit colored attitudes toward city growth and the emphasis on laissez-faire restricted governmental intervention. While the court in the Baroque period tried to construct projects that expressed the glory of the state, the capitalist elite viewed the city more as an investment opportunity. As the profit motive replaced the values of aesthetic design, a highly instrumental attitude toward the city developed: as long as profit could be made, investment in the city would take place. Highest concern was given to the rate of return to investment regardless of what costs this might have on the residents of the city or the shape of the city itself. As profitable investments in the city lasted, city growth occurred. But when possibility or returns on investments became less available and alternatives developed in such places as the suburbs, business and investment money followed. This highly unregulated flow of money and investment into and out of the city frequently left behind a badly used and neglected city structure. Again to quote Mumford:

> Customary morality, corporate standards, traditional evaluations all served as brakes upon speculative enterprise; so likewise was the heavy capital investment in ancient buildings, constructed to endure over the centuries. In order to have a free field for its typical interests, capitalism adopted two methods in relation to existing urban structures: either it sought to escape to the suburbs beyond, free from all municipal restrictions, or alternatively, it sought either to demolish the old structures or to occupy them at a higher density than for which they had been designed. Urban demolition and replacement became one of the chief marks of the new (capitalist) economy. . . . In relation to the city, capitalism was from the beginning anti-historic and as its forces have consolidated over the past four centuries, its destructive dynamism has increased.[7]

Thus, the shift from the princely aristocratic involvement and attachment to the city marking the 17th- and 18th-century Baroque period to the commercial attitudes of the 19th and 20th centuries has led to what the urban historian Sam Bass Warner has called the "private city," wherein the interests of speculators, land developers, and business reign supreme while the role of government and the state is minimized.[8] In the United States, this process of changing attitudes and its results were even more pronounced than in Europe since American cities did not have the historic developments and established growth patterns to act as a brake on speculative activity. As a result, the "private city" and city growth patterns dominated by business and not by the state are more evident in the United States than in Europe. As we have noted, this historical condition is still seen in the relatively lax laws and policies regulating growth in the United States compared to the strictness of such laws in Western Europe. This dominance of the growth process by private motives and the restriction of direct government intervention is a crucial factor in understanding city and suburban growth in the United States, and is a factor which will be repeatedly evident in our investigation.

To return to the concept of "imperatives" with which we began, we can now see that while there may be no explicit "political imperative" evident in the historical growth process in the United States, the role of the government (or rather its absence) helped set the milieux in which demographic technological and economic changes exerted their influence. These other imperatives can be investigated with this in mind.

The Demographics of City Growth

Perhaps the most important characteristic of city growth in the United States during the 1800s and early 1900s was the vast expansion of the size of the population of American cities. The expanding population of cities was fueled by three main sources: farm to city migration, foreign immigration, and "natural increase." By far the most important was the impact that foreign immigration into the United States had on the growth of American cities. Following the prevailing attitudes in the United States toward minimal government intervention in social affairs, the United States allowed itself throughout the 1800s and early 1900s to be inundated by immigrants. Between 1840 and 1920, the period of most intensive immigration, about 33 million immigrants entered the United States. These immigrants shared two important characteristics. First, most settled in cities and not in rural areas. In particular, most settled in the cities of the northeast and the midwest, swelling the size of these cities. Second, most of these immigrants were young and just entering the stage of life where they would form families and have children. As a result of these characteristics, rates of city growth in the United States increased with increases in the rate of immigration. For example, between 1800 and 1840, a period of relatively little immigration into the United States, the rate of urbanization was low (see Table 1). Over the forty-year time span, the percent of the population found in urban areas inched up slowly from 6.1 percent in 1800 to only 10.5 percent in 1840. By 1840, large scale immigration was just beginning. With the arrival of the Irish immigrants in the 1840s, the rate of urban growth increased dramatically. In the single decade, 1840 to 1850, the percent of the population in the United States found in cities, increased by over one-half. From the 1840s onward, supported largely by the flow of

Table 1-1   Growth of U.S. Urban Population, 1790-1920

	Total Population (by 1,000s)	Urban Population (by 1,000s)	Percent Urban	Percent Urban Population	Growth of Total Population
1790	3,929	201	5.1		
1800	5,308	322	6.1	60	35
1810	7,239	525	7.3	69	36
1820	9,638	693	7.2	33	33
1830	12,866	1,127	8.8	82	34
1840	17,069	1,845	10.8	68	33
1850	23,191	3,543	15.3	99	36
1860	31,443	6,216	19.8	75	36
1870	39,813	9,902	25.7	59	23
1880	50,155	14,129	28.2	40	30
1890	62,947	22,106	35.1	61	25
1900	75,994	30,159	39.7	36	21
1910	91,972	41,998	45.7	39	21
1920	105,710	54,157	51.2	29	15

Source: From *Cities and Immigrants: A Geography of Change in Nineteenth Century America* by David Ward, page 6. Copyright© 1971 by Oxford University Press, Inc. Reprinted by permission.

immigrants, the rate of urbanization in the United States remained high.

While not to understate the importance of native American movement into the cities, the greater importance of immigration in fueling urban growth can be summarized by one rather striking fact: by the year 1900, 40 percent of the United States' population was urban but fully two-thirds of these city dwellers were immigrants or the children of immigrants.[9] This rapid and sustained rate of urbanization propelled by large scale immigration is the most basic fact creating the demographic imperative characterizing cities in the last half of the 19th century and the beginning of the 20th. If we accept the basic contention of the demographic imperative and note that the urban population of the United States grew from 1.8 million in 1840 to over 54 million in 1920, it is clear that the late 1800s and the early 1900s were necessarily a period of intense expansion.

Technology and City Growth

Given the large scale population growth, cities had to expand. The direction this expansion could take was theoretically variable and could have been either upward or outward. The balance between outward and upward growth was, according to the notion of the technological imperative, a function of available technical knowledge. As the constraints on growth in one direction eased, growth in that direction would accelerate. For example, severe limits existed on upward growth throughout the early part of the 1800s. These constraints were dramatically eased by two construction innovations. In 1853 the first successful elevator was introduced in the Crystal Palace in New York City. Powered by steam and fairly efficient and reliable, the elevator immediately eased constraints on upward growth. After the Civil War, the use of elevators increased rapidly and buildings were freed from the height restraints imposed by their absence. Thus buildings began to grow upwards.

However, the extent to which they could grow upwards was still severely limited by another fact of the technology of building construction. Throughout the 1800s, buildings were of masonry-bearing wall construction, that is, the weight of higher floors was supported by enlarging the size of the masonry walls of lower ones. The higher the building, the thicker the walls of the lower floors. The usually cited example of the ultimate in this type of construction and its limits is the Monadnock Building in Chicago which, although only 16 stories high, required tapered masonry wall *six feet thick* at the base. Obviously, limits existed to the extent of upward expansion using these available construction techniques. These limits were broken by the introduction of steel frame construction which made the walls of a building only a "skin" hung on the supporting skeleton of a steel frame, eliminating the need for heavy masonry construction. This innovation coupled with improvements in the design and operation of elevators made possible the rapid upward expansion of cities. The introduction of these construction innovations in the late 1800s and early 1900s, especially in the then growing cities of the northeast and Great Lakes regions, dramatically altered their growth patterns and began to produce the highrise skyline we know today.

But the most important technological constraint that shaped the balance between upward and outward expansion did not hinge directly upon building construction techniques, but rather on the nature of available transportation technology. Indeed, the entire shape of city growth and ultimately of suburban growth can be traced to changes in the predominant mode of transportation and the impact that these changes have had on people's ability to move both themselves and their goods in reasonable time and at reasonable cost.

Transportation and the Shape of Cities

The fortunes of cities have always been highly dependent on the nature of the available transportation systems. In studying the relationship between growth and transportation technology, many analysts have tried to indicate what they believe to be the major periods surrounding a dominant mode of transportation and then indicating the changing fortunes of cities during each period. While considerable disagreement exists over the exact dates that act as the boundaries between periods, consensus seems to exist that several major changes in transportation technology have occurred and have affected the nature of city growth.

Drawing on the work of J.R. Borchert,[10] we can identify at least four major "epochs" based on changes in the dominant mode of transportation technology. These are:

Pre-1830: Sailing Ship Trade with Europe

1830-1870: Internal Trade Based on Steamboat and "Iron Horse"

1870-1920: Steel Rails and Electric Power

1920-Present: Internal Combustion Engine and the Shift to Services.

It becomes apparent that the history of transportation technology until about 1920 tended to further the centralized location of people and industry in cities. For example, in the period before the 1830s, virtually all economic activity in the United States was tied to trade with Great Britain and Western Europe. As a result, port cities on the eastern seaboard (e.g., Boston, New York, Philadelphia, and Charleston) grew and prospered by monopolizing trans-Atlantic trade based on sailing ships. Centralized trading facilities found in these cities produced the conditions for early growth. This advantage propelled most of these port cities forward throughout the 1800s and, in fact, by 1860, eight of the nine largest cities in the United States were old port cities that had begun to grow in the late 1700s and early 1800s.

However, while trade with Europe and Great Britain played a major role in early urban growth patterns, internal developments and markets soon began to replace foreign ones. As a result, a new transportation technology designed for this internal trade became important. By the 1830s, trade along the Mississippi and Ohio river system and trade across the Great Lakes was made possible by the successful development of the steamboat. This new technology soon affected urban growth in the United States. Cities such as St. Louis, Cincinnati, and Pittsburgh which could successfully trade along the Mississippi and Ohio, and cities such as Detroit, Cleveland, and Chicago which could benefit from trade along the Great Lakes, began to grow while others not on these waterways did not. Beginning in about the 1850s, primitive railroad systems, the "Iron Horse," began to make a significant impact on the trading patterns in the United States and began to have a major impact on the growth of cities. In particular, the new industrial cities of the United States located in the Northeast and Midwest began to expand their rail links with the outlying regions of the country with the purpose of cementing beneficial trade patterns.

During both these periods, cities in general experienced rapid growth and the importance of central location in cities was becoming evident. But it was really not until the next "epoch," 1870-1920, that railroads became predominant, and no other transportation technology could be as beneficial to the growth of cities and the centralization of activities as the railroad.[11]

In the "epoch" based on the railroad, cities prospered and grew to the extent to which they dominated the best lines of railroad transportation and to the degree to which cities became integrated into the emerging transcontinental railroad network.[12] Thus while New York, Philadelphia, and Boston as old port cities had considerable initial advantages in the competition for new growth, they continued to prosper only insofar as they successfully participated in the new railroad system. Other cities such as Baltimore and Chicago were even more reliant on the railroad. With regard to Chicago, Ward had gone so far as to argue that:

> The rapid growth of Chicago as the leading export assembler for agricultural products and as the leading distributor of imported manufactured goods was based in part on effective credit connections. Eastern capital not only financed the construction of railroads across Iowa, Missouri, Wisconsin, and Minnesota, but apparently was responsible for the development of the city as a marketing and exchange center. The railroads were . . . the instruments of a basic economic nexus which linked Chicago with New York and other eastern sources of capital more closely than any other Middle Western city.[13]

That is, for economic reasons, Chicago was chosen as a Middle Western outpost of eastern industry and capital. The railroads, however, were the means by which the dominance of Chicago was established.

But perhaps the most telling example of the impact of the rails on city growth took place not in the East but rather in California in the competition for growth between San Diego and Los Angeles.[14] Until the late 1800s, Los Angeles was a small town with a population around 5000 people. San Francisco, because of its role as the first major western terminal for a transcontinental railroad, was the major city in the American West. After the Civil War, it became obvious that a terminal for a transcontinental would be needed in southern California. The real question was the location of that terminal. Two cities, San Diego and Los Angeles, competed for this designation. Before the 1800s, it was assumed that San Diego, the only southern California port with a good deep water harbor, would be the terminal and would therefore be the preeminent city of southern California. At the end of the Civil War, it was under the prodding of San Diego that plans for the construction of a new transcontinental were revived. Obviously, San Diego thought it was the logical choice for the western terminal of this new road and would therefore be the major beneficiary. But natural advantages were no longer sufficient in the face of the profit motive. San Diego's plans did not match those of Collis Huntington, Leland Stanford, and a small number of other San Francisco capitalists who monopolized transportation in California. These men had their money invested in the Central Pacific — the western branch of the first transcontinental — and in San Francisco real estate. They did not want competitive transportation lines, and they certainly did not want to encourage the development of a competitive and possibly superior port in San Diego. Such a development would threaten the dominance of San Francisco and thereby reduce the value of their property and business holdings.

Thus, when the first southern transcontinental — the Southern Pacific — started construction in California in the late 1860s, it came under the direction of the larger, more powerful Central Pacific whose board of directors forced the bypassing of San Diego. The new line was routed directly into San Francisco. When, in the 1870s, the demand for the construction of a southern terminal once again intensified, the Southern Pacific, by then firmly controlled by Collis Huntington, finally put a line into southern California but going to Los Angeles, *not* San Diego. The conscious reasoning was that Los Angeles lacked a good harbor and was therefore no possible threat to the trading dominance of San Francisco. So because of the manipulation of a small number of men, and not by the impact alone of any geographic forces or natural superiority in location, Los Angeles became the terminal for the southern thirty-second parallel transcontinental. As a result, Los Angeles began to grow while San Diego stagnated. Between 1870 and 1880, Los Angeles, while still small, almost doubled in size from 5700 to 11,200 people; San Diego, without the benefit of railroad, grew from 2300 to 2600.

In the 1880s, when large scale westward migration began in earnest as both European migrants and native Americans took the new transcontinental lines west, Los Angeles, the southern terminal, grew enormously. For thirty years, from 1890 to 1920, Los Angeles was one of the fastest growing cities in the United States, and by 1920 had a population of almost one-third of a million people.

If the examples of Chicago and Los Angeles are extreme, they nonetheless illustrate the general process of city expansion during this crucial period in American urban history. Railroads had freed the choice of industrial, economic, and population location from the strict reliance on geographic considerations that had existed in the past. The conscious manipulation of investments and the supremacy of the profit motive in the location of rail lines had an inexorable effect of the fate of individual cities. Cities still needed some physical or geographical endowments to be competitive, but their ultimate success depended as much on the ability of city leaders to compete in the fierce battle for the control over rail traffic, and the decisions made by wealthy capitalists regarding that competition.

But if railroads benefited individual cities to different degrees, they in general had a considerable beneficial role in accelerating the concentration of activities in central cities. Railroads are fixed rights of way, that is, they run on predetermined routes that are expensive to construct and to maintain. Once established, these routes are highly inflexible. Given these technological facts, the way to maximize the benefits of the railroad as the dominant mode of transportation is to centralize rail facilities and to concentrate economic and social activity as close to these centralized facilities as possible. The resulting "nodes" in the transportation system thus generated growth in the cities in which they were located. Industry, manufacturing, and commerce competed for city locations seeking to increase their access to the railroads and, through the railroads, to the national marketplace. Thus, in national economic development, the railroads created a concentration of activities in the cities. But just as important, since rail terminals tended to be concentrated in only one part of the city, a definable city core emerged as the central point of business activity in an entire metropolitan area.

Moreover, when railroad technology was modified for use as an *intra*-city mode of transportation, and when, in particular, electric railways were introduced in the 1890s and became the dominant means of moving people and goods within cities, even further centralization of business occurred.

The Impact of Rails on Internal City Growth

Before the introduction of efficient forms of rail transportation beginning in the middle of the 1800s, cities in the United States were "walking cities." That is, all forms of activity were limited by the fact that walking was the predominant mode of transportation. Given that a person could walk only about two to three miles within a reasonable time span (less than 45 minutes is frequently used as a limit), all cities were necessarily limited to a radius of two to three miles. Yet, most of the social, economic, and political needs of the city existed even if the geographic size of the city was limited. The solution was inevitable: the cities of the 1700s and early 1800s were tightly packed areas of intense and mixed land use. The wealthy and the poor, the industrial and the residential, the slaughterhouse and the apartment house, all were in close proximity.

Exactly how tightly clustered was settlement in cities of the early 1800s can be seen in the experience of one of Boston's leading China trade merchants, Thomas Perkins, as he sought to find a new site for his mansion:

> . . . For over thirty years, Colonel Perkins lived on one side or the other of Pearl Street. It was a highly convenient situation. Just a few blocks walk to the east brought him to his counting room. The same distance north and he was on State Street, where he could share in the gossip and schemes of the merchants on 'Change. Beautiful shade trees and lovely gardens gave the street a delightful rural aspect. At the end of the street, across High Street, was the shore. A short after-dinner stroll would bring the Colonel up on Fort Hill from whose height he could scan the harbor for late arriving ships and enjoy the scenic view of Boston Bay. . .
>
> But time was bringing changes to this pleasant area. Commercial Boston was spreading out in every direction from State Street. Gradually Pearl Street was being engulfed. Houses were even being built on Fort Hill. Boston's expanding overseas trade, to which the Colonel himself contributed in no small measure, required warehouses and these were pushing in from the waterfront. . .
>
> As the slums moved toward Pearl Street, as the commercial growth encroached upon it, the Colonel began to get restless and started looking for a better place to live.[15]

The new site that Colonel Perkins finally selected was on Temple Street, less than 1400 feet from his previous Pearl Street residence. This short move was sufficient to escape a declining "neighborhood" and to relocate in one of the best. As a result, while segregation by class did take place, the actual physical space separating the rich and the poor was minimal. Central location was valued by all city residents as the only way to overcome the discomforts and difficulties of prevailing modes of transportation. And central cities were filled with a diverse population living on top of one another.

As a further result of this tight and compact style of settlement, every "metropolitan" area consisted of several cities, each of which was fairly autonomous and contained a wide variety of economic and social activity. Given the absence of good transportation, no city in a region could dominate the entire metropolitan area. For example, in the 1850s, before major improvements in local transportation were introduced, the Boston area consisted of the somewhat larger and more important city of Boston itself. But there also existed the autonomous cities of Roxbury, Dorchester, Charleston, South Boston, and others in close proximity to Boston. In the New York City area, New York City itself was in competition with other autonomous cities such as Brooklyn, Jersey City, and Newark. Other regions surrounding large cities were similarly constituted.

These two characteristics of a walking city, the relatively compact and undifferentiated land use pattern and the existence of multiple cities in a single region, none of which was totally dominant, began to change dramatically with the institution of railways for intracity transportation and mass transit and the subsequent enlargement of the boundaries of cities.

The introduction of improved transit systems based on rails went through several states of evolution. The first significant change occurred in 1852 in New York when an urban horsedrawn street-railway system was successfully introduced. Within several years, other major American cities followed suit. These horsedrawn railways slightly reduced the reliance on walking as the predominant means of transportation and did begin to extend the boundaries of the "walking city." However, horsedrawn railways were in reality not that much more efficient or that much faster than walking. The horsedrawn railway could only average about four to six miles an hour. In addition, horses were also very expensive to keep and maintain.[16] As a result, Warner in *Streetcar Suburbs*[17] estimates that for the 40 years between 1850-1890, when horse railways were dominant in Boston, the edge of reliable transportation increased only from 2½ to 4 miles from City Hall in downtown Boston.

As entrepreneurs began to seek other means of traction, electricity became the most successful alternate. Beginning in the late 1880s and intensifying in the 1890s, horses were rapidly replaced by electrified rails. This change was highly successful and, in fact, produced an incredible transformation in the nature of urbanization and the relationship between the city and its surrounding environment. According to Warner, the electrification of the railroads in the 1880s and 1890s led to a "rate of building and settlement . . . [that] was so rapid that the whole scale and plan of Greater Boston was entirely made over."[18] Details varied from city to city, but the overall impact was the same.

The electrification of intracity railroads greatly increased the geographical city boundaries as the range of reliable transportation pushed outward. Vast new tracts of land were made available and the activities that were tightly packed into the limited space of the walking city could be spread out over a much larger area. As a result, the close proximity of different social and economic activities disappeared. It was replaced by a segregated pattern of land use characterized by the emergence of districts within the city that "specialized" in one kind of activity to the exclusion of others.

Perhaps the best example was the emergence of the Central Business District. As the streetcar railroad systems pushed further outward and increased their range of services, they were still unable to escape the basic fact of technology, that is, that they were limited to fixed rights of way. Just as the steam railroad system found it economically necessary to concentrate service at particular nodes, creating the conditions for city growth in general, electric street railroads also found such concentration of service necessary. The central point of concentration for the streetcars became the center of economic activity in the city — the Central Business District. Moreover, as the lines of local transportation pushed further and further out, they began to connect autonomous cities that had existed in metropolitan areas in the past. As a result, one Central Business District in a region usually became predominant, and many businesses that had once been spread across the autonomous walking cities relocated in the growing dominant Central Business District. The small autonomous cities that surrounded Boston, New York, Philadelphia, and other larger cities, began to lose their importance as well as their separate existence to a growing "downtown" area of the dominant city in that region.

As these businesses began to concentrate in the growing Central Business District and as the benefits for central location in an area increased, premium rents for land in the downtown area became common. Activities that could not pay these high costs were forced out by those which could.

One such high profit activity that could afford the high land costs of central location were office functions that began to define the nature of the Central Business District. Another example of the specialized byproduct of the concentration of transportation at central points in the city was the development of large retail "department" stores which were willing to pay the premiums for central location in the heart of the city. These stores began to develop new city districts such as New York's Fifth Avenue or Chicago's State Street devoted almost exclusively to retail trade:

> After about 1870 . . . the increasing size of the local market and the willingness of people to travel to central locations for apparel, hardware, or drug encouraged many more wholesalers and also new entrepreneurs to establish separate retail establishments.
>
> Yet the emergence of a separate and extensive retail district awaited the organization of variety and department stores. The market for mass produced goods demanded less commodity specialization and for the sake of customer convenience encouraged diversification of the goods offered for sale. Thus, department stores were able to combine in one establishment the local sale of goods previously obtained from separate retail outlets. . . The new retail enterprises built new stores to display their wares and quickly assumed a dominant place in and around the nodal points of the local transportation system.[19]

This centralization of retail trade and office functions in the downtown area had to displace other activities that were once found in the central parts of the walking city. In particular, residential land use and manufacturing activities, neither of which was as profitable as department stores and offices, were displaced from their previous central locations. As these dislocated activities resettled, they too tended to establish more specialized patterns of city growth than was previously evident.

The rearrangement of residential areas in the city was of particular importance. Recall that two separate but related changes were taking place as a result of the introduction of mass transit into the city beginning in the 1890s. First, the mixed residential settlement in the center of the city was being displaced by the concentration of high profit activities in the developing downtown area. Second, new tracts of residential land were being opened up along the expanding mass transit lines leading out into the fringe areas of the city. But the new residential growth along these transit lines did *not* duplicate the mixed residential pattern of the earlier walking city. Instead, a pronounced pattern of residential segregation based on class began to appear. In particular, what Banfield terms the "economic imperative" began to operate as the upper and middle classes began to take advantage of new housing on the fringes while lower classes became restricted to more central locations.

The reshuffling and the resulting class segregation was a direct result of the technological imperatives of the developing electric street railway system. As the street railways pushed outward from the central business district in radial paths leading into the underdeveloped countryside, housing and development along these lines followed. But because these railways were fixed rights of way, the transportation and housing opportunities they produced were beneficial mostly to people with one permanent destination at the business end of the home-to-work journey.[20] These people, usually of upper middle class status, could purchase housing in a newly developing outer area served by a streetcar line that passed their place of employment in the business sector of the city. As a result, the upper middle class segment of the city population was the major consumer of the new fringe housing made available by the expanding transportation system. But the largest segment of the population did not have the fixed place of employment that the upper middle class had. Most artisans, salesmen, clerks, construction workers, manufacturing workers, and others in the lower middle and working classes frequently had changing work destinations and a large proportion of these lower class families had several people in the same household employed at different locations. In short, families in the lower classes frequently had a multiplicity of work destinations, all of which could not be satisfied by a single radial line of transportation. These lower class families required a complete system of crosstown transportation serving a wider range of possible work destinations.

But the logic of radial growth emanating from a central point does not lend itself easily to crosstown transit (see Figure 1). Crosstown lines could only be supported as one got closer and closer to the central terminal point, the point where lines converged and passenger density was highest. In outlying districts, crosstown transit lines would not be profitable because the spaces between the radial lines were too large and passenger density too light to support such lines. As a result, only individuals with fixed work destinations, individuals who were most likely to be in upper and upper middle class occupations, could take advantage of the new housing opportunities the streetcars made available in the outlying districts. Lower class and working class individuals, workers who tended to have variable work destinations, or families with different destinations were forced to live closer to the inner districts of the city, districts where crosstown transit lines could exist profitably.

In addition, the logic of this pattern of development meant that these lower class individuals were competing for land that, because of its more central location, was of higher value than land in the outlying areas. This incongruous situation produced the only solution possible — most residential areas close to the center of the city became intensely crowded as the large working class competed for the limited land available. Many inner city districts built during the late 1800s and early 1900s were built to meet this competition. The housing was built cheaply and was occupied at extremely high density — this being the only way the lower class could meet the costs of segregation in the internal districts of cities. Warner, for example, notes that for all intents and purposes, the Roxbury section of Boston was built as a slum to meet these conditions and even before completion it was already substandard. And, the truth of Mumford's observation can be seen that the three components of the modern industrial city have been the factory, the railroad, and the slum.[21]

Figure 1-1   Radical and Crosstown Transportation Development

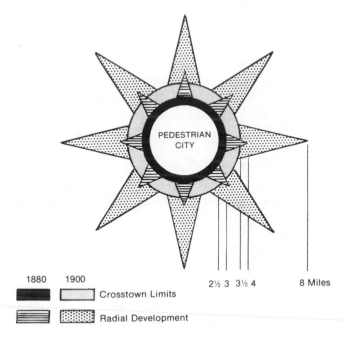

Source: *Cities and Immigrants: A Geography of Change in Nineteenth Century America* by David Ward, page 132. Copyright ©1971 by Oxford University Press, Inc. Reprinted by permission.

The end result of these changes was that the pattern of the walking city was turned upside down. Central residential location was no longer desirable. The ideal of low density development became the sought-after goal for the wealthy and the middle class. Areas on the fringes of the city, many of which were previously inhabited by the poor who could not compete for desired location in the city, became highly valued. Conversely, "downtown" central residential location became the burden of the lower classes who could not afford to locate further out. Thus, the "economic imperative" implying that the well-to-do occupy the fringe areas and the not so well off occupy the center is really a direct result of other factors, especially the "technological imperative" relating to the logic of intracity transportation systems based on fixed rights of way.

E.W. Burgess and the Classic Model
of City Growth

Perhaps the best way to understand the results of these changes is to look at the classic model of growth in American cities, that put forward by E.W. Burgess of the "Chicago School" in 1929.[22] According to Burgess, American cities and their growth could be understood by conceptualizing the city as a series of "concentric zones" (see Figure 2). Briefly stated, these zones were:

Zone I: The Central Business District. According to Burgess, cities had a major area in which office activities were concentrated. As we have seen, this was the result of the concentration of transportation lines into a central location and the premium rents thus produced. To Burgess, this central business district was the dynamic core of the city. The overwhelming expectation of Burgess and, indeed, of most of his contemporaries was that the central business district would continue to expand dynamically and continue to require larger tracts of land. This new land would be acquired through the conversion of land on the fringes of the central business district to business use.

Zone II: The Zone in Transition. Given the expansion of the central business district and the expectation of continued growth, the land immediately surrounding the central business district would not be a site for investment. Instead, the buildings in this area would be allowed to deteriorate awaiting the expansion of the central business district and the conversion of this land to high profit business activities. In addition, much of this zone was comprised of old residential neighborhoods left over from the "walking city." Since these areas were close to the downtown area, they could support crosstown traffic. As a result, this zone was a prime area for intensive residential development by lower class individuals. And, in fact, Burgess' model notes that in most cities, Zone II was peopled by first generation immigrants and other poor groups who were crowded into deteriorating housing.

Zone III: The Zone of Independent Workingmen's Homes. According to Burgess, this next zone was populated mostly by second generation, lower middle class ethnics who were beginning

Figure 1-2   Concentric Zones of Urban Growth:
The Classic Model of E. W. Burgess

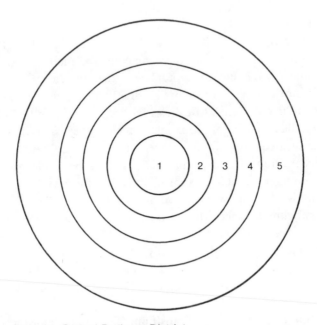

Zone 1:   Central Business District
Zone 2:   Zone in Transition
Zone 3:   Zone of Independent Workingmen's Homes
Zone 4:   Zone of Better Residences
Zone 5:   Commuter Zone

Source: Adapted from E.W. Burgess, "Urban Areas," in T.V. South and L.D. White, eds., *Chicago* (Chicago: University of Chicago Press, 1929).

to establish themselves and whose income enabled them to move out of Zone II into better housing. Thus, Zone III was of higher social status than Zone II.

Zone IV: The Zone of Better Residences. According to the model, this outermost zone of city residential development was the area in which the upper class lived. The best housing and the most expensive and modern residential development occurred in this zone and was available only to the wealthiest city residents.

Thus, a clear social status gradient exists in the model with distance from the central downtown area being the key to higher social status residential development. Burgess also extended his model beyond the central city to include a Zone V, the Commuter Zone. According to the model, residents who lived in this zone and commuted into the central business district for employment were of even higher status than those found in any of the city zones themselves.

The basic underlying structure of the Burgess model indicates concisely the two most important characteristics of city growth in the era of city development when railroads were the dominant means of transportation. These two characteristics were (1) the social gradient of increasing status with distance from the downtown area and (2) the growth process being dependent on the expansion of the central business district. According to the model, as the central business district expanded and displaced residents from Zone II, these displaced residents would "invade" Zone III, setting up outward ripples through the entire urban system. Outward pressure and city growth are then conceived as resulting from a dynamically expanding central business district.

While considerable debate has ensued since Burgess postulated his model in 1929, there is an enduring accuracy of Burgess' description of the conditions of developing industrial cities in the United States during the transportation epoch dominated by railroads.[23]

The End of Central City Expansion in Older Metropolitan Regions

But the overwhelming supposition found in this classic model is that the central business district and central cities in general were going to continue to be the nucleus of growth and expansion. Yet even as central cities were reaching their peak of dominance and their greatest concentrations of wealth and power in the early Twentieth Century, and even as their dynamic growth process was being detailed by Burgess, changes in technology and shifts in social attitudes were taking place that would eventually eclipse the growth of central cities. Three broad categories of changes can be identified, all of which contributed to the end of centralized urban development.

The Escape from Immigrants

As the immigrant populations swelled in the cities of the northeast and midwest making the populations of these cities more and more heterogeneous, both industries and older established residents of the cities became anxious over the impact these "aliens" would have on the environment. Starting with the Irish in the mid-1800s, immigrants began to control increasing shares of urban political power. The bosses and machines that characterized this period were usually marked by corruption, graft, and financial mismanagement. For example, Boss Tweed of New York's Tammany Hall is reputed to have stolen several hundred million dollars from the city treasury with his ring of "Forty Thieves." The reaction to this immigrant power was widespread.

On one level, corporate leaders and middle class professionals sought to minimize the impact that the immigrant population could have on city policy through its control of politics. It was in the early 1900s that the "Reform Movement" in the United States, weakening political parties and increasing professional management in the cities, had its greatest impact. This reform movement was led by corporate managers and not by immigrant politicians.[24] According to Zane Miller, the reform movement went through two distinct phases. In the first phase, between 1880 and 1900, Miller argues that reformers concentrated on voluntary groups that studied municipal problems and offered privately financed services to remedy poor conditions of the inner city. According to Miller, by the turn of the century, each pinpointed problem of the inner city became the province of one or another private philanthropic organization. This approach had its limits and by the turn of the century, with the growing power of the new professional class, reformers turned their attention more directly to government and politics.

A second phase of the reform movement tried to minimize immigrant control by "purifying" city government of bossism and corruption and by introducing concepts of business efficiency into city government.[25] This course of political reform was frequently a long, hard battle and the durability of immigrant-based political machines may have seemed unquestionable to many observers in the early 1900s (see, for example, Lincoln Steffens, *The Shame of the Cities*). Given these conditions, businesses increasingly chose to leave the city. After the turn of the century manufacturing and other business concerns began a move to the more "orderly" suburbs where it was felt that business would be protected from the immigrant-based machines of the cities and the uncertainties represented by that style of politics. As the Mid-Chicago Development Study noted: "Heterogeneous and constantly changing, urban life defied the kind of order that scientific management was placing on manufacturing concerns."[26] Thus, the cities began to represent a questionable investment opportunity. As businessmen and professionals found it difficult to fight the power of the machines and immigrant politics, they increasingly left the city.

Changes in Technology and Industrial Practices

Cities also began to lose their attractiveness for investment and growth as industrial development proceeded and as new manufacturing techniques emphasizing the assembly line were introduced. Assembly line methods worked best on a single floor rather than in multi-story buildings.[27] However, single-story plants obviously consume large tracts of land, land that was not available at reasonable cost in the central cities. Since the economies of assembly line manufacturing were overwhelming, firms began to move to virgin land on the outskirts of the city, abandoning the central city as too expensive.

Initially, cities tried to keep pace with this decentralization of activity and tried to convert vacant land within the city boundaries to industrial use. The case of Chicago was typical. As the trend toward decentralization became apparent, the City of Chicago organized industrial districts within the city. Thus, in 1890, Chicago established a Central Manufacturing District, north of the Union Stock Yards. But this area soon was filled and other large districts in the city were not available. Thus, industrial districts outside the city began to appear. The development of the Lake Calumet area in South Chicago and that of Gary, Indiana, by U.S. Steel (named, incidentally, after Elbert Gary, the president of U.S. Steel) were indicative of the growing industrial and manufacturing development occurring outside the city's boundaries.

In addition to the change in production techniques, changes in the transport system began to occur that lessened the centrality of the city. First, railroads began to diversify their routes and develop transportation activities in areas other than the central city. Again, to use Chicago as an example, the Chicago Belt Line helped make possible the intensive development of industrial satellites such as Aurora, Elgin, and Waukegan and thus furthered the decentralization of activity outside Chicago.

But on a much more fundamental level, there were the beginnings of the new epoch in the transportation technology. This new epoch was characterized by a shift in the dominant transportation technology from railroad to trucks and automobiles — a shift with severe consequences to cities.

The new transportation technology had two distinct dimensions; one, the shift in *intra*city transportation, and the other, the shift in *inter*city transport. As noted, a decentralizing trend in intracity growth patterns was introduced into city growth when the boundaries of the "walking city" were broken by electric railroads. Specialized neighborhoods and districts became evident and some wealthy individuals began to move entirely out of the central city. But in general, electric railroads had a centralizing effect on growth and, in fact, helped create a distinct central business district and the concentration of wealth in an identifiable downtown. But between 1910 and 1920, cars and trucks began to compete with and eventually replace rail transport systems. Moreover, cars and trucks were nowhere as kindly toward central city dominance as was rail transport.

Robert Fogelson's description of Los Angeles is perhaps the archetypical example with regard to the competition between electric railways and cars.[28] Los Angeles had experienced considerable development of its downtown area and the concentration of business activity that was typical of the early 1900s. This concentration was supported in part because its "scattered suburban population did not form a large enough market for outlying retail enterprises, and the radial electric railways, which did not supply crosstown service, provided swift and inexpensive transit in and out of downtown."[29] Established businesses did not have the incentives to relocate out of the central business district despite growth in the suburbs and despite the fact that increasing numbers of suburbs were making land available to businesses. Thus, as long as the railroads provided the means for rapid entry and exit to the central business district, central location was prized. But the eventual failure of the electric railways did produce a rapid decentralization of business activity. The reasons for the failure of the electric railways are complex, relating to rising costs of labor and power; but these rising costs were aggravated by growing automobile ownership and usage.

Between 1914 and 1919, automobile registration in the City of Los Angeles quadrupled to 60,000 and doubled in the county to more than 100,000. This rate of increase quickened, and between 1920 and 1925 more than 500,000 cars were registered in the Los Angeles area — more than half of them traveling in and out of downtown every day. This influx of cars crowded the streets. Since the electric railways ran on rights of way that were not separate from automobile traffic, the railways became tied up in larger and larger traffic jams. As this occurred, the electric railways began to experience decreases in the mileage traveled per kilowatt hour of energy and per manhour of labor. Faced with these rising costs, the electric railways in Los Angeles adopted a response that is known to anyone who has any familiarity with modern day mass transit systems: the railways cut services and raised their fares. Given higher fares for less service, Los Angelenos of the Twenties adopted the same response that urban residents of the 1960s and 1970s now adopt. They abandoned the rails and shifted even more to the use of cars. More cars meant more downtown congestion; more congestion meant a less pleasant downtown environment; eventually lower profits for downtown businesses became the norm as people began to refuse to travel downtown for shopping excursions. As a result, businesses were "pushed" into leaving central city locations to relocate or expand activity in the outskirts of the city.

This shift in commercial activity was accompanied by a growing investment by state and local governments in the construction of highways — an investment necessary for the development of non-central locations. But ultimately it was the shift in transportation systems from railroads to trucks that allowed the attraction of non-core areas to grow. The shift to trucks at first freed businesses from central city location in the conduct of intracity business. Businesses could now locate on the fringes of the city and truck their goods cheaply and efficiently into the central city either for sale or for transfer to the railroads which could then handle intercity shipping. But highways improved and expanded in their coverage of the country and trucks began to increase their share of intercity transport. Thus, as highways and trucks improved, business and manufacturing became increasingly freed of reliance on central city facilities and services.

While many of these developments were undoubtedly the result of technological advances and, in particular the growing efficiency of cars and trucks compared to railways, considerable political and social activity reinforced this shift toward a system totally dominated by cars and trucks. The testimony of Tom Bradley, Mayor of Los Angeles, before the U.S. Senate Subcommittee on Antitrust and Monopoly in 1974 is instructive on this point:

> In 1970, the Automotive Manufactures Association stated that, "converted urban transit lost its market to the automobile, because it lacked the speed, convenience, and flexibility of the car." What the Association neglected to add was that the auto and allied interests played an important role in assuring that mass transit would lack that speed, convenience and flexibility.
>
> Thirty-five years ago Los Angeles was served by the world's largest interurban electric railway system. The Pacific Electric System branched out from Los Angeles for more than 75 miles, reaching north to San Fernando, east to San Bernardino and south to Santa Ana. The "big Red cars," so-called to distinguish them from the narrow-gauge street railway, ran literally all over the Los Angeles area. At its point of greatest extension, it operated 1,164 miles of track in fifty-odd communities, which pretty well defines Los Angeles as it is today. Not only did the P.E. outline the present form of Los Angeles, it also filled in much of its internal topography.
>
> In 1938, General Motors and Standard Oil of California organized Pacific City Lines (PCL) as an affiliate to the National City Lines (NCL, a national firm) to "motorize" West Coast electric railways. The following year PCL acquired, and substituted bus lines for three northern California electric rail systems in Fresno, San Jose, and Stockton. In 1940, G.M., Standard Oil and Firestone, took the reins of management of Pacific City

Lines, in order to supervise its California operations more directly. That same year, PCL began to acquire and "scrap" portions of the $100 million Pacific Electric system including rail lines from Los Angeles to Burbank, Glendale, Pasadena, and San Bernardino. Subsequently, in December 1944, another NCL affiliate — American City Lines — was financed by G.M. and Standard Oil to "motorize downtown Los Angeles." At the time, the Pacific Electric shared downtown Los Angeles trackage with a local electric street car company, the Los Angeles Railway. American City Lines purchased the local system, "scrapped" its electric cars, tore down its power transmission lines, up-rooted the tracks, and placed G.M. diesel buses fueled by Standard Oil on Los Angeles city streets. By this time, Los Angeles' 3,000 quiet, pollution free, electric train system was totally destroyed. With the destruction of the Pacific Electric System, one historian has stated, Los Angeles may have lost its best hope for mass rapid transit. "The Pacific Electric," he remarked, "could have comprised the nucleus of a highly effective rapid transit system, which would have contributed greatly to lessening the tremendous traffic and smoke problem that developed from the population growth." The substitution of G.M. diesel buses, which were put on the streets, apparently benefited G.M., Standard Oil, and Firestone considerably more than the riding public. The Pacific Electric system with its extensive private right of ways, provided a more efficient system than buses on crowded streets.

By 1949, General Motors had been involved in the replacement of more than 100 electric transit systems with G.M. buses in 45 cities including New York, Chicago, Philadelphia, Detroit, St. Louis, and Baltimore, besides Los Angeles. In April of that year, a Chicago federal jury convicted G.M. of having criminally conspired with Standard Oil of California, Firestone Tire, and others to replace electric transportation with gas or diesel-powered buses to monopolize the sale of buses and related products to local transportation companies throughout the country. The court imposed a sanction of $5,000 on G.M. In addition, the jury convicted H.C. Grossman, who was the treasurer of General Motors. Grossman had played a key role in the "motorization" campaign and had served as a director of the Pacific City Lines, when the Company undertook the dismantlement of the $100 million Pacific Electric System. The court fined Grossman the sum of one dollar.

But despite its criminal conviction, General Motors contrived to acquire and dieselize electric transit systems through September 1955. By that time, 88 percent of the nation's electric street car systems had been eliminated. In 1936, when G.M. organized National City Lines, 40,000 street cars were operating in the country, at the end of 1955, only 5,000 remained. In 1961 the last train ran on the Pacific Electric Lines, through Watts to Long Beach. In December 1955, Mr. Roger Kyes of G.M. observed before your Committee: "The motor coach has supplanted the inter-urban system and has for all practical purposes eliminated the trolley (streetcar)."

All of these actions took place without evaluation of the merits of the electric street railway and electric trolley bus as an effective mode of mass transportation. Rather than interrelating the rail system with diesel buses, the rail systems were all but totally eliminated. This left the public with little alternative but to use what G.M. and the oil companies produced.

Since these activities we have seen the displacement of bus transportation by the automobile. By 1952, there remained only one major company which produced buses and one concerned with operating buses in the intercity market. Since 1925 more than 50 firms have withdrawn from city bus manufacturing including Ford, International Harvester, Studebaker Twin Coach, and Chrysler (Dodge). Since 1952, when the bus market was limited to practically one manufacturer, city motor bus ridership had declined to 4.5 billion and intercity motor bus ridership had fallen to 125 million, or a combined loss of 3.8 billion passengers. Consequently bus production and sales have declined from 8,480 in 1951 to only 3,700 in 1972 or about 56 percent.

As you can see from these series of historical events, the destruction of a system in Los Angeles with over 1,000 miles of tracks took place in a very calculated fashion. The fact that a handful of giant corporations determined the form of ground transportation for the country's three largest cities — and for a hundred other cities — should not be easily forgotten. It may be both relevant and highly significant to our contemporary situation.[30]

Thus electric railways, and eventually steam railways, modes of transportation that benefited central cities, suffered decline and frequent destruction from a combination of technological changes and politically and economically motivated decisions.

Annexation

Yet a third change was occurring in the relationship of central cities to their fringe areas that would eventually dramatically alter the balance between central city and suburban growth; this is a severe restriction in the ability of central cities to expand their boundaries through annexation.

Since the end of the walking city most growth in American cities has occurred on the fringes of current urban development. Until the early Twentieth Century this fringe growth was constrained by the dominant modes of transportation and manufacturing technologies. But just as importantly, fringe growth was regulated by the ability of central cities to expand their physical boundaries to encompass that growth. The figures on the growth of American cities through annexation as reported by the Advisory Commission on Intergovernmental Relations summarizes the crucial developments:

Of the 42 most populous cities in 1958, only nine covered more than ten miles at the time of incorporation. However, by 1958, 32 encompassed more than 50 square miles, and 14 included more than 100.[31]

This growth in physical size was due to the ability of central cities to annex fringe areas that became the site of growth. Yet most of the growth of the large cities through annexation actually took place between the Civil War and the turn of this century.

Chicago, for example, in the year 1889 added 120 square miles of territory to itself, enlarging its size from less than 30 square miles. This huge annexation included two entire towns (Lake and Jefferson), part of the town of Cicero, the city of Lake View, and the large village of Hyde Park. In 1893, additional annexations occurred bringing the total area of Chicago to 185 square miles. But just as important as the expansion of physical size is the fact that within the boundaries of this newly annexed territory most population growth was occurring. Thus, within the original city between 1880 and 1890, the population grew from 503,000 to 792,000. But this rate of growth was dwarfed by the 650 percent increase over those same years in the population of the surrounding area (up from 40,000 to 308,000). It was then only through its large annexations that Chicago's population exceeded 1 million making it the second largest city in the country.[32] However, after the 1890s the rate of annexation slowed dramatically.

Similarly, Boston grew by spurts over a relatively short time span through annexing the independent towns of Roxbury in 1868, Dorchester 1870, and Charlestown, Brighton, and West Roxbury in 1873. However, after 1873, the annexation movement was effectively completed and by the 1880s, with but one minor exception, no town again seriously considered annexation to Boston.[33]

The timing of the growth of Los Angeles through annexation was somewhat later than its counterparts in the east. In 1895, Los Angeles was about 31 square miles, virtually the same size it was at its founding 200 years earlier. In the 20 years between 1895 and 1915 it had succeeded in growing to 108 square miles. This annexation activity was a result of its development as the terminal of the southern transcontinental railroad and its subsequent need to develop a good harbor to advance its position in trade and manufacturing. Thus the annexations between 1895 and 1915 included Wilmington, San Pedro, and the Shoestring that connects these harbor areas to the bulk of the city. Yet it was after 1915 that Los Angeles entered its period of most rapid growth through annexation. Between 1915 and 1925, L.A. annexed over 300 square miles of territory (including the San Fernando Valley which was almost twice the size of the city of Los Angeles itself). However, even if the period of most rapid growth was two or three decades later than that of Boston or Chicago, Los Angeles also lost its ability to grow through annexation and its rate of growth after 1925 slowed dramatically.

As a result of the expansion of their borders through annexation, many cities in the United States for a time were able to capture growth on their fringes and grow at a rapid rate. Suburbanization, as we understand it, i.e., the existence of small autonomous communities existing beyond the boundaries of a central city, could not exist since central cities kept absorbing many suburban communities. But this ability to annex surrounding territory of cities in the United States, especially the older, larger ones in the northeast and midwest, was severely restricted during the early part of this century, thereby laying the seed for contemporary patterns of suburban growth.

The historical causes for this end of annexation are important to note. We have seen that the central cities of the United States represented a centralization of wealth and economic activity that was occurring throughout the 1800s. This control of resources gave the central cities the fiscal capabilities to develop services (sewers, water, roads, etc.) necessary to support a higher quality of urban life than available in other, non-central city areas. In order to gain access to this higher level of wealth, communities on the fringes of central cities frequently had to join the central city.

Thus, as Warner points out in discussing the growth of Boston through the annexation of Roxbury:

> Though Roxbury had a high school and many towns did not, Boston Latin School was better. Though some of Roxbury's main streets had curbs and sidewalks, most of Boston did, and Boston even had some fully paved streets besides. Though Roxbury had a water company, Boston had a great

waterworks which served the whole city and could serve all of Roxbury too. So the comparisons went.[34]

Eventually the lure of the services controlled by Boston was so strong that Roxbury was annexed to Boston. Similarly, the great annexation of surrounding territory by Chicago in 1889 was prompted by the desire of fringe residents to gain access to the high levels of police and fire protection given Chicago residents as well as their desire to utilize Chicago's growing and efficient sewer and water systems.[35]

Related to this control of services was the fact that cities usually were founded at the most advantageous geographical location of a region, most frequently a location that maximized access to waterways. As cities grew they frequently gained exclusive control over access to water supplies and often used this control to further their own growth. Most notable is the case of Los Angeles which was founded on the Los Angeles River, originally the only regular water supply for the entire Los Angeles Basin.[36] Under its charter in Spanish law, Los Angeles derived prior rights to the water in the Los Angeles River. Through its control of this water, Los Angeles gained a crucial advantage in the arrid climate of Southern California. Indeed, if the selection of Los Angeles as the terminal for the southern transcontinental railroad produced the population and economic growth that led to the push for the expansion of the city, it was control and manipulation of its water rights that gave Los Angeles the ability to expand. Thus, Los Angeles experienced several rapid expansions in its physical size, most of them related to crucial developments in its water supply system. For example, in the 1890s, L.A. grew from 29 square miles to 43 square miles in area, largely in response to a California Supreme Court ruling that Los Angeles City property had a prior claim to L.A. water over all extra-territorial demands, regardless of whether or not these outlying territories had been previously served. In other words, the greatest certainty in obtaining water in the arid region came with being legally part of the city. As a result outlying communities joined Los Angeles.

However, the Los Angeles River rapidly proved to be inadequate to supply a growing population. In response during the early 1900s, Los Angeles aggressively undertook an expansion of its water supply trying to preserve its preeminence in Southern California. This was done through the purchase of land in the Owens Valley and the construction of an aquaduct to carry water from the Owens River to the city. With the completion of this aquaduct in 1905 and the subsequent increase in the water supply, Los Angeles again began a period of rapid growth — from 43 square miles in 1906 to 108 square miles in 1910. But the greatest rate of growth was yet to come. The growth resulting from the "Great Annexation Movement" between 1915 and 1927 increasing the size of L.A. from 108 to 441 square miles was the result of changes made in laws governing the distribution of water. In 1915 the Municipal Annexation Commission recommended that annexation to or consolidation with the city of Los Angeles be made a prerequisite to the continued supply of water from city sources. As a result of that policy decision water-short communities in the L.A. basin had hardly any choice but to join the city.

Thus, older central cities controlled wealth and/or physical resources that fringe communities needed. In many instances, the only way in which suburban communities could gain access to these resources was to become part of the city proper. But the annexation movement came to a halt around the turn of the century. In Boston the annexation movement ended in the 1870s, in Chicago in the 1880s, in New York in the 1890s, and in Los Angeles in the 1920s. While the precise timing may have varied between cities, the general causes were the same. These reasons included a growing hostility to the central city, a desire for suburban autonomy, the desire for a suburban community free from the perceived evil of city politics, and a growth in the political power on the part of suburban communities that allowed them to develop alternate mechanisms to supply essential services without annexation to central cities.

As the central cities in the northeast and midwest became more immigrant dominated, as these immigrants began to develop control over elective politics through political machines, and as the general style of life in the city began to respond to these changes, middle and upper class native Americans sought to increase their distance from the central city and to seek to create a political barrier between themselves and the immigrants. Moving beyond the political boundaries of the city was the most obvious way of doing this. But just as essential was to ensure that those political boundaries did not expand.

Middle class suburbanites were thus presented with a dilemma: they wished to protect themselves from the central cities by containing the city, yet for a time the central cities had resources that were attractive and that suburbanites needed. The lure of these services was at first strong enough to overpower that suburban resistance. But eventually suburbanites developed ways of eating their cake and having it too, that is, they eventually gained access to the services they needed without becoming part of the city. Two major mechanisms were used.

First was the creation of metropolitan districts to supply services to fringe communities and thereby replace one major incentive of city annexation. For example, in the 1880s and 1890s, the Massachusetts state legislature created three specialized state agencies which began to provide water, sewers, and parks on a metropolitan wide basis for the Boston area. The towns in the region were thus provided these services by the state and no longer had to rely on Boston to supply them. As a result, communities in the Boston area stopped considering annexation.

Similarly, in Chicago the creation of the Metropolitan Sanitary District in 1889 severely weakened Chicago's control over water drawn from Lake Michigan and the disposal of sewage into the lake. For decades, Chicago had drawn water from Lake Michigan for both its own purposes and to supply inland communities. It had also used the lake for dumping its sewage as well as that of other communities. Partly as a result of its access to the Lake for both purposes, suburbs had an incentive to become part of Chicago. However, in the 1880s, the sewage dumped into the Lake had begun to pollute the water supply. The first response was to construct intakes for fresh water further away from the shore. However, this proved inadequate and the death rate from typhoid alone was close to 200 per 100,000 people in the late 1880s. Thus, a more comprehensive plan for sewage disposal was needed. The solution devised was to take the Chicago River which flowed into Lake Michigan, to turn the flow of the river around and have it flow into the Mississippi. The Chicago River would then carry Chicago's sewage west with the hope that the cleansing action from the flow of the Mississippi would dissolve the sewage before it reached downstream communities. But Chicago itself did not possess the political authority to undertake this task. It was the Illinois legislature that created the Metropolitan Sanitary District, including the city and all its western suburbs. The district then broke Chicago's monopoly on water and sewage disposal and deprived the city of one of its major attractions to the growing fringe areas.

These examples are indicative of the general process that was occurring. Fringe residents no longer desired to become part of the larger city and sought mechanisms to provide essential services while at the same time preserving their autonomy and identity apart from the city. Most frequently it was the state that provided the legal and political means to do so, usually through the creation of special metropolitan districts for the provision of services.

Concurrent with these events, a second related series of changes was occurring. Many states in which the largest cities were located began to change their laws to make annexation to the central city more difficult. During the late 1800s and even into the early 1900s, annexation was legally uncomplicated. Frequently the state legislature or a city council could unilaterally annex territory to a city. Alternatively, annexation could be accomplished by a simple majority of voters in the *combined* population of the city and area to be annexed thus making the population in a suburban community, small in relation to the size of a city's population, totally dependent on the will of city residents.

But with the growth of hostility toward cities, and with the growing desire on the part of suburbanites to protect themselves from the city, annexation laws became more stringent. Many states gave the exclusive right to begin annexation proceedings to fringe communities, and some states required that a majority in *both* the city and in the area to be annexed vote in favor of annexation. In addition, and a point which will be considered in more detail in the next chapter, states frequently limited annexations to unincorporated areas only, thereby giving fringe communities a major incentive to incorporate.[37] This helped stop city expansion but created a multitude of small autonomous suburbs on the city's rim.

Most of these changes occurred in a relatively short time period at the beginning of this century. Coupled with state actions in the provision of services through metropolitan districts, the older cities of the United States, mostly concentrated in the northeast and midwest, lost their ability to expand their boundaries. This laid the seeds for a major suburban explosion in the largest metropolitan areas of the country.

In the post-World War II period, however, annexations began to increase in number again. This new annexation movement resulted from some of the same reasons as earlier annexation — the desire of suburbs for access to city wealth and services. But this new spurt of annexations was in new metropolitan areas in the South and West and not in older metropolitan regions.

Thus, in 1970, 55 percent of the population of Gainesville, Florida lived in territory annexed in the preceding decade. In Little Rock, Arkansas 27 percent lived in recently annexed territory, in Columbus, Georgia, 31 percent. In the West, over 11 percent of Denver's population lived in such territory, while in Las Vegas the proportion was over 18 percent and in Phoenix just less than 11 percent. A considerable part of the growth of Southern and Western cities can thus be accounted for by annexation.

Compare this to the fact that Los Angeles between 1960 and 1970 annexed areas containing less than one-half of one percent of its 1970 population while New York, Detroit, Philadelphia, Boston, and other large northeastern and midwestern cities experienced no population growth at all due to annexation. Thus, major regional differences in the rate of central city growth and suburban growth resulting from differences in recent annexation experiences are important to keep in mind.

In general, since the replacement of the walking city by a city based on faster modes of transportation, growth in the American city has been more active on the fringes than at the center. The shift from walking to railways started this trend, and recent developments such as the shift from railways to cars and trucks allowed the decentralization of business and population to the fringes to accelerate. Newer central cities in the South and West have been able to expand their boundaries to capture some of this fringe growth, and hence show considerable growth. However, older cities in the north and midwest can no longer do so and as a result are now entering a period of population decline. While growth in the suburbs of these large cities still occurs, this growth and expansion escapes these older cities which are frozen into their current fixed boundaries.

This, then, is the general environment of city growth/suburban growth.

Summary: Demographics, Technology, and the Metropolitan Community

The size, the vitality, and indeed the very existence of cities have been influenced and dependent upon certain "imperative" forces generated by the political, economic, and technological systems prevailing at any given point in time. The cities of the United States have been the beneficiaries of the major population expansion of the past 150 years. Fueled by natural increase, by heavy farm to city migration, and by an extremely liberal immigration policy, urban areas in the United States experienced rapid and intense population growth. Moreover, until about 1910, existing technology overwhelmingly favored the centralization of economic and social activity in core locations. The combination of these ingredients created by the turn of the century many vital, vigorous, expanding, and wealthy central cities.

But eventually technological innovations began to erode the dominance of the central cities. As early as 1920 decentralization of jobs and industry was evident. With the development of light weight materials, with the increasing ability to use cars and trucks for the movement of people and the shipment of goods, with the shift toward assembly line production techniques that favored one story factories, the decentralization of industry from the central city into the underdeveloped areas on the fringes proceeded.

Similarly, just as industry decentralized, people also left the central city. Most of these people took advantage of the automobile rather than mass transit and have thus been able to avail themselves to a wider range of suburban housing opportunities than in the past. With this shift in population into the fringes, retail and service functions have also left the cities and followed the population into the suburbs.

Central cities have also lost their political advantages and many have been restrained from growing to capture development beyond their borders. Thus a host of functions central cities once served are now taken care of elsewhere in the metropolitan region and central cities no longer monopolize the satisfaction of the needs of the metropolitan area.

Yet we know that this deconcentration is not uniform across all types of activities. Cities tend to lose the most modern and often the most profitable businesses. They often also lose the wealthiest people. Central cities suffer correspondingly. If the industrial city of the United States in the 1800s and early 1900s was characterized, as Mumford put it, by: "the factory, the railroad, and the slum," the central city at the present time is increasingly characterized by only one of these: the slum. But this rearrangement of people and jobs has also severely affected the nature of suburban growth, which we now examine.

Notes

1. Brian J.L. Berry and Yehoshua Cohen, "Decentralization of Commerce and Industry: The Restructuring of Metropolitan America," in, Louis Masotti and Jeffrey K. Hadden, eds., *The Urbanization of the Suburbs* (Beverly Hills, Calif.: Sage Publications, 1973), pp. 431-455.

2. Edward C. Banfield, *The Unheavenly City Revisited* (Boston: Little, Brown and Co., 1974), p. 25. Copyright © 1968, 1970, 1974 by Edward C. Banfield used by permission of Little, Brown and Company.

3. James L. Sundquist, "A Comparison of Policy-Making Capacity in the United States and Five European Countries: The Case of Population Distribution." A paper delivered at the IPSA Congress, August 16-21, 1976. Edinburgh: p. 1.

4. *Ibid.*, p. 2.

5. *Ibid.*, p. 13.

6. Louis Mumford; *The City in History* (New York: Harcourt Brace and World, 1961), pp. 378-379.

7. *Ibid.*, p. 413.

8. Sam Bass Warner, *The Private City* (Philadelphia: University of Philadelphia Press, 1968).

9. David Ward, *Cities and Immigrants* (New York: Oxford University Press, 1971), ch. 1,2.

10. J.R. Borchert, "American Metropolitan Evolution," *Geographical Review* 57 (July 1967), pp. 301-32.

11. Kenneth T. Jackson and Stanley K. Schultz, ed., *Cities in American History* (New York: Knopf, 1972), Introduction.

12. A.R. Pred, "Industrialization, Initial Advantage and American Metropolitan Growth," *Geographical Review* 55 (April 1965), pp. 158-85. Zane L. Miller, *Urbanization of Modern America* (New York: Harcourt Brace Jovanovich, 1973).

13. Ward, *op. cit.*, pp. 36-37.

14. This account is drawn from Robert M. Fogelson, *The Fragmented Metropolis: Los Angeles 1850-1930* (Cambridge: Harvard University Press, 1968), ch. 3.

15. Carl Seaburg and Stanley Paterson, *Merchant Prince of Boston: Colonel T.H. Perkins, 1764-1854* (Cambridge: Harvard University Press, 1971), pp. 375-76. ©Harvard University Press.

16. K.H. Schaeffer and Elliot Sklar, *Access for All: Transportation and Urban Growth* (Baltimore: Penguin Books, 1975), p. 22.

17. Sam Bass Warner, *Streetcar Suburbs* (Cambridge: Harvard University Press, 1962).

18. *Ibid.*, p. 22.

19. Ward, *op. cit.*, pp. 94-99.

20. Warner, *op. cit.*, ch. 4.

21. Mumford, *op. cit.*, p. 458.

22. E.W Burgess, "Urban Areas," in T.V. South and L.D. White, eds., *Chicago: An Experiment in Social Science Research* (Chicago: University of Chicago Press, 1929). Also, "The Determination of Gradients in the Growth of the City." Publications of the American Sociological Society, 21 (1927), pp. 178-184.

23. R.J. Johnston, *Urban Residential Patterns* (New York: Praeger, 1971), ch. IV.

24. Samuel Hays, "Municipal Reform in the Progressive Era." *Pacific Northwest Quarterly* 15 (October 1964), pp. 157-169.

25. Miller, *op. cit.*, pp. 104-108.

26. The Center for Urban Studies, *Mid-Chicago Development Study*, reprinted in Brian J.L. Berry and Frank E. Horton, *Geographic Perspectives on Urban Systems* (Englewood Cliffs: Prentice Hall, 1970), p. 463.

27. *Ibid.*, pp. 463-464.

28. Fogelson, *op. cit.*, ch. 8.

29. *Ibid.*, p. 151.

30. Testimony presented to the Subcommittee on Antitrust and Monopoly of the Committee on the Judiciary, United States Senate, 93rd Congress, February 26-March 1, 1974.

31. Advisory Commission on Intergovernmental Relations, *The Challenge of Local Government Reorganization*; vol. 3; Substate Regionalism and the Federal System, Washington, D.C.: Advisory Commission on Intergovernmental Relations, 1974.

32. Harold M. Mayer and Richard C. Wade, *Chicago* (Chicago: University of Chicago Press, 1969), pp. 176-177.

33. Warner, *op. cit.*, pp. 163-164.

34. *Ibid.*, p. 113. ©Harvard University Press.

35. Mayer and Wade, *op. cit.*, p. 176

36. This discussion draws heavily on Vincent Ostrom, *Water and Politics* (Los Angeles: Haynes Foundation, 1953).

37. Ira R. Kaufman and Leo F. Schnore, "Municipal Annexations and Suburbanization, 1960-1970" (Madison, Wis.: Center for Demography and Ecology, March 1975).

Chapter 2

Inequalities in Metropolitan Growth: Demographic and Economic Development of Suburbia

The change from railroads to cars and trucks as the dominant form of transportation created the conditions for the suburbanization of population and of business activity. The reorganization of metropolitan America began as early as 1920 as wealthier central city residents no longer needed nor desired central city location and as businesses began to take advantage of the large tracts of cheap, undeveloped suburban land made available by the improved road system. As this reorganization took place, state legislatures, especially in many northeastern and midwestern states, responded to the wishes of the new suburbanites by restricting the ability of central cities to expand their boundaries to encompass the new suburban growth. This helped divide metropolitan areas into two separate and unequal segments.

The resulting inequalities between city and suburban residents, evident since the 1920s, increased with the rapid suburbanization following the Second World War, especially as large numbers of blacks left the South and migrated into the cities of the North and West and as "white flight" to the suburbs accelerated. The post-War suburbanization involved a relatively more heterogeneous population than earlier suburban movements, transforming suburbia permanently away from the upper-class domination still popular in many stereotypical images. But suburbanization still involved only the relatively more affluent segments of central city populations, leaving the central cities with a disproportionate share of the poor and the needy, both white and black. The results of this pattern of metropolitan development have been described as a "white noose" of wealthy white suburbs surrounding and strangling black dominated central cities. Just as graphically, developments have been seen as producing a "donut" — a white suburban ring surrounding a center dominated by minorities.

The resulting racial and class differences between cities and suburbs are thus basic facts of metropolitan development in the United States — especially in the older and larger areas of the northeast and midwest. These unequal conditions between cities and suburbs have helped produce some of the most controversial issues in the public arena — issues such as cross-district busing to achieve school desegregation, the development of an appropriate national urban policy, the use of local property taxes to finance public services, and indeed concern for the continued viability of local government structure itself. Each is related to present patterns of city/suburban development. These inequalities thus merit detailed investigation and will be the first topic of investigation in this chapter.

City/Suburban Differences
Black Suburbanization: The Racial Difference

The "donut" and the "white noose" conceptualizations of city/suburban differences are founded largely on the image of a black dominated central city surrounded by a white suburban ring. In contrast to this prevailing image, some speculation now exists hypothesizing a growing black suburbanization that over time will diminish the racial inequalities in metropolitan growth patterns.[4] However, the overwhelming force of existing data does not point toward significantly greater equality among the races in access to suburbs, but rather shows a clear and persistent racial split between cities and suburbs, with "suburban selectivity" choosing whites over blacks as suburban residents. This is readily seen when considering the distribution of blacks in cities and suburbs.

Of basic importance in this analysis is the historical fact that the American black population was rapidly transformed from a predominantly rural people to a predominantly urban one, in a relatively short time span of about 25 years, beginning in about 1940. Despite earlier black migrations out of the South, especially the "Great Migration" of World War I, at the opening of the 1940s well over half of the black population in the United States lived in rural areas and was still a largely Southern population. However, a significant urban movement began in earnest among Southern blacks in the 1940s and continued for well over two decades. As a result of this movement, Census data show that by 1960 a larger proportion of blacks than whites lived in metropolitan areas. As seen in Table 2-1, in 1960 about 64 percent of the black population lived in metropolitan areas, about 1.4 percent more than the comparable figure for whites. By 1970, the proportion of the population of both races living in metropolitan areas increased, but blacks concentrated in these regions at a faster rate. By 1970 about 74 percent of the black population lived in metropolitan areas compared to only 68 percent of whites. Even more striking is the change documented between 1970 and 1974. For the first time in half a century, the relative size of the white population living in metropolitan areas actually *decreased*, reflecting a new rural (or "ex-urban") movement away from *both* cities *and* suburbs on the part of the white population. Yet over those same four years, the proportion of the black population living in metropolitan areas continued to increase.

It must be noted that some of the recent growth in black metropolitan population was the result of changing definitions of metropolitan areas and that a significant number of blacks living on the outskirts of Southern cities became part of the metropolitan population as these cities expanded in the 1950s and 1960s. These growing cities became the core of new Standard Metropolitan Statistical Areas (SMSAs) or else caused surrounding counties to be redefined as metropolitan, bringing blacks into the metropolitan population by definition rather than resulting from new black residential patterns. But most of the change in black population settlement was real. Pushed out of the South by the mechanization of Southern agriculture and attracted to the higher paying jobs of the cities of the North and West (and to the cities of the South itself), the decades following the 1940s were ones of remarkable movement of American blacks.[5] On one level, this intense movement to urban areas is reflected in the data showing the great concentration of blacks in metropolitan areas. But even more striking is the pattern of racial settlement *within* metropolitan areas — differences that show the clear segregation of blacks in the central cities of the United States.

For whites, metropolitan settlement has increasingly meant residential location outside the central cities. Again taking just the 14 years covered in Table 2-1, note how rapid the deconcentration of the white metropolitan population has been. In 1960, just less than half of all metropolitan whites (48 percent) lived in the central cities. During the 1960s, this relative proportion dropped almost 7 percent, so that the 1970 Census showed just more than 41 percent of metropolitan whites living in central cities. But just as important is that in the first four years of the 1970s alone, the relative proportion of metropolitan whites living in the central cities decreased an additional *3 percent*, showing the continued rapid flight of whites from central cities into suburbs. As a result, less than forty percent of the white metropolitan population now lives in the central cities.

In contrast, metropolitan blacks are much more highly concentrated in the central cities. While they, too, have shown some deconcentration, the limited rate at which blacks partake of residential growth in the suburbs is quickly seen. In 1960, almost 80 percent of metropolitan blacks lived in the central cities. By 1970, 79 percent lived in cities. And, while in 1974 less than four in every ten persons of the white metropolitan population lived in the central cities, the comparable figure for blacks was 78 percent. Thus while almost ten percent less of the metropolitan white population lived in the central cities in 1974 compared to 1960, the decrease among metropolitan blacks was just 2 percent.

These divergent trends in central city settlement show that the deconcentration of America's metropolitan population has been overwhelmingly a white population movement. While it is certainly true that blacks have made some marginal gains in suburban settlement, taking the figures shown in Table 2-1, a

Table 2-1   Distribution by Size of Place and Race, 1960, 1970

Whites*	1960	1970**	1974
SMSA as percent of total	62.9	67.9	67.1
Central city as percent of SMSA	47.8	41.1	38.2
Non-SMSA	37.3	32.1	32.9
Blacks			
SMSA as percent of total	64.3	74.1	75.2
Central city as percent of SMSA	79.5	78.9	77.5
Non-SMSA	35.2	25.9	24.8

*The actual basis for this computation is the subtraction from the total population of population Negro. Except in cases such as California where a large Oriental population exists, the term white is acceptable over the more accurate term non-Negro.

**Part of the changes between 1960 and 1970 are the result of the inclusion of areas defined as metropolitan between 1960 and 1970. Using the 1960 SMSAs only, the respective figures show the same pattern.

Source: U.S. Bureau of the Census, Social, and Economic Characteristics of the Population in Metropolitan and Non-Metropolitan areas: 1960 and 1970.
   U.S. Bureau of the Census, Social, and Economic Characteristics of the population in Metropolitan and Non-Metropolitan Areas: 1970 and 1974.

racial split in metropolitan growth is clearly evident.

Black Suburbanization and the South

Another aspect of black metropolitan settlement must be noted that gives even further support to the image of suburban growth as being white dominated. In 1974, only about 5 percent of the suburban population of the United States nation-wide was black. This compared to over 11 percent of the nation's population black. Yet even this obvious imbalance remains an exaggeration of the degree to which blacks have participated in suburban expansion as usually understood. The percentage of suburban population black is inflated by the inclusion of the South in the nation-wide figure. There is, in fact, a large black suburban population in the South, but it is a suburban population with a difference. Black residence in rural areas surrounding Southern cities is of long historical standing, predating recent growth. However, Southern cities lately have grown, and as a result many

Southern rural areas have become "suburbs" by Census definition. Blacks in these rural areas became "suburbanites" also by definition. Yet the blacks in these newly designated suburban areas frequently inhabit the most isolated, poorest communities in the entire metropolitan area. Moreover, until recently, Southern cities were smaller and probably more agreeable places to live than Northern cities. As a result, a suburban push was not as evident in the South as elsewhere. Therefore, the black "suburban" population in the South lives on large tracts of land for which upper class white central city residents have had no use. Thus, a large Southern black "suburban" population exists — but it is a poor suburban population concentrated in fringe areas not really subject to urban growth pressures, and a population found in suburban communities that do not resemble the relatively desirable suburbs of the north.

As an indication of the impact of this large and different type of suburban population, it should be noted that until 1960, because of the inclusion of this poor black Southern suburban population in Census calculations, the average social status (as measured by income and education) of black suburbanites was *lower* than the social status of black central city residents. By 1970, because of the outmovement of blacks from the southern fringes to the cities, and because of an increase (however small) in higher status black suburbanites in northern and western areas, black social status differences began to resemble that of whites, and black suburbanites are now of higher social class than black central city residents.

Further, even in terms of the relative size of the Southern black suburban population, considerable change is occurring. As the cities in the South grow and become subject to the same "imperatives" earlier found in Northern cities, the surrounding urban fringe will likely become more desirable as a place to live and work. If this occurs, and evidence exists that this process is already under way, the South may begin to resemble other regions of the country with higher status whites competing for suburban land to the exclusion of racial minority groups. In fact, the percent of suburban population in the South that is black has been declining throughout recent years as blacks left for cities both north and south, and as white suburbanization in the South accelerated. Nonetheless, in 1970, about 10 percent of the suburban population in the South was black. This figure was substantially higher than the black percentage in the other regions of the country: 2.8 percent in the north central, 3.2 percent in the west, and 3.6 percent in the northeast. As such, the larger black suburban population in the South inflates the national average, even though the Southern brand of black suburbanization does not represent access to the better housing or community services usually assumed to be part of suburbia.

Segregation of Blacks in Suburbia

A second aspect of black suburbanization must also be noted. Even the small proportion of the suburban population that is black is not evenly distributed across the suburbs in a metropolitan area. Instead, blacks tend to be concentrated in suburbs which are predominantly of two types. First, blacks are frequently found isolated in suburbs that have traditionally been defined as black enclaves. As Farley shows, Kinlock, outside of Saint Louis, was defined as a black suburb before 1900; Robbins, near Chicago, became a black suburb before World War I; other suburbs similarly experienced an early conversion and have been traditionally defined as areas for black settlement.

More recently, blacks have expanded into a second type of suburb. These are suburbs which are aging and frequently rapidly deteriorating inner suburbs such as East Chicago Heights or Yonkers, New York. This type of suburban community experiencing black suburban growth usually represents the most disadvantaged suburb, and a community frequently abandoned by whites.[6] Such a suburban community represents, at best, only a marginal improvement over conditions found in the central cities.

As a result, much of black suburbanization cannot be seen in any way as an integration of suburbia. Rather, black suburban enclaves emerge, many of which are low status suburbs abandoned by whites. To use the image developed by Frederick Wirt and his colleagues to describe this process: "Enveloped by predominantly white suburbs, then, the spatial distribution of these black suburban enclaves resembles patches of coal on a snowfield."[7]

While some isolated examples of significant black suburbanization do exist, and while black population increases in the suburbs do occur, the general pattern is of only incremental expansion of the black suburban population — about 1-2 percent in most metropolitan areas over the past decade. Suburban selectivity has obviously included a very clear racial component.

Class Inequalities in Metropolitan Growth

If suburban selectivity has selected whites to be the racial group most likely to expand into the suburbs, it has also been equally careful in the selection of the social status of suburban population — choosing, in general, the more well-to-do. The 1970 Census documents some of the substantial differences in social class between central city residents and suburbanites. Most indicators of social class indicate uniformly the higher social status and greater personal wealth of suburbanites. Several such measures for central city and suburban residents are shown in Table 2-2 for 1960, 1970, and 1974.

First, with regard to family income, a basic measure of wealth, the differences between city and suburb are clear. In 1969, the U.S. Census reported the median income for all central city families as $9500, while in the suburbs it was $11,800 — a difference of $2300 in favor of suburbs. While this in itself is indicative of major gaps between the general level of economic well-being in the city compared to the suburbs, even more striking is the concentration of poverty in the central cities compared to the suburbs. The 1970 Census reported that 11 percent of all central city families were under the officially designated poverty level. This is more than double the percentage of such families in the suburbs. This difference in personal wealth is naturally reflected in the value of houses in the central city and suburbs. The average home value in the suburbs was reported to be almost $21,000 compared to $16,400 in the central city. Thus, central city residents have on the average lower levels of income, are more likely to be poor, and, in general, own less expensive housing than suburban residents.

A similar pattern of advantage for the suburbs holds for education. While it is true that in 1970 the median years of education completed for central city adults and for suburban

Table 2-2 Social Status Differences, Cities, and Suburbs: 1960, 1970, 1974

	1960		1970		1974[6]	
	Cities	Suburbs	Cities	Suburbs	Cities	Suburbs
Income						
Median Family Income[1]	$ 5,945	$ 7,114	$ 9,519	$11,771	$11,343	$14,007
Percent of Families Below Poverty Line[2]	10.0	5.6	11.0	5.0	10.2	3.9[7]
Home Value						
Median Home Value[3]	$12,300	$14,400	$16,400	$20,700		
Education[4]						
Median School Years Completed: Adults 25 Years or Older	10.7	12.0	12.0	12.3		
Percent With Less Than 5 Years of Education	8.4	4.6	6.1	3.2	5.2	2.6
Percent With 4 or More Years of College	8.0	10.9	10.0	12.2	10.9	13.1
Occupation[5] (Percent of Work Force in Each Category)						
Professionals	12.4	15.4	16.2	18.9	15.6	17.9
Managers	8.7	10.9	8.0	10.3	10.5	12.7
Sales	10.0	9.4	7.8	9.1	7.0	17.9
Clerical	19.7	18.2	22.9	21.2	22.5	19.5
Crafts	13.3	16.9	12.8	14.9	12.7	15.0
Operators	21.0	17.7	13.7	11.7	12.5	11.3
Laborers	5.1	3.9	4.8	3.7	5.0	4.5
Service	11.0	7.0	13.7	10.2	14.3	11.5

Sources:
[1] U.S. Census, Volume 1, General Studies and Economic Characteristics. 1960: Table 100; 1970: Table 105.

[2] U.S. Census of Housing, U.S. Summary, Figure 516.

[3] U.S. Census, Volume 1, General Social and Economic Characteristics. 1960: Table 100; 1970: Table 2.

[4] U.S. Census, Volume 1, General Social and Economic Characteristics. 1960: Table 100; 1970: Table 99.

[5] U.S. Census, General Social and Economic Characteristics. 1960: Table 100; 1970: Table 102

[6] 1974 estimates are from U.S. Census, Social and Economic Characteristics of the Population in Metropolitan and Non-Metropolitan Areas. 1974-1960. Not all measures appear in this report.

[7] The 1974 report does not use the exact same basis for computation as do the 1970 and 1960 Census. This figure is percent of families receiving public assistance, a reasonable approximation.

adults are similar (12.0 to 12.3 years), this figure understates some important differences. In central cities, more than 6 percent of the adult population had less than 5 years of schooling, in the suburbs this figure was 3 percent. On the other end of the education spectrum, 11 percent of city residents completed four or more years of college compared to more than 12 percent of suburban residents. In 1974, this difference in educational achievement remained. In short, across all metropolitan areas in the United States, suburban residents are in fact better educated than central city ones. This education gap is mirrored in the figures for occupational distribution. Note that suburban residents tend to be more highly concentrated in the higher status occupations (professional and managerial positions), while they are less concentrated in the lower status work of operators, laborers, and services.

Moreover, across the nation as a whole, there is evidence that these socioeconomic differences are increasing. Reynolds Farley in an important study in 1964 comparing central city and suburbs in the aggregate, showed a *growing* gap between central cities and suburbs, emerging as early as 1920 and increasing since then. His 1976 study confirms the continuation of this trend through 1970,[8] as do the data reported in Table 2-2. The way in which this gap appears and increases is conceptualized by Farley as highly dependent on the flow of migrants into and across metropolitan areas.

Research has consistently shown migrants to be of higher social status than non-migrants. Yet as people move, the majority of them, at present, decide to settle in suburbs rather than in central cities. Thus, suburbs attract proportionately more higher status migrants than do central cities, and as a result the status of suburban communities increases. Amos Hawley and Basil Zimmer also show that central cities not only fail to attract as many migrants as the suburbs, but the ones they do attract are of the lowest status.[9] Indeed, between 1970 and 1974 the average family income of city-ward migrants was $1300 less than families leaving the cities. Why lower status migrants locate in the central cities while higher status migrants tend to locate in the suburbs is a complex question. The answer combines the personal preferences of migrants with differences in the cost and availability of suburban housing compared to central city housing. It is probably true that most people would at present prefer to live outside central cities. However, because of the operation of the housing market, suburban housing tends to be more expensive than central city housing. This is in part because costlier housing exists in the suburbs when compared to the older housing stock of many central cities. Thus, the "natural" housing market would by itself produce some class inequalities between cities and suburbs since more upper class migrants would have the money necessary to purchase higher cost suburban housing. But this market consideration is reinforced by public policy decisions made by suburbs, policies that increase the cost of suburban housing even higher than the market might dictate. In particular, suburbs enact zoning laws and building codes that make the construction of suburban housing artificially expensive. At the same time, suburbs frequently prohibit the construction of multi-family housing and subsidized housing that might increase the opportunities of low or moderate income families to find housing, forcing these lower class families to remain in the central cities (see Chapter 3 for a fuller discussion of these issues). As a result, suburban growth policies in part help to explain the differences in the settlement patterns of low and high status migrants and in part to help explain the growth of class inequalities between cities and suburbs. Nonetheless, it is important to note that differences in migration flow and, in particular, the residential location of upper class versus lower class migrants help explain the growth of inequalities between cities and suburbs.[10]

Regional Differences in Inequality

The data just presented then show that across the nation as a whole, the prevailing image of city/suburban inequalities appears true: central city and suburban inequalities exist and point uniformly to higher status suburbs. But while this image may be valid in the nation in general, considerable variation in the extent of inequalities exists across metropolitan regions, and, in fact, some metropolitan areas do not at all conform to the expected pattern of class bias favoring the suburbs.

These regional differences can be seen first in the detailed data on income for 15 cities and their suburbs shown in Table 2-3. Across these fifteen areas the patterns reported for the national sample of all metropolitan areas is repeated. In 1960, the suburban rings had an average family income of $11,300 which was considerably higher than the $9500 average for central city families. By 1970, the gap between suburban and central city family income in these 15 areas grew — suburban families averaged $15,200 which was fully $3500 more than the average central city family income (note that while the income level found in these fifteen large metropolitan areas is higher than the national average, the pattern is the same as in the nation as a whole).

But closer inspection of Table 2-3 shows considerable variation between metropolitan areas. For example, the differences between average family income in cities and suburbs were greatest in Cleveland, St. Louis, and Chicago. These are all older northern areas. On the other hand, differences were smallest in Los Angeles, Houston, and Dallas — all newer western and southern metropolitan areas. This pattern begins to imply an important condition of current suburban growth; a significant variation in the extent of class inequality between cities and suburbs is found across regions in the United States. And, in particular, newer metropolitan regions show less inequality between cities and suburbs than older ones.

These regional variations in income distribution and class biases in metropolitan growth become even clearer when we inspect the patterns of city/suburban differences in another measure of social class, the distribution of educational achievement as documented by the work of Leo Schnore.[11]

In his investigation of inequalities between cities and suburbs, Schnore divided the population of metropolitan areas into distinct social "classes" based on different levels of educational achievement. The distribution of these classes across 200 central cities and their associated suburban fringe was then charted. Schnore postulated that based on the concept of the social gradient and the usual expectation of bias in favor of the suburbs, a consistent concentration of higher educational classes in the suburbs should be found. However, instead of finding this pattern

Table 2-3 Differences Between City and Suburban Rings in Average Family Income, 1960-1970: 15 Large American Metropolitan Areas

Average Family Income ($ Thousand)

Area	City	Ring	Difference
New York			
1960	9.3	12.9	3.6
1970	12.1	16.2	4.1
Los Angeles			
1960	10.8	10.8	0
1970	13.4	13.8	0.4
Chicago			
1960	9.9	13.7	3.8
1970	12.0	16.8	4.8
Philadelphia			
1960	8.4	11.3	2.9
1970	10.9	14.6	3.7
Detroit			
1960	9.0	11.1	2.1
1970	11.6	16.0	4.4
San Francisco			
1960	10.0	11.2	1.2
1970	12.7	14.9	2.2
Boston			
1960	8.3	10.8	2.5
1970	10.8	14.3	3.5
Washington			
1960	10.1	14.7	4.6
1970	12.8	16.9	4.1
Cleveland			
1960	8.2	12.6	4.4
1970	10.2	15.8	5.6
Saint Louis			
1960	7.5	10.6	3.1
1970	9.6	14.3	4.8
Pittsburgh			
1960	8.4	9.6	1.2
1970	11.2	12.5	1.3
Minneapolis			
1960	9.2	11.0	1.8
1970	12.0	15.5	3.5
Houston			
1960	9.6	9.0	−0.6
1970	12.4	13.3	0.9
Baltimore			
1960	8.4	10.3	1.9
1970	10.6	14.3	3.7
Dallas			
1960	9.3	10.1	0.8
1970	13.2	13.9	0.7
Total			
1960	9.2	11.3	2.1
1970	11.7	15.2	3.5

Source: Adapted from Reynolds Farley, "Components of Suburban Population Growth," in Barry Schwarz (ed.), *The Changing Face of the Suburbs* (Chicago: University of Chicago Press, 1976), pages 16-17.

in all 200 areas studied, Schnore found at least 5 types of city/suburban differences. These five types were: Type (1) a "perfect reversal" of the suburban stereotype in that people with the lowest level of education were concentrated in the suburbs, while people with the highest level of education were overrepresented in the central city. Of the 200 areas examined, 24 were of this type. Albuquerque and Tucson were cited by Schnore as the "ideal types" in this category, and most of the 24 areas in this category were newer and smaller metropolitan areas.

Type (2) the concentration of both high and low educational classes in the central city, and the suburban ring containing a higher than expected proportion of middle class people. Seventy of the 200 areas were in this category, with Los Angeles cited as the typical case.

Type (3) the "expected pattern" of lower educational classes concentrated in the city and higher class individuals in the suburbs. This type of area is the perfect match to the social gradient model and perfectly matches the stereotypical image of American metropolitan development. Fully 90 cases fit into this category and included were most of the major metropolitan areas of the United States such as New York, Philadelphia, Chicago, Detroit, and Baltimore.

Type (4) the expected social gradient but with even more extreme concentration of low income individuals in the central city than expected. Four cities fell into this category, of which Miami was the most important.

Type (5) no consistent pattern of social status differentiation between city and suburb. There were 12 such areas that escaped classification.

Several important conclusions can be drawn from Schnore's investigation. First, the stereotypical image of high status suburbs and low status cities has considerable support in empirical evidence. Note that 94 (types 3 and 4) of the 200 areas studied by Schnore fit the expected pattern. Among these 94 metropolitan regions are the largest and most visible in the country. But just as important is the fact that in empirical terms, the majority (106) of the areas did *not* meet the expected social gradient model. But despite this surprising finding, Schnore's work may indicate an evolutionary process in metropolitan areas that will convert many of these higher status cities into the expected pattern of disadvantage relative to their suburbs.

Schnore argues that the extent of status differences between central city and suburban rings tends to vary systematically with at least three aspects of the metropolitan region. First, status differences between cities and suburbs are a product of the age of the region (measured by how long the central city has had a population greater than 50,000). According to Schnore, older metropolitan areas exhibit the greatest status differences in favor of the suburbs. Second, status differences also vary directly with the size of the metropolitan area, with larger areas more likely to exhibit clear biases in favor of suburbs. Third, status differences also vary according to the region of the county in which the metropolitan area is found, with status differences in favor of the suburbs most clearly found in the north and midwestern sections of the country.

These facts lead Schnore to propose an evolutionary schema to describe American metropolitan development. According to Schnore, the data suggest that:

> 1) smaller and younger central cities in the United States tend to be occupied by the local elite, while their peripheral suburban areas contain the lower strata; 2) with growth and the passage of time, the central city becomes the main residential area for both the highest and lowest strata, at least temporarily, while the broad middle class are overrepresented in the suburbs; and 3) a subsequent stage in this evolutionary process is achieved when the suburbs become the semiprivate preserve of both the upper and middle strata, while the central city is given over the lowest strata.[12]

Thus, in the north and midwest, where the largest and oldest cities are concentrated, and where annexation laws are most restrictive of central city expansion, most metropolitan areas have "achieved" the pattern predicted by Burgess and detailed in Chapter 1 — the central cities are poorer than their suburbs and grow increasingly disadvantaged. In newer cities such as Dallas, Houston, Phoenix, and to some extent Los Angeles, the expected pattern has not yet emerged. But if Schnore is correct, the evolutionary process of American metropolitan development will slowly draw a similar white dominated, high status "noose" around them too.

However, there now exists some speculation that recent events and changes in patterns of suburban growth may change the conditions underlying the processes Schnore postulates. In particular, Thomas Murphy and John Rehfuss identify several changes that may undermine the seeming inevitability of Schnore's conceptualization.[13] Just as the emergence of the social gradient combined elements of personal preferences, market forces, and public policy, the undermining of these evolutionary processes may similarly combine all three ingredients. Thus, Murphy and Rehfuss argue that personal preferences of high income families may be changing and that some city-ward movement of high status families is evident especially into the most desirable sections of central cities such as Georgetown in Washington, D.C., Park Slope in Brooklyn, New York, or the preserved downtown sections in Philadelphia near Rittenhouse Square. Furthermore, given the current high cost of single family housing, increases in the availability of multiple family dwellings, including condominiums and townhouses in suburbia, will be inevitable. This new housing may expand the range of suburban housing opportunities to a wider income range, although the price of some of this new construction is comparable to single family construction.

Further, it is possible that more forceful regulation of the exclusionary actions of suburbs in barring access of low and moderate income groups may be forthcoming. To the extent that these artificial public policy barriers are removed, the social gradient favoring suburbs may be restricted, and greater class and racial equalities between cities and suburbs achieved.

Yet, as the data through 1974 show, the patterns of central city/suburban inequalities have long historical roots. These inequalities seem to have survived unabated the changing mores and life styles of recent years and the series of government attacks on suburban exclusivity embodied in several laws and policies adopted by the Federal and state governments during the 1960s and early 1970s.

The Rearrangement of Jobs and Employment in Metropolitan Areas

The arrangement of people by social status is one of the major developments in metropolitan America at the current time. But we know that not only people, but also businesses and jobs are changing location. The data presented in the previous sections document a growing concentration of less educated, low status people in the central cities, and a corresponding concentration of more highly educated, higher status individuals in the suburban ring. Yet the rearrangement of jobs in metropolitan America areas is a perverse reflection of these residential patterns.

With the improvement of transportation and other supporting services in suburban areas, businesses began to take advantage of the newly available tracts of suburban land. Many types of businesses moved to the suburbs, but most important for our present discussion is the fact that a great number of manufacturing concerns took advantage of the changing environment and moved to the suburbs. The extent of this changing location of jobs can be seen by the fact that between 1947 and 1976, the number of manufacturing jobs in suburban areas of the United States increased by more than 3.9 million (from 4.1 to 8 million jobs), while the central cities of the United States lost almost 300,000 manufacturing jobs (7.4 down to 7.1 million). As a result, by 1967 more than half of the manufacturing jobs in metropolitan America were located in suburbs and not in cities.[14]

Furthermore, inspection of the way in which this movement of manufacturing jobs took place across areas of different size, age, and region (Table 2-4) shows that larger, older northern and midwestern central cities lost the most jobs while the smaller, newer southern and western cities either lost the least or actually gained jobs. If we assume realistically that these manufacturing jobs could be filled by less educated workers, consider just how perversely Schnore's findings and these data on the movement of manufacturing jobs interact: the cities in which the lowest education population is concentrated are the same cities which are losing possible employment opportunities at the fastest rate. This obviously creates major social problems to which there are at least three possible solutions.

Table 2-4   Mean Change in Manufacturing Employment
Within 245 SMSAs, Their Central Cities, and Suburban Rings
by SMSA Size, Age, and Region 1947-67*
(in hundreds)

Metropolitan Characteristic	N	SMSAs	Central Cities	Suburban Rings
Size				
Under 250,000	113	3,457	307	3,150
250,000-500,000	63	7,800	-619	8,419
500,000-1 million	36	12,741	-1,993	14,734
Over 1 million	33	68,739	-6,584	75,323
Inception date (age)				
After 1950	80	6,321	659	5,662
1930-50	53	9,846	1,857	7,989
1900-20	63	13,142	1,934	11,168
Before 1900	49	35,785	-11,609	47,394
Region				
Northeast	42	11,040	-8,216	19,256
Northcentral	68	11,350	-6,827	18,177
South	98	11,935	2,646	9,289
West	37	32,513	6,939	25,574
Total	245	14,731	-1,197	15,928

*Constant SMSA boundaries with adjustments for annexation.
Source: John D. Kasarda, "The Changing Occupational Structure of the American Metropolis." Reprinted from *The Changing Face of the Suburbs* edited by Barry Schwarz by permission of the University c f Chicago Press, copyright 1976, page 121.

First, the concentration of low status individuals in the central cities could be reversed by government and the present forces (or "imperatives") creating the socioeconomic stratification between city and suburbs curtailed. In fact, people have argued in favor of "opening up the suburbs," and we will investigate some of the major possibilities for the containment or reversal of the current evolution of metropolitan regions in later chapters.

In the absence of such action on the part of government, an increase in "reverse commuting" is possible. That is, lower status central city workers could somehow absorb the costs of commuting into the suburbs and they could live in the city while reverse commuting to the suburbs. But consider the nature of this reverse commuting. Low cost mass transit facilities exist in many metropolitan areas. However, these are best suited for delivering a somewhat scattered residential population to a concentrated workplace such as the Central Business District. While this is particularly true of rail transit, this fact helps structure the efficiency of bus transit too. The distribution of suburban employment by no means conforms to this kind of development. Instead, suburban employment opportunities are far flung without any single significant concentrations. This makes the use of mass transit facilities difficult, if not impossible. As a result, reverse commuting becomes expensive as the central city resident must either own and operate his own car or else make arrangements for a car pool. Despite the expense, growing numbers of blue collar workers are doing just that. John Kasarda notes that "commuting streams" from city residence to suburban jobs increased between 1960 and 1970, and that, in general, blue collar workers are forced to commute over large segments of the metropolitan area to get to their place of employment[15]

The Fiscal Crises: Low Resources and High Demands

But this second option is costly to individuals, and despite its growing importance, is short of satisfactory. This leaves the third "option," one which unfortunately characterizes many metropolitan areas. This is the course of growing unemployment in the central city and its associated ills: high welfare costs, growing social service demands, declining tax base. The recent fiscal crises in New York City and the emerging ones in other older cities are part and parcel of the ongoing rearrangement of people and jobs in metropolitan areas — two divergent movements that increasingly isolate low status people in the city from possible jobs in the suburbs.[16]

But again, the extent to which this separation has occurred differs from metropolitan area to metropolitan area. Perhaps the best summary statement of this variation is found in the work of Kevin R. Cox, a "social geographer."[17] Cox investigated patterns of resource concentration and service demands across cities and suburbs in 35 metropolitan areas of the United States. He argued that empirically the service demands a community experiences can be tapped by 8 basic measures:[18] the relative size of the black population; the proportion of community housing that is owner occupied; the general soundness of community housing stock; the community unemployment rate; the community crime rate (burglaries and robberies); the size of education expenditures; and the relative tax rate compared to community income. Some communities represent a concentration of a population with high service demands; other communities have populations with low demands.

Similarly, communities can be measured with regard to the degree to which they have at their disposal the resources to meet these service demands. Cox argued that the level of resources can be tapped by measuring community conditions across several basic measures: the relative size of the community population black; the education and income levels of the community; and the value of its housing.

In general, Cox's investigation showed a high concentration of service demands in the central cities coupled with a low concentration of resources to pay for those demands. This outlines the conditions for a fiscal crisis. Suburban municipalities, on the average, represented a reverse, much more beneficial mixture of resources and demands. This pattern is of course predictable from our previous discussion. But Cox also tried to plot out geographically the extent of inequalities between cities and suburbs, and it is this attempt that is of interest. Cox computed a single composite "Fiscal Disparities Index" combining differences between demands and resources in cities compared to their surrounding suburbs. These fiscal disparity scores showing the extent of fiscal disparities between cities and their surrounding suburbs have been broken down by quartiles in Table 2-5, and their geographic distribution is displayed in Figure 2-1.

The data, and the map in particular, quickly summarize the regional variation in the inequalities between cities and suburbs. Note that following the rearrangement of people and of jobs across different size and different aged regions, the fiscal disparities problem, as expected, is greatest in the major older metropolitan areas in the northeast and midwest, and is least severe in the newer metropolitan areas such as San Diego, Dallas, and San Bernardino.

But if these newer areas have until now escaped the

Figure 2-1   The Geography of the Central-City-Suburban Fiscal Disparities Problem

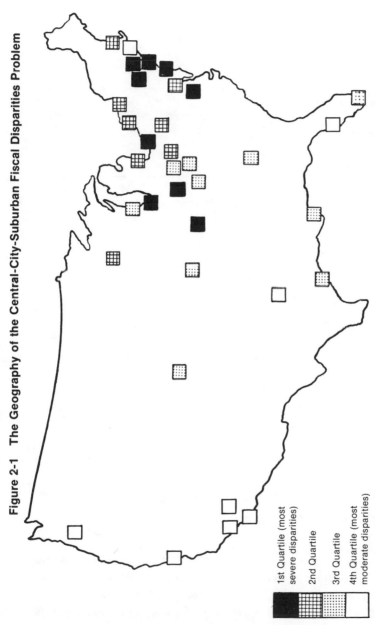

This map is based on the composite disparity index discussed in the text. The Northeastern-Western and Southern regional dichotomy is clearly apparent.

1st Quartile (most severe disparities)

2nd Quartile

3rd Quartile

4th Quartile (most moderate disparities)

Source: *Conflict, Power and Politics in the City: A Geographic View* by Kevin R. Cox. Copyright 1973 by McGraw-Hill, Inc. Used with permission of McGraw-Hill Book Company.

Table 2-5   Fiscal Disparities Between Cities and Suburbs:
35 Large Metropolitan Areas

First Quartile: Worst Central City/Suburban Imbalance

Newark	Chicago
New York	Philadelphia
Cleveland	Indianapolis
St. Louis	Paterson
Washington, D.C.	

Second Quartile

Columbus	Pittsburgh
Detroit	Baltimore
Miami	Buffalo
Boston	Minneapolis
Rochester	

Third Quartile

Louisville	Denver
Kansas City	Cincinnati
Milwaukee	Dayton
New Orleans	Houston
Atlanta	

Fourth Quartile: Least Central City/Suburban Imbalance

Tampa-St. Petersburg	Providence
San Francisco	Portland
San Diego	Los Angeles
San Bernardino	Dallas

Source: Adapted from Kevin R. Cox, *Conflict, Power, and Politics in the City* (New York: McGraw-Hill, 1973), page 41.

development pattern and its inherent problems that now plague their older counterparts, the continued existence of an uncontrolled "economic imperative" may make the pattern of disparities found in the oldest metropolitan areas more universal.

Intra-Suburban Differences

Inequalities Within Suburbia

The inequalities between cities and suburbs just described have significant impact on the functioning of metropolitan areas and are an undeniable characteristic of contemporary patterns of metropolitan growth. Yet these inequalities between cities and suburbs have often been an exclusive focus of concern, neglecting an equally important facet of contemporary metropolitan development concerning differences *between suburbs* themselves. Just as the reality of city/suburban class differences is more complex than the stereotypical image of poor cities and rich suburbs, the reality within suburbia is more complex than is frequently assumed. Far from being composed only of high status, fiscally sound communities, many metropolitan areas contain suburban communities with severe financial and fiscal problems, and with levels of services worse than found in central cities. Indeed, the Advisory Council on Intergovernmental Relations has gone so far as to argue that:

> Of growing significance are the fiscal disparities among rich and poor suburban communities in many of the metropolitan areas — disparities that often are even more dramatic than those observed between central cities and suburbia in general. Many of the older suburban communities are taking on the physical, social and economic characteristics of the central city. This type of community is especially vulnerable to fiscal distress because it lacks the diversified tax base that has enabled the central city to absorb some of the impact of extraordinary expenditure demands.[19]

If across the nation as a whole it is true that suburbs are wealthier, "whiter," and more fiscally sound than central cities, it is also true that not all suburbs share these characteristics. Inequalities between suburbs exist and may be growing. These disparities between suburbs have become an important characteristic of current patterns of metropolitan growth and, we will argue below, are a direct outgrowth of the desire of suburbanites to exclude lower class residential development as well as certain practices of local government finance. Thus, in the first half of this chapter we were mostly concerned with detailing the inequalities between cities and suburbs, the causal factors being noted in Chapter 1. We are concerned in this part of the chapter with both detailing the existence of inequalities between suburbs, and also with a discussion of its causes.

The Bases for Suburban Differentiation

Recall that in Chapter 1 we saw that advances in transportation technologies allowed the emergence of specialized districts within the central city. Before improvements in mass transportation, the walking city was characterized by tightly packed and mixed land uses with the poor and the rich, the factory and the apartment house located in close proximity. More advanced transportation systems produced a spatial rearrangement in the metropolis, a rearrangement most noted for the creation of specialized districts and a resulting segregation between different kinds of economic activities and social classes.

Most of the impetus for this segregation was economically motivated. Once wider locational choices resulting from the improved transportation system became available, it was natural for industrial, commercial, and residential activities to separate from each other. For example, residential property located near the congestion, noise, and dirt characterizing many factories would lose value as residential property and eventually convert to industrial use. Conversely, a factory located in a residential area might find existing services designed for residential purposes inadequate for its industrial needs. Thus, a factory might find itself located in a neighborhood with narrow streets and inadequate power, water and sewer services. Such a factory would find it disadvantageous to remain in such a location and discover location in an industrial district to be more profitable. Given such conditions over time, a "natural" segregation between different kinds of residential, business, and industrial land uses would develop.

In addition, *within* any given category of land use continued specialization might occur. Most notably, between residential districts of a metropolis, we might find that people segregate themselves further. Research on the ecology of cities shows that residential neighborhoods in most American cities are distinguishable in terms of ethnicity, race, social class, and stage of life cycle (young families with children, older families, etc.).[20] Much of this segregation is the result of the similar preferences held by people in like circumstances, i.e., families with children need different types of housing than unmarried people or childless couples. The "economic imperative" would reinforce the natural segregatory processes, as would the existence of racial discrimination. But the existence of specialized residential districts seems, nonetheless, to be largely a product of the desire of people to live in communities composed of people like themselves.[21]

As a result, segregation by economic function and by "life style" has become a characteristic of modern urban settlement. This segregation is largely a natural process, based both on economic forces and on the desire of people to form homogeneous residential districts, occurring in all American metropolitan areas, and made possible by advanced transportation technologies. But the meaning of this segregation differs in the central city and suburban parts of the metropolis.

The Institutionalization of Differences: Suburban Fragmentation

Note that regardless of how specialized or segregated districts become within a central city, *one* city government is still ultimately responsible for governance and for such particular government functions as raising local taxes and allocating resources and services. This single city government can provide coordination and focus in the provision of local services in the city.

However, compared to the overarching structure of central city government, the most frequent description applied to the system of government found in suburbia is "fragmented." Instead of there being a single central government, suburban areas are divided into multiple government jurisdictions, each one of which is considerably autonomous, and each of which has responsibilities for raising taxes, for providing services, and for governance within its particular jurisdiction. The extent of fragmentation found in most metropolitan areas is indicated by Wood's title for his investigation of the New York metropolitan area: *1400 Governments*,[22] and is given further meaning in Lineberry and Sharkansky's discussion of fragmentation:

> If a cartographer were to color every municipality in each metropolitan area a different color, he would need 474 different colors for the St. Louis SMSA . . . As a matter of comparison, there are approximately four times as many local governments in the St. Louis area alone as there are nation states in the world.[23]

In contrast to the unified structure of cities, suburban fragmentation makes the development of coordinated policies in suburbia difficult.[24] Furthermore, the small size of most suburban governments interacts with the natural segregatory processes of metropolitan development to make the governance of suburbia even more difficult than just the sheer number of local governments alone implies. The creation of specialized areas occurs in both city and suburban portions of the metropolis. But in the central city, these diverse socioeconomic districts coexist under a single political structure. In the suburbs, however, the system of small political jurisdictions, when superimposed over the specialized patterns of development, institutionalizes socioeconomic differences into separate political ones.

This occurs as follows: As in the central city, specialized districts emerge in suburbia. Residential enclaves develop, as do commercial and industrial ones. The rich separate from the not so rich. Racial concentrations develop. But in contrast to central cities, suburban political boundary lines get drawn around these specialized areas, creating artificial walls between them. Suburban governments often come into existence specifically to protect these specialized areas from outside pressures, frequently enacting policies that exclude types of activity other than already existing ones.[25] This exclusionary use of local government powers can be motivated by the desire to preserve a homogeneous settlement pattern, excluding, in particular, low status people perceived to have a different life style; by the desire to preserve the level of community fiscal wealth by barring poor people who would demand services but could not pay for them; or, by the desire to preserve a community's tax base by attracting taxable business development (see Chapter 3 for a fuller discussion of these alternative motives). Political boundary lines in suburbs then divide a metropolitan region into a number of specialized, separate, and autonomous political units. As a result of the exclusionary actions of local government, motivated by social status and/or fiscal concerns, socioeconomic differentiation found to occur becomes more rigid through the system of local government. As Michael Danielson states:

> Political fragmentation in the metropolis is a suburban phenomenon, as is the institutionalization of socioeconomic differentiation along local political boundaries.[26]

Since the distribution of wealth and resources varies from area to area, the institutionalization of these differences implies that some suburbs will be well-off, while others will not be. To use Richard C. Hill's terminology: suburban regions become marked by a large number of local governments which are "separate *and* unequal."[27]

The concept of fragmented metropolitan growth thus implies two distinct but related phenomena. First, is simply the proliferation of the number of governments found in suburbia. This makes governance difficult because of the large number of actors that are involved in local government. The small size of many of these local governments frequently makes them haphazardly governed and may produce low quality local services. But, in addition, fragmentation implies the institutionalization of socioeconomic difference by political boundary lines. This institutionalization of differences makes the governance of suburbia more complicated. The separate and unequal nature of fragmented metropolitan development gives neighboring suburban jurisdictions incentives not only to be uncooperative, but to be outright competitive with one another.

The Basis for Competition: Local Property Taxes

If, in part, the institutionalization of socioeconomic differences in suburbia results from the desire of people to exclude lower class settlement from their communities on social or "life style" grounds, this motive is reinforced by concerns for the impact of lower class residents on the level of local government services and the taxes needed to pay for them. Thus, the incentives for suburban competition and for the institutionalization of differences between suburbs are built into the system of financing local government services, a system of finance based overwhelmingly on the local property tax.

Of all levels of government, local governments account for the largest share of direct government expenditures on domestic programs. In recent years, over 40 percent of all such government expenditures has come from localities.[28] Money to meet the costs of such services comes from several sources: local taxes; intergovernmental aid and transfers from states and national government; user charges for public services; and borrowing. But historically by far the single most important source of revenue for local governments is the property tax.

In the early 1970s, local government raised about $40 billion per year through the property tax. This accounted for about 80 percent of their total tax revenue.[29] The general result is high property taxes. But considerable variation in tax rates between neighboring communities is common in metropolitan regions. Table 2-6 shows the tax rates found in 60 suburbs greater than 2500 population in the Long Island, New York suburban region in 1970, and is typical of most suburban regions.[30] Of the 60 Long Island suburbs shown, 16 communities taxed themselves at less than $.50 per $100 of computed market valuation for the property within their borders. In contrast to these low tax communities, 13 Long Island suburbs charged more than $1.00 per $100 of market value, and of these high tax suburbs, the most highly taxed used a rate more than 4 times the average of the least taxed communities. The range between the highest and lowest taxing communities is even more striking. Great Neck Plaza had a village tax rate of only $0.22, while Long Beach had a tax rate more than *10 times* greater ($2.30). This variation in tax rates is mostly dependent on the value of the property tax base found in a given community. Communities with strong property tax bases can tax themselves at a lower rate yet still generate sufficient revenue to cover necessary municipal service costs. In contrast, suburbs with weak tax bases need higher rates to provide such revenue.

Thus, low taxes do not necessarily mean inadequate governmental services or "poor government." A low tax rate applied to a strong local tax base can provide high revenues, while a high tax rate applied to a weak fiscal base may provide revenue for only a modicum of services. This inequality in tax burdens and local services helps provide some of the incentives for suburban competition.

Communities can create a strong local fiscal base by either of two strategies. First, suburbs can try to attract high income families whose expensive houses yield high tax revenues in relation to service demands. This, historically, is the traditional "winning" strategy in suburban competition. Alternately, given

Table 2-6 Tax Rate in Long Island Suburbs, Fiscal Year 1969

Tax Rate Less Than $0.50 per $100 Computed True Market Value[1]

Babylon*	Huntington*
Bellport	Manorhaven
Brookville	Munsy Park
East Hills	North Hempstead*
Flower Hill	Oyster Bay
Great Neck	Port Jefferson
Great Neck Plaza	Port Washington
Hempstead*	Southampton*

Tax Rate Between $0.50 and $0.75 per $100

Bayville	Lindenhurst
Brightwaters	Massapequa Park
Brookhaven*	Mineola
Cedarhurst	New Hyde Park
East Hampton*	Roslyn
East Rockaway	Sandspoint
East Williston	Smithtown*
Farmingdale	Southold*
Islip*	Westbury
Kings Point	Williston
Lake Success	

Tax Rate Between $0.76 and $1.00 per $100

Babylon	Riverhead*
Islepark	Sea Cliff
Lawrence	Shelter Island*
Lloyd Harbor	Southampton
Old Westbury	Valley Stream

Tax Rate Between $1.01 and $1.50 per $100

Amityville	Lynbrook
Garden City	Malverne
Glen Cove**	Patchogue
Great Neck Estates	Rockville Center
Floral Park	

Tax Rate More Than $1.50 per $100

Freeport	Long Beach**
Hempstead	Northport

*In terms of government organization, Long Island is divided into towns marked by an (*), cities (**), and villages.

[1]Tax rates are computed by taking assessed valuation and dividing this figure by the "equalization rate" set by New York State. This is necessary since local governments set assessed value at a fraction of true market value. The computed figure estimates true market value of community property. Property tax revenue divided by estimated market value determines the effective tax rate for the local community. The necessary data in New York are found in the *Special Report on Municipal Affairs* by the State Comptroller, April 1970. The data are for municipal functions only, and do not include school district taxes which are levied by separate independent school districts.

the decentralization of employment and business activities characterizing suburban growth since the 1950s, and given the concentration of taxable wealth such activities represent, suburbs can try to build a strong fiscal base by attracting business firms that represent commercial property tax base.

Taking Long Island as an example, the impact of these two growth strategies can be examined. We can arrange the suburban communities in the region into three separate categories: first, exclusive residential suburbs — those communities which specialize in high income, high cost housing while excluding employment; second, employing suburbs — those communities which are characterized by a high concentration of business and employment; and third, "mixed" or "balanced" suburbs — those communities with neither asset.[31] This classification allows us to inspect the relationship between economic activity, personal wealth, community fiscal wealth, and local government revenues, providing evidence for the incentives that exist for competition between suburbs.

Table 2-7 shows measures of personal wealth (average home value, average family income) and community fiscal strength (assessed valuation per capita, tax rate, government revenues per capita) for each of the three types of communities.[32] Consider first the exclusive residential communities. The average home value in these communities was $44,000, 50 percent higher than that in the other two types of communities. Moreover, the family income in exclusive residential suburbs was almost twice that of employing suburbs, and more than twice that of balanced communities. In short, rich people live in these exclusive residential communities.

But the concentration of personal wealth is also reflected in measures of community fiscal well-being. The average assessed valuation per capita in exclusive residential communities was $12,350, substantially higher than in the other two types of communities. Given this concentration of fiscal wealth, these exclusive residential suburbs were able to tax themselves at the lowest rates of all types (an average of $0.60 per $100) yet still produce about average government revenues ($120 per capita) to pay for municipal government services.

Compared to the concentration of personal wealth in exclusive

Table 2-7 Personal and Community Fiscal Wealth By Type of Community:* Long Island, 1970

	Average All Suburbs	Average Exclusive Residential Suburbs	Average Balanced Suburbs	Average Employing Suburbs
Personal Wealth	(N = 40)	(N = 12)	(N = 16)	(N = 12)
Home Value	$35,057	44,071	28,278	30,988
Family Income	$19,816	28,448	13,962	15,402
Fiscal Wealth				
Assessed Valuation per capita	$10,110	12,350	7,120	10,160
Tax Rate	$0.82	0.60	0.94	0.96
Revenue per capita	$130	120	110	160

Source: Adapted from John Logan and Mark Schneider, "The Political Economy of Suburban Growth," a paper presented at the XVII Annual Convention of the International Studies Association, Toronto, Canada, February 25-29, 1976.

*Communities are divided into categories depending on their employment/residents ratio, a standard measure of the development found in a community (see, e.g., Victor Jones, "Economic Classification of Cities and Metropolitan Areas," *Municipal Yearbook 1953*, 49-57). In this study, residential suburbs had an E/R ratio equal to 0; balanced suburbs a ratio greater than 0 and less than 1.0; employing suburbs had a ratio of greater than 1.0.

residential suburbs, employing suburbs are significantly poorer in terms of the personal wealth of their residents. Average home value was only $31,000 and average family income about $15,000. But, because these suburbs have concentrations of commercial property tax base, their assessed valuation per capita ($10,120) is higher than might be expected. While they do tax themselves at the highest average rate of all three types of communities ($0.98 per $100), this high tax rate produces by far the highest government revenues per capita ($160).

From these data, exclusive residential suburbs seem the most well-off. These wealthy residential communities have low taxes *and* sufficient government revenues to purchase necessary services. Employing suburbs appear somewhat less advantaged, taxing themselves more heavily but at least producing high revenues for local services. However, consider the plight of the last type of suburb — that is the "balanced" suburb with neither concentration of wealthy residents nor of taxable business property. As a result of the failure to attract taxable resources, the "balanced" communities have the lowest levels of personal wealth and the lowest per capita assessed valuation of any type of community in the region. Moreover, they tax themselves at a rate just fractionally lower than employing suburbs ($0.94 per $100 compared to $0.96). Yet, compare the yield of the taxes in these communities to that of the other communities — their per capita revenues are by far the lowest. In short, these "balanced" communities, lacking a strong tax base, must tax themselves at high rates just to produce the lowest revenues to support local services. It is for this reason that Wood[33] refers to this type of community as the "unannointed."

Individuals and government officials in each of the independent suburbs in a region obviously have strong incentives to regulate the kinds of people or businesses that settle within the boundaries of their community. To the extent that a suburb succeeds in attracting "productive" resources into its borders (i.e., people or businesses that generate more tax revenue than they demand in services), it can reduce taxes, increase the level of local services, or both! To the extent that a suburb fails to attract such resources, it must increase its taxes to pay for even minimal services.

As a result, suburbs compete with other neighboring suburbs for desirable residents. The independence and autonomy inherent in fragmented suburban growth means that the losers in this competition are separated from the tax resources concentrated within the borders of their more successful neighbors, and produces a system of suburban governments that are, indeed, separate and unequal.

Incorporation of Suburban Governments: The Role of Government in Institutionalizing Differences

It is important to understand the role of local government policy in creating and furthering suburban competition. Suburban communities may be either incorporated or unincorporated — that is, they may exist as a formally recognized government corporation granted certain powers by the state, or they may exist as unincorporated areas of settlement without such formal government powers. Incorporation by suburban communities serves several purposes. On one level, incorporation is often a necessary response by a concentrated population newly emerging in a suburban area in need of additional governmental services. Many services, such as parks or sewers, are not needed before intense development occurs. Thus, while a sparsely populated rural area may find its need for local government minimal, more intense suburban development frequently produces greater service demands. Incorporation by suburban communities is often necessary before services can be provided to satisfy these demands. But this process of incorporation also increases the power of local suburban communities to control growth and to further inequalities in metropolitan development. While we have previously shown that incorporation was used to prevent the expansion of the central city, and to institutionalize differences between central cities and suburbs, we are here concerned with the use of incorporation to institutionalize differences *between* suburbs.

Inherent in the increased control over services, incorporation gives a suburb new tools of government to protect itself from changes in the environment and to regulate entry into that community. Most important, incorporation gives a suburb increased control over zoning and land use policy, tax and budgeting decisions, and planning and promotional activities. As a result, incorporations are frequently motivated not only by the need to provide services, but also by the desire of communities to gain government powers to protect some value or resource held by the community.

This protective role of incorporation (as compared to the "service delivery" role) can be inferred from the data presented in Table 2-8. Over 2,000 incorporated communities found in the 1970 Census are arranged by decade of incorporation. Note how closely the pattern of incorporations corresponds to changes in the nature of suburbanization. In particular, note how closely increases in the rate of incorporation parallel developments in transportation technologies that changed the environment of suburban growth by increasing the number and widening the range of potential suburban residents. By 1880, only 586 incorporated suburbs existed in the United States. But beginning in the 1880s and accelerating in the 1890-1910 period, the rate of suburban incorporations increased dramatically. These incorporations were in response to the expansion of the central

Table 2-8   Dates of Incorporation of American Suburbs

Incorporated by	Number	Percent of Total
1880	586	24.9
1890	219	9.3
1900	263	11.2
1910	269	11.4
1920	177	7.5
1930	190	8.1
1940	81	3.4
1950	177	7.5
1960	232	9.8
1970	162	6.9
Total	2,356	100%

Source: Avery M. Guest, "American Suburban Development," Seattle, Washington: Center for Studies in Demography and Ecology (unpublished).

cities' boundaries made possible by the transportation improvements of those decades, particularly the expansion of electric streetcar lines. As noted, these incorporations were frequently an explicit attempt to protect native dominated, upper middle class communities from encroachment by the immigrant dominated central cities and from a more diverse population seeking entry into the suburbs.

Between 1910 and 1920, the rate of incorporations declined considerably. However, the decade of the 1920s represents another increase in incorporations, this spurt most likely in response to the growth of truck transportation and the expansion into suburbia of new industries. It is also important to note that it was in 1926 that the Supreme Court gave its approval in a landmark case, *Euclid v. Ambler*, to the local use of zoning, and Seymour Toll[34] notes that suburbs were among the first communities to adopt this powerful tool of regulating growth. It is likely that some of the incorporations of the 1920s were done specifically to gain control over land use through now validated zoning laws.

However, the most serious change in suburban growth patterns did not occur in the 1920s, but in the post-World War II era. Not only did the number of people moving to the suburbs increase, but so did the range of socioeconomic status represented by those suburban migrants. A considerable number of working class and lower class people sought suburban housing. In response to this expansion of suburban migration, beginning in the late 1940s and intensifying in the 1950s, suburban communities adopted the same strategy that was found in the past, that is, they incorporated to gain increased control over growth. As a result, the 1950s showed the largest number of incorporations since the 1890s. But the most blatant examples of the exclusionary, protective uses of incorporation are buried in these aggregate statistics. Consider, in particular, the case of Black Jack, Missouri, a town of less than 5000 residents, most of whom were white. Black Jack incorporated in 1970, and one of its first actions as an incorporated community was to adopt a one-acre, single family zoning ordinance. By so doing, Black Jack sought to prevent the construction of a multiple-family, low and moderate income subsidized housing project planned for the area. Because the use of this new power, and indeed the impetus for the very incorporation, was so blatantly racially motivated, the Federal courts eventually struck down Black Jack's zoning ordinance. But Black Jack's actions, in particular its desire to incorporate to gain more control over its growth, were only the extremes of common practice.

The powers that communities gain upon incorporation are wide ranging and as noted earlier include zoning, subdivision regulation, development timing ordinances, local control over budget and service allocations, and greater discretion in setting tax rates. And the ways in which these powers are used is similarly wide ranging. Robert Warren has documented the range of purposes of incorporation among suburbs during the 1950s in the particular case of Los Angeles. In response to the growth of the 1950s, suburbs incorporated: to avoid annexation by the city of Los Angeles or by a neighboring suburb; to slow the rate of population increase; to preserve the residential character of the community; to protect a wealthy or commercial property tax base among other reasons.[35] But the one common theme involved in all these incorporations was the desire of suburbs to gain government powers to protect some value or resource held by the community and to exclude development or land uses that would threaten the community. While this use of incorporation and local government powers is a general process that has been visible in the historical development of suburbs since the first suburban expansions of the 1890s, we now want to consider the range of values that may be held by suburbs and what they may seek to protect. In particular, we wish to argue that at present, the predominant value held by suburbs in their competition with their neighbors may be undergoing a considerable redefinition.

Rich People v. Commercial Development: The Changing Object of Suburban Competition

Given the dominant image of suburbia as a semi-rural retreat devoted to residential development, historically, commercial development in the suburbs has frequently carried with it a negative connotation. Suburban communities which developed as commercial centers have been documented to be relatively unattractive places and have been populated by the least desirable of suburban residents. Schnore's work examining differences between "employing suburbs," that is, suburbs with a high concentration of industrial-commercial development, and "residential suburbs" is the classic statement of this historical pattern.[36] Schnore showed that employing suburbs were in many ways central cities writ small. Employing suburbs had inexpensive housing, a concentration of multi-family dwellings, and a resulting high density. Further, the residents of employing suburbs were of lower social status than those of more exclusively residential suburbs. And, in addition, just as many central cities showed a relative stagnation in terms of population growth, similarly, employing suburbs grew at a much slower rate than residential suburbs. In short, suburbs which were employing centers were not attractive to high status, wealthy suburbanites, and by implication, business development was not a value to be maximized in suburban competition.

Schnore's carefully documented research findings based on data generated through the 1950s coupled nicely with the prevailing image of suburbia. Residential suburbs were where people wanted to live, and, as the data from Long Island and other regions indicate, the fiscal benefits of an exclusive residential development strategy successfully followed could be considerable.

But speculation now exists concerning a change in the relative worth of residential and commercial development in suburbia. Several conditions found in current suburban growth have led to the belief that, at present, the value of commercial development in suburbs is being reevaluated and up-graded as a goal in suburban competition. The first relevant change is the rapid decentralization of business and manufacturing from the central cities into the suburbs that has been found since 1950. Since this is a recent event, the firms relocating will be housed in new buildings of modern design, many planned with concern for the environmental impact of their activities. Many of these new firms are involved in light industry, electronics, or in services such as banking and insurance. As such, they are already inherently "cleaner" and more pleasant than the older types of manufacturing that may have in the past sought the cheap land of suburbia. Further, local governments have been able to negotiate with firms seeking entry into their boundaries concerning arrangements to either regulate the firm's demands for public services, or to find ways for the firms more directly to pay for the costs for such services. To the extent that industries and businesses are clean and their service costs controlled, such development can represent an addition to local tax base considerably in excess of strictly residential development.[37]

Thus, the physical and fiscal attractiveness of business may have been undergoing reevaluation. At the same time, throughout the 1960s and 1970s, the costs of local government have been skyrocketing and along with these costs, the taxes necessary to pay for them. This alone may have made suburbs cast more favorable eyes on business development with the concentrated taxable resources it represents.

In addition, it was also becoming evident that the exclusive residential strategy based on the personal wealth of high income suburbanites could not be successfully followed by all suburbs. The suburban explosion of the 1950s and 1960s was fueled by a wider range of social classes than previous suburban expansion, and working class and lower class suburbanites were found in growing numbers. This segment of the suburban population did not lend itself to the exclusive residential strategy of community fiscal well-being. The income levels and the taxable home values of this lower strata of suburbanite would simply not be high enough to allow low taxes to produce revenues sufficient to cover the increasing costs of local services. In addition, numerous planning studies also began to show even the most expensive housing did not automatically produce sufficient tax revenues to cover services.[38]

In short, suburbs were faced with a changing social milieux — an influx of new suburbanites who demanded services but could not easily pay for them, a growing cost of local government and upward pressure on taxes, and the decentralization of business that represented a potentially lucrative addition to local tax base. As a result, industrial and commercial development may be emerging as the most important focus of new suburban competition. The benefits of successfully attracting such development can be seen in the data from Long Island; employing suburbs had by far the highest per capita government revenues from a tax rate that was only marginally higher than the "balanced" suburbs.

It is also possible that the most successful suburbs now use their powers of government to entice taxable firms into their boundaries while at the same time excluding the lower income workers these firms may employ.[39] These "undesirable" lower income workers then must find housing either in the central cities and "reverse commute" to the suburbs, a phenomenon noted above as increasingly common, or else these workers must find housing in a less attractive and less successful suburb. In either case, the most successful employing suburbs wind up ahead; they get the taxable resource represented by the business and exclude the workers who could otherwise be demanding local services.

John Logan[40] further suggests that as this process unfolds over time, the relatively low taxes and high service levels found in successful employing suburbs eventually makes them increasingly attractive as residential communities. He shows that between 1960 and 1970 the employing suburbs of Santa Clara County, California were the site of the most rapid influx of wealthy suburbanites as reflected in family income levels and in home values. Avery M. Guest[41] presents somewhat complementary data and argues that employing suburbs concentrating on retail and wholesale trade, but *not* manufacturing, are the most attractive places now found in suburbia. Guest shows that these "trade centers," as a subset of employing suburbs, are now increasingly found to contain high status residents. This may imply that even if manufacturing development represents a net fiscal plus to suburbs, the negative image of manufacturing and its effect on the suburban environment may be so adverse as to outweigh possible fiscal benefits. Since such detriments do not attend commercial development to the same degree, it is possible that suburbs would prefer such developments as regional shopping centers and its attendant tax benefits, rather than compete for manufacturing development. But nonetheless, business development may now be a positive value for suburbs and may now become associated with residential locational choices of the wealthiest and most desirable suburbanites, frequently because of the tax incentives and fiscal benefits associated with such growth in the system of suburban competition that now exists.

But note that as this process unfolds, inequalities in suburbia may increase. If, in fact, the taxable resources of both high income suburban residents and commercial development become concentrated in the *same* communities, the fiscal wealth of these "successful" communities will improve dramatically but only at cost to surrounding communities deprived of the increasingly concentrated taxable resources of the region.

The Regional Milieux of Suburban Competition

The process of competition for taxable resources with its subsequent pattern of winners and losers is a widespread phenomenon in American metropolitan development, but recent research has indicated considerable variation between different regions in the country. The preconditions for the existence of suburban competition have been mentioned above: the existence of multiple autonomous suburban governments in a region, the desire for exclusion of low class residents, local government responsibility for financing services, reliance on the local property tax, and changes in the environment that cause suburbs to try to restrict entry into its borders with some suburbs more successful than others.

While the factors promoting competition exist to some degree in all suburban regions, the extent to which these conditions are found does vary significantly from region to region. Researchers have also noted that the range of inequality found between suburbs also varies from region to region.[42] By relating the degree to which the different conditions creating competition match the degree of inequality found across regions, researchers have tried to identify those factors which are most likely to promote competition and subsequent inequality.

Richard C. Hill's study is perhaps the best example of this type of investigation. Hill measured the inequality resulting from suburban competition using the standard deviation around the average family income for all municipalities of a given region. Given the nature of the standard deviation, one can argue that larger standard deviations indicate greater inequality (i.e., some municipalities are further above average, others further below than in regions with smaller standard deviations). Using this measure, Hill seeks to find the conditions related to variation in the standard deviation across 63 SMSAs in 1960 (unfortunately the only year for which he had complete data. His findings, however, closely parallel those of Eric Branfman and his colleagues,[43] who use both 1960 and 1970 data). Across the 63 SMSAs studied, Hill finds greater income inequality between suburban associated with the following:

1) the percent of families in a region with incomes greater than $10,000.

2) the degree of income inequality found among families in a region.

3) the percent of the population in a region, nonwhite.

4) the number of municipalities per capita.[44]

In regions where there are more governments and more rich families, greater inequalities between suburbs are found. In regions where there is a larger population nonwhite and where there is a greater degree of income differences between families, inequality between suburbs is also greater. Hill argues that it is not coincidental that it is in the regions where the potential threats to the lifestyle and isolation of the wealthy are the greatest (that is, in regions with the greatest concentrations of the poor and the nonwhite) that inequalities between communities are more severe. Indeed, Hill argues that as threats to the well-being of wealthy suburbanites increases, they use the fragmented system of local government to protect themselves from the poor and nonwhite by barring these groups from exclusive suburban enclaves, enclaves maintained and protected by local government powers. As Hill notes:

> Advantaged classes and status groups in the metropolitan community seek to maximize control over scarce resources and maintain life-style values through homogeneous and complementary residential groupings. In the context of the fragmented system of governments in the metropolis, municipal governments become an institutional arrangement for promoting and protecting the unequal distribution of scarce resources.[45]

Thus, inequalities in family income, and racial and class segregation are encouraged and institutionalized by the existence of fragmented suburban governmental structure. The system of local government in the United States helps to further inequalities in fiscal resources, tax burdens, and service levels in metropolitan areas, and helps to create differences between cities and suburbs and between neighboring suburbs in the metropolis.

But, as seen throughout this chapter, the conditions associated with greater inequalities vary from region to region, and are more concentrated in the oldest and largest SMSAs where greater government fragmentation and a greater diversity of population in race and class terms exist.

Summary: Cities versus Suburbs and Suburbs versus Suburbs: Inequalities in Metropolitan Development

Inequalities are an enduring and common characteristic of current forms of metropolitan development. In the most frequently discussed form, inequalities take the shape of significant differences between central cities and their suburbs with regard to racial settlement patterns and in the level of social class of city and suburban residents.

Such race and class inequalities appear to be part of the evolution of the American metropolis and a result of the desire of a large segment of the American population to escape the central cities. The extent of inequalities is greatest in the oldest metropolitan regions in the United States but may be the end product of the evolution of all American metropolitan areas.

The concept of the "social gradient" most frequently used to explain the emergence of these inequalities traces back to the 1920s and the work of the "Chicago School" of demography. Central to the concept is the belief that economic competition for the most desirable land in the central business was the dynamic force propelling metropolitan development. However, these economic forces were clearly reinforced by political intervention. This is most notable in the drawing of rigid city boundary lines that created an "artificial wall" between cities and suburbs. This wall separates lower class residents at the beginning of the social gradient from higher class residents further from the center. Furthermore, local government policies may have artificially reinforced any such gradient by restricting access of the poor to the housing markets of suburbia.

These politically reinforced social status differences between cities and suburbs seem remarkably durable. Research traces a city/suburb dichotomy back to at least 1920 and shows a continuation of such differences through the 1970s. While the massive suburbanization of the post-World War II period has increased the relative heterogeneity of suburbia by introducing more lower and middle class families, central cities in many parts of the country still have, by far, the lowest status populations in the metropolitan region. Government policies enacted in the 1960s to redress such imbalances have had no measurable impact as of yet.

The rapid decentralization of jobs from the central cities may exacerbate further central city/suburban differences. Central cities are not only losing higher status residents, but are also suffering from the loss of taxable commercial and industrial activity.

Inequalities between suburbs also occur. In examining this phenomenon, a natural segregatory impulse was postulated as operating in metropolitan development. This segregatory impulse is on one level economic — conflicting land uses in close proximity (e.g., the factory and the home) make little sense economically. This creates an incentive for segregation by economic function. In addition, social science literature and studies of human ecology in particular repeatedly demonstrate a preference by people to segregate into districts of like situated families or individuals. But just as political forces acted to exacerbate central city/suburban differences, political forces reinforce segregation within suburbia. The drawing of political boundary lines around specialized suburban communities, and the use of local government powers to regulate entry into the suburbs furthers segregation. Moreover, the system of local government finance, a system based mostly on the property tax, creates incentives for communities to seek desirable (that is, taxable) residents and exclude undesirable ones.

This process at one time operated almost exclusively with regard to competition for high status residential development, but has recently expanded to include competition for industrial and commercial development. There is accumulating evidence that this new form of competition reinforces segregation along class lines — the most successful suburbs in the future may be those that attract both high status residents *and* taxable commercial development. Thus, many suburbs now welcome business and employment growth but bar the entry of lower income employees who could work in the new firms. These lower income families then must seek housing in other, less successful suburbs. This process will produce some very well-off communities, but leave others with a poor tax base relative to service demands. To the extent that this process becomes characteristic of suburban growth, inequalities between suburbs will intensify.

Thus, even *if* Federal or state policy can reverse the trend toward inequalities between cities and suburbs, the communities into which a more heterogeneous suburban population moves must be a concern. If racial minorities and the lower income groups escape the central cities only to inherit the most disadvantaged suburbs, have we as a society accomplished much in terms of equal treatment of our citizens?

Throughout this discussion we have seen a combination of economic and ecological forces interacting with government powers to institutionalize inequalities. In the next chapter, we 'ook at managing metropolitan growth and see how zoning, a specific government power, has developed as a means to produce inequalities and what reforms have been suggested to make the suburban development process more equitable.

Notes

1. Basil G. Zimmer, "The Urban Centrifugal Drift," in Amos H. Hawley and Vincent P. Rock, eds., *Metropolitan American Contemporary Perspective* (New York: John Wiley & Sons, 1975).

2. William G. Colman, *Cities, Suburbs, and States* (New York: The Free Press, 1975), ch. 4.

3. John J. Harrigan, *Political Change in the Metropolis* (Boston: Little, Brown, 1976), p. 38.

4. Reynolds Farley, "The Changing Distribution of Negroes Within Metropolitan Areas: The Emergence of Black Suburbs," *American Journal of Sociology* 75 (January 1970), pp. 512-529. Also see Thomas P. Murphey and John Rehfuss, *Urban Politics in the Suburban Era* (Homewood, Illinois: Dorsey Press, 1976), ch. 1; and, David R. Goldfield, "Limits of Suburban Growth," *Urban Affairs Quarterly* (September 1976), pp. 83-102.

5. Francis Fox Piven and Richard Cloward, *Regulating the Poor* (New York: Pantheon 1971).

6. Farley, *op. cit.* Also see Harold X. Connolly, "Black Movement into the Suburbs," in James Hughes, ed., *Suburbanization Dynamics and the Future of the City* (New Brunswick: Center for Urban Policy Research, 1974).

7. Frederick M. Wirt, Benjamin Walter, Francine F. Rabinovitz and Deborah R. Hensler, *On the City's Rim* (Lexington, Mass.: D.C. Heath and Company, 1972), p. 40.

8. Farley, "Suburban Persistence," *American Sociological Review* 29 (February 1964), pp. 38-47. Also see Avery M. Guest, "Suburban Social Status: Persistence or Evolution," unpublished manuscript, Center for the Study of Demography and Ecology, University of Washington, Seattle; and Farley, "Components of Suburban Population Growth," in Barry Schwarz, ed., *The Changing Face of the Suburbs* (Chicago: University of Chicago Press, 1976).

9. Also see Farley, "Components," p. 27; and Hawley and Zimmer, *The Metropolitan Community* (Beverly Hills: Sage Publications, 1970).

10. Zimmer, *op. cit.;* Also see Karl E. Taeuber and F. Taeuber, *Negroes in Cities* (Chicago: Aldine, 1965).

11. Leo F. Schnore, "The Socioeconomic Status of Cities and Suburbs," *American Sociological Review* 28 (February 1963), pp. 76-85.

12. Schnore, *Class and Race in Cities and Suburbs* (Chicago: Markham 1972) p. 72. Note that Schnore's work implies that on the average central city residents will be less educated and of lower social status than suburbanites. But this may be somewhat misleading in one regard. In many cities, people recognize a sharp class structure emerging in the city with both the very high income people *and* the very poor living in the central city with the suburbs occupied by the middle classes. The emergence of a rigid class structure within the city is not inconsistent with Schnore's empirical findings — the low level of education of the larger numbers of poor in the city would in fact make the central city of lower status than the suburbs, even if a number of extremely wealthy individuals still retained residence in the city.

13. Murphy and Rehfuss, *op. cit.*, pp. 19-22. See also David R. Goldfield, *op. cit.*

14. John D. Kasarda, "The Changing Occupational Structure of the American Metropolis," in Schwarz, ed., *The Changing Face of the Suburbs, op. cit.*

15. *Ibid.*, p. 127. Also see the National Committee Against Discrimination in Housing, *The Impact of Housing on Job Opportunities* (New York, 1968).

16. Zimmer, *op. cit.*, p. 53. Also see A.R. Weber, "Labor Market Perspectives of the New City," in Benjamin Chinitz, ed., *City and Suburbs* (Englewood Cliffs: Prentice Hall, 1964).

17. Kevin R. Cox, *Conflict, Power and Politics in the City* (New York: McGraw Hill, 1973).

18. The technical argument supporting Cox need not concern us in great detail. Basically, Cox took a variety of Census data for his sample of communities, variables that logically relate to service demands and community wealth. These variables were factor analyzed, and the most characteristic of these variables used for further analysis.

19. Advisory Commission on Intergovernmental Relations, *Fiscal Balance in the American Federal System* (Washington, D.C.: Government Printing Office, 1965), vol. 2, p. 6.

20. For a good recent summary of this literature see R.E. Johnston, *Urban Residential Patterns* (New York: Praeger, 1971).

21. See Herbert Gans, *The Urban Villagers* (New York: The Free Press, 1962) and *The Levittowners* (New York: Vintage, 1967). Also see Nathan Kantrowitz, "Ethnic and Racial Segregation in the New York Metropolis, 1960," *American Journal of Sociology* 74 (May 1969), pp. 685-695.

22. Robert C. Wood, *1400 Governments* (Cambridge: Harvard University Press, 1961).

23. Robert Lineberry and Ira Sharkansky, *Urban Politics and Public Policy* (New York: Harper and Row, 1974), p. 24.

24. Committee for Economic Development, *Reshaping Government in Metropolitan Areas* (New York: CED, 1966).

25. Robert O. Warren, *Government in Metropolitan Regions* (Davis, California: Institute of Governmental Affairs, 1966).

26. Michael Danielson, "Differentiation, Segregation and Political Fragmentation in the American Metropolis," in A.E. Kier Nash, ed., *Governance and Population*, vol. 4, Research Reports of the Commission on Population Growth and the American Future (Washington, D.C.: Government Printing Office, 1972).

27. Richard C. Hill, "Separate and Unequal: Governmental Inequality in the Metropolis," *American Political Science Review* 68 (December 1974), pp. 1557-1568.

28. Advisory Commission on Intergovernmental Relations, *Trends in Fiscal Federalism 1954-1974* (Washington, D.C.: Government Printing Office, 1975), p. 11.

29. Henry J. Aaron, *Who Pays the Property Tax?* (Washington, D.C.: The Brookings Institution, 1975), p. 8-12.

30. See, for example, John Riew, "Metropolitan Disparities and Fiscal Federalism," in John P. Crecine, ed., *Financing the Metropolis* (Beverly Hills,

California: Sage Publications, 1970); Advisory Commission on Intergovernmental Relations, *Urban America and the Federal System* (Washington, D.C.: Government Printing Office, 1969); Harrigan, *op. cit.*, pp. 186-188.

31. This classification of communities has a long tradition in ecological studies. The classification is based on an index called the employment/residents ratio (E/R ratio) which relates the number of employees in retail and wholesale trades plus manufacturing work found in a community to the number of residents in the community so employed. A high E/R ratio indicates a relative high concentration of employment or an "employing suburb," while a low E/R ratio indicates a residential suburb.

32. This analysis includes only certain larger villages since the U.S. Census does not report all necessary data for smaller villages or for towns. But the process and principle discussed applies to them as well — it is a *general* condition of contemporary suburban development.

33. Wood, *Suburbia — Its People and Their Politics* (Boston: Houghton-Mifflin, 1958).

34. Seymour I. Toll, *Zoned America* (New York: Grossman Publishers, 1969).

35. Warren, *op. cit.*, ch. 10.

36. Schnore, "Satellites and Suburbs," *Social Forces* 36 (December 1957), pp. 121-127.

37. James W. Hughes and Franklyn James, "The Dispersion of Employment," in James Hughes, ed., *New Dimensions of Urban Planning* (New Brunswick, New Jersey: Center for Urban Policy Research, 1974).

38. See, for example, Franklin J. James with Duane Windsor, "Fiscal Zoning, Fiscal Reform, and Exclusionary Land Use Controls," *Journal of American Institute of Planners* 42 (April 1976), pp. 130-141; this point is also discussed in more detail in ch. 3.

39. Hill, *op. cit.*, page 1559.

40. John Logan, "Industrialization and the Stratification of Cities in Suburban Regions," *American Journal of Sociology* 82 (Sept. 1976), pp. 333-48. Also John Logan and Mark Schneider, "The Political Economy of Suburban Growth," a paper presented to the Annual Meeting of the International Studies Association, Toronto, Canada, February 25-29, 1976.

41. Avery M. Guest, "Employment and Residential Character," unpublished manuscript, Center for Demography and Ecology, University of Washington, Seattle.

42. See Logan and Schneider, *op. cit.*, for a two region comparison. Eric J. Branfman, Benjamin I. Cohen and David M. Trubek, "Measuring the Invisible Wall: Land Use Controls and Residential Patterns of the Poor," *Yale Law Journal* 82 (Jan. 1973), pp. 483-508; and Hill, *op. cit.*, report multiple region comparisons.

43. See Branfman *et al., Ibid.*

44. Hill, *op. cit.*, p. 1567.

45. Richard Child Hill, "Separate and Unequal: Governmental Inequality in the Metropolis," *American Political Science Review* 68 (December 1974), p. 1559. Copyright© 1974, American Political Science Association.

Chapter 3

Controlling Community Growth and Development: Land Use and Zoning

The use of local government powers to produce inequalities in suburban development was discussed in Chapter 2. We now turn more fully to an examination of one specific power of growth control used by suburbs to produce inequalities in metropolitan areas. The major focus of this chapter will be on zoning and associated land use controls, powers of local governments often thought directly to affect suburban community development.

In the following pages, we will look at the historical development of zoning in the United States, inspect more fully the various land use and development policies formulated by suburbs, and note recent decisions of the courts, the federal government, and the states that are altering the environment in which suburban land use and community development policies are made.

The History of Zoning and Land Use Control

Zoning is a fundamental power available to local governments for controlling growth and community development. Through zoning, local governments can regulate, among other things, the quantity of housing built, the amount of land available for residential construction, the mix of single family and multiple family dwellings, and the size of such housing units. Similarly, through the manipulation of zoning laws, local communities can also affect the amount of business growth in the community by regulating the amount of land zoned for commercial and industrial uses. In short, through the successful manipulation of zoning laws, it is possible for a community to exercise significant control over the rate and composition of its own development.[1]

Yet, despite this fundamental importance, the use of zoning to control growth and development is not explicitly recognized in law. Instead, because of the peculiarities of American legal history, zoning is based on the broad grant of power to local governments to enact laws that protect the "general welfare" of its citizens — a grant of authority generally known as the "police power" of the state.

The roots of zoning in the police power has created certain constraints that help define the role of zoning in controlling suburban growth. Because the police power is not an unlimited grant to local governments, communities must show that the actions they are undertaking bear a direct relationship to the protection of the health, safety or general welfare of the area. Zoning regulations affecting the use of private property and the types of development that may take place within local government borders are therefore legally and constitutionally justifiable only insofar as they serve the legitimate needs of the community to protect its residents from unsafe or threatening growth.

However, in its present use by suburbs, zoning has been widely condemned for going far beyond such valid concerns for the preservation of the general welfare. Instead, it is frequently argued that the use of zoning has created inequalities in metropolitan areas through the exclusion ("zoning out") of the poor and racial minority groups from suburbia in general and from the wealthiest suburbs in particular. The use of zoning as an exclusionary tool barring low and moderate income groups from suburbs can be seen in the details of a zoning ordinance enacted by Glassboro, New Jersey and recently subject to court challenge because of its highly tenuous link to the protection of the general welfare of that community.

The zoning regulation in question controlled multi-family construction in Glassboro and required that the following conditions be met in any new apartment house construction in the suburb: that central air conditioning and an automatic garbage disposal be in each apartment; that a master television antenna be built for each building; that an average of just only one bedroom per unit be maintained; that a clothes washer and dryer be available for every 8 bedrooms; that at least 8 square feet of swimming pool or tennis court area be constructed for every 100 feet of living space; and that 2 off strect parking spots be available for every apartment.

The challenge to the ordinance was based on the argument that such zoning requirements bore no relationship to health or safety needs and thereby went beyond the legal justification for zoning in the police power. Instead, it was argued that, in this instance, Glassboro's use of its zoning powers was designed to force up the cost of housing and thereby exclude lower income individuals from the community.[?]

Glassboro's zoning ordinance is far from unique. To the contrary, critics of metropolitan growth almost invariably talk of suburban zoning as "exclusionary zoning," implying the general transformation of a legitimate government power to protect the welfare of a community to the illegitimate use of zoning to exclude low income individuals from suburban housing opportunities. In the following pages, we examine this transformation of zoning power, highlighting three basic characteristics of land use regulation in the United States that seem most germane to an understanding of the growth of "exclusionary zoning." These are (1) citizen attitudes restricting government regulation of private property; (2) the active role of the courts in the development of zoning law and practices; and (3) the American system of Federalism. Each of these three characteristics has had an independent effect on the development of exclusionary zoning, but perhaps more important they have served to reinforce one another in the historical development of zoning.

Historic Attitudes and Policies Toward
Land Use Regulation

The support of private property is deeply rooted in Anglo-American law and practices. Concerning the fundamental and almost inviolate sanctity of private property, the famous jurist Blackstone went so far as to write: "regard of the law for private property is so great that it will not authorize the least violation of it, not even for the general good of the whole community."[3] Many observers have argued that logically paralleling such a set of beliefs is a general predisposition to reject or limit public policies that interfere with the use of private property.[4]

On the most fundamental level, the sanctity of private property from public control is reflected in the dominant system of land ownership in the United States. Under this system of "fee simple" contracts, a system that developed and expanded dramatically during the 1700s,[5] a property holder owns his land extending from the center of the earth to the sky, and can use and dispose of the land in any way he chooses. Under this system of land ownership, the only justifiable restrictions are generally characterized as "nuisance laws," meaning that an action of a property owner causing harm to a neighbor's property could legitimately be regulated. Even then, courts have historically taken a dim view of this minimal responsibility and regulation.[6]

When land was abundant and neighboring properties far removed from one another, the fee simple system of land ownership was understandable. In fact, fee simple ownership probably served society's purposes very well — under this system of land tenure and minimal control, a rapid settling of the vast and empty American continent took place. Yet, at present, when high density settlement and concentration of the population in metropolitan areas are the dominant characteristics of American society, the fee simple system of land ownership, and the deep respect for the unrestricted use of private property, still predominates, placing restrictions on the ability of society to control metropolitan growth and development.

Similarly reflecting the prevailing attitudes toward land use regulation is the historical record of all levels of government in the

United States in controlling the vast tracts of land they once owned. Through purchases of such territories as Louisiana, Florida, and Alaska, or through treaties with countries such as England and Mexico, the United States federal government, at one time or another, owned over 75 percent of the land in the continental United States, and almost 100 percent of Alaska. The states owned other large tracts of land; in addition many cities such as New York, Detroit, Savannah, and Austin, Texas also owned land near what is now their centers.[7] However, rather than retaining ownership of these lands, and regulating their development and use, or instead of imposing future use restrictions at time of sale, most government lands were literally given away or sold to private users without government restriction on future use or development. While this policy of land transfer was predominant in the 1800s, when rapid development was the goal, its effects are still felt today. On the most concrete level, an opportunity for government to regulate future growth on most of the land in the United States was forever lost. But this is a question of hindsight, and given the hostility toward government regulation and the overwhelming need for development in the U.S. during the 1800s, perhaps more forceful government regulation of land would have been impossible. Yet, the historical residue of this land conversion process still exists to the present, and it has been shown by Sundquist[8] among others that of all the advanced industrial countries in Europe and North America, the United States, by far, has the most minimal government policies regulating land use and community development (see Chapter 1).

The Courts and Land Use Control

The courts in the United States have also been major actors in defining zoning. The courts have set the historical limits on what can be accomplished through zoning by defining the guidelines and boundaries within which zoning can be held as a legitimate use of the police power. Historically, the involvement of the courts in zoning has centered largely on the question of property rights and what is known as the "taking issue."[9]

Theoretically, local governments have a wide range of powers by which to regulate growth. They can purchase land outright from its owners and then decide how to develop it. Similarly, local governments can condemn privately owned land through their power of eminent domain and then compensate the owner for the loss. This condemned land then becomes public property which can be developed as the government sees fit. In either case of eminent domain or purchase, the private property owner has received compensation for his property and the land now belongs to the public.

In contrast, under the system of zoning, land is retained in private hands. Through zoning, the community tells the private property owner that, for the good of the community, only certain kinds of development and use of that land are now allowed. As a result of zoning regulations, a private property owner may be deprived of full use of his land and may be effectively deprived of its most profitable use. But recall that the private property owner received *no* compensation for his loss. As a result, land owners frequently appeal to the courts claiming that their property has been "taken" by government and that they have been deprived of property without due process of law. In response, the local government must show that the zoning regulation actually furthers the public welfare and that a "compelling state interest" has been served by the zoning regulation.

Since a private property owner is unlikely to find most reasons sufficiently compelling to justify the loss of the unrestricted and perhaps most profitable use of his property, court battles over the legitimacy and legality of local zoning laws have been common. The decisions rendered by courts have helped to set the limits on how far local governments can go in regulating property and land development.

Further, while most of the involvement of the courts in zoning has focused on the issue of property rights, the courts have also been involved in zoning and community development on other levels as well. In the United States, courts have the authority to judge whether rights other than property rights (such as equal protection of the law, or the right to travel) have been infringed upon by local zoning laws and policies. As a result, the courts can and do intervene frequently in zoning law on a variety of issues, and much of zoning practice reflects this intervention.

Federalism and Land Use Control

A final factor conditioning zoning and growth policy in the United States is the presence of a multi-tier system of government. Under present constitutional arrangements, it is the governments of the individual states that have the most power, constitutionally, to regulate growth. Historically, however, the states have almost completely delegated this power to local governments allowing individual municipalities the right to formulate and implement zoning and growth policy virtually unrestricted by state guidance.[10] As a result, most growth and zoning policy is really formulated by the large numbers of individual local governments found in metropolitan regions. The tensions between local governments, which desire to retain control over zoning and community development, and state governments (and to a somewhat lesser extent, the federal government) desiring more integrated and coordinated growth has become a fairly common ingredient of the zoning and community development policy arena.

These three factors, respect for private property, the intervention of the courts, and American federalism, have all had individual effects in creating zoning law and community development policy as practiced by local governments. But a historical investigation of the growth of zoning and an identification of the specific components of zoning law most widely employed by suburbs at the current time, shows that these three factors have interacted over time to further create the broad outlines in which zoning takes place.

The Origin and Growth of Zoning

In the late 1800s, we know that there was a rapid explosion in the size of the American urban population. Moreover, this population growth was fueled mostly by immigrant expansion (see chapter 1). On the east coast, this immigrant population was mostly of Europeans; while on the west coast, there was also a significant number of Orientals. Zoning developed as one means of controlling the location and lifestyle of these immigrants, and of regulating disruptions immigrants were producing in cities.

The earliest and most blatant use of zoning to regulate

immigrant lifestyles and location occurred in San Francisco in the 1880s, and concerned the regulation of the sizable Chinese community. Previous attempts explicitly to regulate the location of the Chinese population by passing legislation dealing with them as an identifiable race were declared unconstitutional under the Fourteenth Amendment to the United States Constitution. As a result, an alternate constitutionally acceptable means of regulating the Chinese was sought. It was observed by San Franciscans that laundries were a focal point in the Chinese community. It was reasoned that the distribution of the Chinese population could be controlled by regulating the location of these laundries. As a result, San Francisco adopted a series of local ordinances banning laundries from most parts of the city — eventually shutting down about 300 such businesses. These laundries were, however, allowed to remain in the areas ("zones") of the city that the white population was willing to tolerate as a Chinese ghetto. The legal justification of such regulation was that the laundries were a public nuisance, represented a significant threat to the public's safety, and had to be restricted to areas where they would do the least damage. In 1886, the California Supreme Court upheld this regulation as a legitimate exercise of the police power of the state, neglecting the clear racial implications of the policy. Thus, San Francisco had used zoning laws to achieve segregation, and the exclusionary impact of such regulation was given judicial blessing whereas a specific segregatory policy had previously failed.

After this California court decision, San Francisco, followed by Los Angeles and other California cities, quickly adopted a series of ordinances restricting the location of a growing variety of land uses. The restrictions were, as in the case of the Chinese laundries, based on the police power and supposedly designed to protect the health and safety of the population from noxious and dangerous land development. In actuality a variety of social goals, including racial segregation, was also served.

While these events were taking place in California, the cities in the east were also experiencing the rapid influx of an immigrant population. In response to this, large-scale tenement districts were being created. These tenement districts were uniformly characterized by disease, crowding, and social disorder. To control such conditions, cities began to draft regulations on the size and height of buildings — regulations designed to increase ventilation and light in apartments and to decrease crowding. These regulations were justified under the police power of the state as attempts to improve the health and safety of the population. As such, they were legally acceptable.

These local laws regulating the location of businesses, building size, hazardous land development, and density were all early prototypes of the more comprehensive zoning laws that would soon emerge. But all these early regulations were piecemeal, dealing with one condition at a time and usually covering only a geographically small section of the city. The development of a more comprehensive approach to zoning and growth regulation awaited a social and political movement that could articulate the need for comprehensive growth controls in the cities, and a movement that could successfully fight for a comprehensive approach to growth. The Progressive Reform Movement of the early 1900s provided such an opportunity.

Progressives and the City Planning Movement

As the quality of urban life in the United States appeared to deteriorate under the pressure of urban expansion, and as the government of most cities proved incapable of dealing with the problems of governing an expanding metropolis, a Progressive Movement stressing good government and the reform of social institutions emerged. The Progressives were interested in a variety of issues concerning urban life and government, including the question of planning and regulated growth. In their general approach to government and the problems of cities, Progressives emphasized a scientific and rational search for solutions. The city planning movement provided such a rational, scientific approach to the specific question of urban growth. As a result, the Progressive Movement and the infant city planning movement intertwined frequently.

Consider as an example of the concern for rationality of city growth one of the very first acts of the modern city planning movement, the Chicago World's Fair of 1893. As part of the Fair, the leading architects in the United States had collaborated to produce the "White City" — a closely planned and integrated group of buildings portraying the best results of rational city planning. By all accounts, the results were nothing less than spectacular. As a direct outgrowth of this display, a "City Beautiful Movement" emerged calling for planned growth and the replication of the results of the White City elsewhere. Indeed, springing out of this set of events, in 1901 the first meeting of American planners was held in Washington, D.C. and rationally planned and scientifically sound growth became a much talked about goal. This "planning" approach to growth management struck responsive chords among Progressives.

Other important forces supporting city planning also appeared in the early 1900s. The experiences of European countries, Germany in particular, in regulating growth through a system of zones restricting building size and construction styles became known to American planners and became part of their approach to growth management.

At about the same time in England, Ebenezer Howard published a seminal work entitled "Garden Cities of Tomorrow." This book had an enormous impact on the American planning movement. In his work, Howard stressed the need for limited and balanced community development and the conscious control of growth to preserve community health and well-being. Howard called for the construction of "garden cities" — carefully planned and balanced communities in which all growth and development would be integrated with existing activities. In 1903, following the surge of interest in Howard's work, construction of the first garden city actually began in England, the city of Letchworth about 35 miles north of London.

The impact of these events on the American city planning movement can be imagined. The status and importance of planners increased and their ability to actually control growth and development in a rational and planned manner seemed great. As their status increased, city planners also became increasingly influential in the Progressive Reform Movement stressing rational government of urban areas. It was only a matter of time before the ideas of city planners began to have an impact on existing laws governing growth.

But in fact, while these general social and political movements might have produced a comprehensive growth plan in any number of large American cities, the drafting of the first comprehensive zoning law in the United States finally took place in New York City between 1913 and 1916. And the actual impetus for comprehensive zoning in New York was produced by two problems specific to New York that magnified the general problems other cities were facing.

New York and the Birth of Comprehensive Zoning

In the early 1900s, not only was New York experiencing rapid population growth, but it was also experiencing a vast increase in the rate of skyscraper construction, intensifying the general problems of urban growth. Between 1890 and 1910, following the introduction of steelframe construction and efficient elevators, the entire skyline of lower Manhattan was transformed as larger and taller buildings appeared in rapid succession.

But the rush to the construction of skyscrapers was unplanned and often had adverse effects on surrounding properties. Skyscrapers invariably cast their shadows on neighboring buildings, depriving them of light and air. This was a direct threat to the property values of smaller, overshadowed buildings, as well as a threat to the health of the people who worked in them. Furthermore, the concentration of large office buildings in a small area around Wall Street in lower Manhattan began to create problems resulting from congestion and the intense demand for transportation, water, fire protection, and other services. As a result, calls for the regulation of skyscrapers began to emerge. Eventually these demands would help produce the first comprehensive zoning plan to be drafted.

However, an additional set of conditions also was at work in New York. As the mass transportation system improved in American cities, exclusive shopping districts began to emerge (see chapter 1). In New York City, this district was concentrated on Fifth Avenue. A substantial part of the sales in these department stores were of ready-made clothing, one of the major innovations in the life style of turn-of-the-century America. This ready-made clothing was manufactured by small-sized firms constituting the garment industry. To minimize shipping costs these firms wanted to be as close as possible to their retail outlets. As a result, garment firms located in the lofts and buildings bordering Fifth Avenue. This inevitably caused congestion on the Avenue, to the consternation to the proprietors of the exclusive department stores. But even worse, the workers in the garment firms, mostly first or second generation immigrants, had the audacity to walk on Fifth Avenue during their lunch breaks. This presented an appalling image problem to the Fifth Avenue stores, all of which catered to the "carriage trade" and which desired to spare their elite customers the degradation of rubbing shoulders with the masses. As a result of the congestion caused by the garment industry, the exclusive department stores began to move further north up Fifth Avenue seeking escape. But following the understandable desire of the garment industry to be close to its retail outlets, the garment firms marched up Fifth Avenue right alongside the department stores.

Recognizing the inexorable forces contained in the economics of the situation, retailers and department store owners in particular formed the Fifth Avenue Association in an attempt to pressure local government regulation of the garment industry and to prevent the industry's further spread. This Fifth Avenue Association, acting out of its own selfish needs to protect the image of its member stores, provided the organization and financial support for the zoning movement that culminated in New York City between 1913-1916.[11]

Thus, the developing desire for increased land use regulation grew out of the general conditions of city growth at the turn of the century — immigrant population expansion, rapid increases in the physical heights of buildings, the development of conflicting land uses in cities that had not yet burst outwards. In addition, a conscious concern for regulating and planning growth and development was also part of a growing Progressive Reform movement and a newly developing city planning movement.

In New York City, these general problems were made more

intense by the construction of large skyscrapers and by the growth of a garment industry. Thus, it is not really surprising that when municipal reformers finally captured control of New York City government in 1910 and faced the problems associated with New York's growth, they turned to zoning as a possible solution. In 1913, reformers created a Heights of Buildings Commission charged with formulating a government response to the problems of growth. In 1913, the Commission issued a report calling for zoning and this report eventually led to the passage of the nation's first comprehensive zoning law in 1916.

Yet, if zoning was the child of reform, when the ordinances were finally drafted between 1913 and 1916, the product was more the work of lawyers than of planners. This had significant impact on the future of zoning and caused major changes in zoning's rationale and use. While planners believed in the need to regulate growth as a legitimate function of government, the lawyers drafting the zoning legislation, acting with an eye toward eventual court challenge, based zoning on the police power and the right to regulate land use to protect health and safety. Further, while planners believed in the integrity and worth of their plans for the general citizenry, the political justification for zoning devised by lawyers was the need to protect the property values of Fifth Avenue merchants and the owners of downtown skyscrapers. This limited political base was expanded eventually by appealing to home owners throughout the city by the extensive designation of single family zoning districts in which multi-family housing was barred. In fact, one could argue that comprehensive zoning was formulated to protect property interests in Manhattan but included the entire city just to make it legally defensible and more politically acceptable.[12]

The history and development of the 1916 zoning ordinances in New York City is interesting in its own right, but more important is the impact that New York's experience has had on zoning law and municipal growth policy in the more than 50 years since zoning's inception. Much of subsequent zoning law and regulation has adhered surprisingly closely to the original guidelines set forth in New York City in 1916.[13] This can be seen in a simple enumeration of some of the characteristics of the 1916 law that have prevailed to the present.

First, and perhaps most important, was the justification of
zoning in the police power rather than in any inherent right of
government to control growth itself. This has reinforced the
system of public regulation of private land, rather than public
ownership. Second, was an emphasis on single family homes. In
New York City, this took the form of "cumulative zoning,"
implying a hierarchy of land uses. Residential land use was the
"highest" category of development, a category within which single
family development was the pinnacle. Following this residential
category were commercial zones. And last, was an unrestricted
category of land, reserved mostly for industrial development.
Under this system, higher uses could locate in lower zones, but not
vice versa. Thus, a single family home could locate anywhere,
while a factory was limited to just an industrial district. While
zoning codes actually based on cumulative zoning are not all that
widespread, the emphasis on single family homes is quite common
in zoning law. Further, zoning ordinances specified permitted
land uses and set "use standards." Under this concept, things not
specifically permitted, especially in the residential and
commercial zones, were denied development rights. But these
standards and zones were not to be applied to existing buildings
and development but only to future ones. Thus a business or
factory already in a residential zone did not have to close down,
and the rights and property interests of existing owners were only
marginally affected. Finally the 1916 law included extensive
appeals procedures both administrative and judicial to allow the
future application of zoning laws to be challenged.

Yet there is one basic deficiency in the 1916 zoning law seen in
each one of these above provisions, and it is a failure that persists
to the current time. This failure is that in 1916, as in most zoning
ordinances following, zoning was formulated without a guiding
growth plan for future development. In other words, zoning was
reactive to change and to political demands rather than trying to
lead or guide growth. Zoning was, therefore, not conceived and
implemented as a planning tool for balanced and controlled
growth, the concept as originally conceived by the city planning
movement and by municipal reformers. Instead, zoning law
reflected the existing power of private property owners and the

hesitance of American government to try to regulate effectively those interests.

Yet despite these major deficiencies, or perhaps because of them, in New York in 1916, and other places since, the cooperation and agreement of business and government officials, along with the support of reformers, was forthcoming. In New York, the system of zoning was rapidly given legal authority by required enabling legislation on the part of the New York State legislature. Upon this political success in New York, zoning spread rapidly throughout the United States. Demand by local governments for information about zoning was so phenomenal that in 1924 the United States Department of Commerce drafted a Standard State Enabling Act designed to quicken state legislative action necessary to enable localities to zone. Further, many of the provisions of this Standard Act borrowed heavily from the New York City experience, helping to institutionalize the inherent weaknesses of zoning.

Despite its rapid spread, a major question concerning the constitutionality of zoning still remained. After all, even if minimally, zoning still regulated private property and was therefore conceivably a violation of the due process clause of the Constitution. However, in 1926 in *Euclid v. Ambler*, the U.S. Supreme Court held that zoning was a legitimate use of the police power and hence constitutional. Following this decision, the already rapid spread of zoning accelerated even further. Many of the communities to adopt zoning ordinances after the Supreme Court's ruling in *Euclid* were newly formed suburbs seeking to gain greater control over their development in one of the decades of most rapid suburbanization of this century.

Zoning in the Suburbs

Zoning thus became a basic government power to regulate and control community growth. Without doubt, when used properly, zoning gives metropolitan communities and their planners tools to regulate undesirable growth and to promote more harmonious and pleasing patterns of development than may be produced by the unfettered workings of the land market and economy. However, at present, significant problems attend the use of zoning laws in suburbia.

As we have seen, while established originally in response to the problems of big city expansion, zoning diffused rapidly throughout the metropolitan area. Yet, if zoning in the city sought to protect property values of both business and home owners, once zoning moved from the city to the suburbs, it began to be used almost exclusively for the protection of single family residential development from other land uses. Early suburban zoning ordinances began to exclude business and industry from locating in many suburban communities and also began to exclude multiple family dwellings. This exclusionary use of zoning may have distorted the economically efficient development of suburbia by overly restricting the operation of a free land market and by denying land to business expansion,[14] but more importantly, the establishment and reinforcement of class and race segregation between cities and suburbs, and among suburbs, became a part of zoning practice.

While explicit segregation through zoning was, of course, unconstitutional, segregation through zoning was nonetheless achieved in suburbs by the careful use of small, closely defined zoning districts in which only high cost housing was permitted. This expensive housing then could only be afforded by white middle and upper class residents, and segregation was accomplished through legally accepted land use policies.[15]

Thus, what has emerged in zoning practice is a system of laws written and administered by local governments operating under state government authority, but with only minimal state guidance. Further, this system of laws has been used for exclusionary purposes to further inequalities in metropolitan growth. It is the actual components of zoning law that accomplish this exclusion to which we now turn.

The Tools of Growth Control: Zoning Mechanisms

Zoning provides a variety of means through which suburbs try to regulate growth and control the composition of development. The usual provisions of zoning ordinances that affect the cost, the timing, and the composition of growth have been identified as have their intended purposes. Briefly they are as follows.[16]

(1) Large lot zoning. The specification of minimum acreage per home is probably the most common attempt at controlling suburban growth. Setting minimum lot sizes of one acre is not uncommon — one study found that over ¾ of available land in northeastern New Jersey suburbs was zoned for one acre or more. Such a large lot zoning strategy has various intentions, the most frequently noted are exclusionary and fiscal. Suburban communities, it is argued, establish zones with high minimum acreage to force up the cost of housing. This supposedly increases the residential tax base. At the same time, low density development hopefully minimizes demands for increased services that might occur with more rapid population growth. Concurrently, by keeping home costs high, a social exclusion of low income groups may also result. In addition, large lot zoning is often seen as an attempt to preserve a rural community character, one of the major social values embodied in suburban expansion.

(2) Minimum floor space or minimum building size. Local zoning ordinances frequently require that new construction be of a certain minimum size, that is, the zoning law sets the minimum square feet that a house must contain. Since there is a direct relationship between increased size and increased cost, suburbs try to keep the cost of housing and subsequently the income and class levels of its residents high by using this zoning mechanism. Indeed, partly as a result of such zoning regulations the average size of suburban houses in the United States has increased by over 50 percent in the last two decades, pushing up the cost of housing beyond the means of most low and moderate income families.

(3) Bans on the construction of multiple family dwellings. A survey by the U.S. Department of Housing reported that 99 percent of undeveloped land in the United States zoned for residential use is zoned for single family homes. A similar survey in northeastern New Jersey showed only ½ of 1 percent of residential land zoned for multiple family dwellings. These studies further show that while some additional land may be available for multiple family construction, this land was located in commercial and industrial districts and not residential areas.[17] This is not to say that multiple family dwellings are not being built in suburbia.

In fact, since 1957 the rate of increase of multiple family construction in the suburbs has been unprecedented.[18] However, these surveys do show that land *already* zoned for multiple family use is almost impossible to find. As a result, *rezoning* for suburban multiple family housing construction must take place. Suburbs can then regulate the type of multiple family construction by rezoning for only the most exclusive and expensive proposed developments and refusing to rezone for the construction of low income housing.

(4) Restrictions on bedrooms. Even when multiple family dwellings are approved, it is frequent to find zoning restrictions on the number of bedrooms allowed, as in the Glassboro zoning ordinance discussed above. One or two bedroom maximums for apartments are common. Fiscally, the intention of such restrictions is to minimize the number of school age children found in an apartment complex and reduce service demands that might necessitate increased taxes. The zoning also excludes from the community larger families that cannot afford to purchase single family housing with more bedrooms.

(5) Prohibitions on mobile homes. These prohibitions are in part socially motivated, that is, suburban residents may be offended aesthetically by mobile homes ("trailer parks") and by the image of the types of people who live in them. But part of the objection is also based on fiscal grounds, the low value of mobile homes seems to imply that they would create a negative fiscal impact if allowed. However, since mobile homes can be built and sold at a fraction of regular housing costs, the prohibition on mobile homes has an escalating effect on suburban housing cost, thereby excluding low and moderate income groups from suburbia.

(6) Prohibitions on subsidized housing. The intention of such prohibitions is obvious — these zoning laws are designed *specifically* to exclude low income people from a community. However, the legality of these explicit bans has been the subject of judicial scrutiny[19] and the continued ability of suburbs to maintain such bans is questionable. Furthermore, the construction of subsidized housing has recently become of greater concern to the U.S. Department of Housing and Urban

Development and pressure on suburbs to accept subsidized housing may increase (see the section on Federal government responses to exclusionary zoning below).

(7) Administrative delays. Complex administrative requirements for such things as permits for construction are frequently embodied in zoning laws. These delays may have a considerable impact on housing prices by increasing accumulated interest costs. In large multiple family construction projects, delays are usually the most severe and can in fact make such development unprofitable, if not impossible.

(8) Frontage requirements and other subdivision standards. Such requirements regulating sewer lines, sidewalk paving, and street paving all have an impact on housing. Municipalities can require stringent subdivision regulations and thereby force up the cost of housing.

While zoning may have been originally designed to protect neighbors from the nuisances of unrestricted land use, and to protect the health and safety of community residents, many of the above provisions of zoning law have obviously moved beyond these valid concerns to produce exclusionary and unbalanced patterns of suburban development. Moreover, in addition to these zoning laws, other government powers have been used for exclusionary purposes through the manipulation of housing cost.

A Further Road to Exclusion: Building Codes

While zoning regulates the availability and cost of land and to an extent the construction of buildings, a more direct effect on actual construction costs is through municipally enforced building codes.

The specific effect of certain building code regulations on the cost of housing can be seen immediately by a single condition that a local building code may require: a full basement, if required by law, can add upwards of $3000 to the cost of a new house. Similarly, building codes specifying an additional ⅛ to ¼ inch of external wall thickness can add between $2200 and $4500 to construction costs. The list goes on.[20] These code requirements having an immediate effect on housing costs can be manipulated by communities to keep housing costs high and as a result, keep low and moderate income families out.

In general, building codes have been indicted for being outmoded and retarding the development of an efficient home building industry by preventing mass production of cheaper housing. But despite these long-standing complaints, changes in building codes have been slow in coming. Thus, most suburbs still require on-site inspection of new construction, and most suburbs have building codes that differ from those found in neighboring jurisdictions. Mass construction techniques, making possible cheaper housing, are barred by such patterns of code enforcement. Similarly, building codes frequently prohibit the use of new building materials or the use of prefabrication procedures that would also reduce the cost of housing. An example is that of plastic pipes (pvc) for waste water and drainage. Such pipes are light, flexible, and much cheaper than metal pipes, yet they are just as durable. However, the building codes of most suburbs ban their use, thus adding to the cost of housing, and again, such high costs having necessary exclusionary impact on class and racial segregation.[21]

In fact, given these costs, Anthony Downs[22] singles out building codes and not zoning as the single most important factor forcing up the cost of suburban housing and helping to create the economic and social inequalities in metropolitan areas. According to Downs, building codes make it impossible to build new low quality but perfectly safe and acceptable housing in most suburbs, especially the most exclusive suburbs with the most stringent codes. As a result of the prohibitions and restrictions of zoning and building codes, virtually all unsubsidized new housing is out of reach of most Americans. Indeed, estimates run as high as 75 percent of the total population, and of course 100 percent of low and moderate income families may be excluded from new housing in suburbia.[23].

Fiscal Exclusion vs. Social Exclusion
Suburban Motives and Community Development

In explaining the patterns of suburban inequalities and the use of zoning laws and building codes to produce them, there exists a common assumption that these are created by the actions of suburban governmental officials concerned mostly with the *fiscal base* of their local communities and the adverse impact of services and on taxes of an influx of low or moderate income people. This belief is usually termed, "fiscal zoning," and implies that suburban development policies are made with an eye on the local fiscal situation. According to this belief, suburbs formulate growth policy to maximize tax revenues in relation to service demands. The argument in support of fiscal zoning is compelling, and has been developed in some detail in Chapter 2. The basic components of the argument can be simply restated: (1) there is a multiplicity of independent suburban jurisdictions in metropolitan areas; (2) these suburbs must use the property tax extensively to pay for local services; (3) the property tax rate varies according to the level of wealth in a community; and (4) poor communities frequently tax themselves heavily to finance even minimal services, while rich communities tax themselves at lower rates to provide much better services. As a result, the argument continues, communities have incentives to plan and regulate growth on fiscal grounds rather than on the basis of broader considerations such as environment, balanced community growth, etc.[24] While this development strategy is most frequently referred to as "fiscal zoning," more colorfully it can be viewed as "fiscal mercantilism" — the effort to export service costs to other municipalities while importing tax resources.[25] Perhaps equally concisely, the system of zoning based on local taxes and associated fiscal considerations has been described as designed to maximize the incentives of communities to "kick the poor around."[26]

Empirical Evidence for Fiscal Zoning

Given the strong support in logic for fiscal zoning, it is surprising that empirical data documenting the widespread use of fiscal motivations is quite sparse. Some examples of empirical evidence supporting fiscal zoning occur in the following works:

First, studies of the location of taxable business and industrial property show inequalities produced by fiscal zoning. These studies usually begin by analyzing the "profitability" of different kinds of development to suburban governments, and by indicating a "pecking order" of fiscally attractive development. With regard to business growth, studies show that commercial development usually generates more tax revenues than it costs to service, while industrial development is less attractive. With regard to residential development, high cost housing is usually viewed as more fiscally attractive than low cost housing.[27] In a concrete fashion, suburbs now reflect this fiscal reasoning by vastly overzoning for large lot, expensive single family homes. But even more interesting is that suburbs now overzone for industrial and commercial development (a reverse of earlier patterns of excluding industry and commerce). As an example, Princeton, New Jersey has zoned enough land for business use to create 1.2 million jobs in that suburb alone while restricting the supply of housing.

A recent study by William A. Fischel[28] gives more meaning to the relationship between fiscal zoning and business location. Using the case of Northeastern, New Jersey, and focusing on the relative impact on taxes and services of business development, Fischel tries to estimate the relative tax advantage accruing to communities by attracting either commercial or industrial growth. His analysis shows that both commercial and industrial property taxes enable communities to lower residential property taxes, raise service levels, in particular school expenditures, or do both. However, comparing industrial to commercial development, Fischel estimates that about 70 percent of commercial property tax payments can be used to lower taxes or improve services, while only about 50 percent of industrial tax payments are so available. (The remaining tax revenues are apparently used for other than local educational services, particularly for those services related to controlling the environmental impact of development. Assumably, since the environmental impact of industrial development is greater than the impact of commercial development, more tax money generated from industrial growth must be devoted to environmental protection, leaving less money left over for tax relief or increased educational expenditures.) As a result of such differentials in fiscal impact, Fischel argues that commercial development is more attractive to suburbs than is industrial development.

But where Fischel makes his most interesting observations concerns the competition between suburban communities for the location of more desirable commercial development in comparison to the less attractive industrial development. Fischel shows that in this competition, the richest suburbs experience the most success — that is, they attract the best commercial development. On the other hand, the poorest suburbs lose out and attract only the less fiscally attractive industrial development. The explanation presented is simple given the system of local taxes and fiscal zoning — richer suburbs already have lower tax rates and are hence in a more competitive situation to attract the more desirable commercial development. In contrast, poorer suburbs have higher taxes and are therefore less competitive.

But consider the implications of this pattern of fiscal zoning over the long run — the richer suburbs, already with lower taxes, attract the most fiscally productive development. Their fiscal base improves, their taxes stay low, and they remain in a position competitive to attract even more fiscally productive development. Poorer suburbs, suburbs already with higher tax rates, can attract only industrial development that is not as fiscally productive. As a result, their taxes stay high, and they continue to fail to attract more productive commercial development. In short, the manipulation of fiscal differences allows the rich to get richer and the not-so-rich to fall further behind. In this regard, note that Fischel does not even deal with the least competitive suburb, the type that may fail to attract either kind of development, communities that would fall into the "balanced" or "unannointed" category discussed in Chapter 2. Nonetheless, Fischel's argument does give empirical support for the position that a fiscal motivation operates in zoning and development decisions, and the argument does show how inequalities based on fiscal mercantilism can emerge.

A similar process of fiscal zoning can be implied from data gathered in a comparative analysis of suburban development in Santa Clara County, California and Long Island, New York between 1960 and 1970.[29] The study shows that the most significant improvements in community fiscal wealth (as measured by assessed valuation per capita and tax rate) occurred in communities with concentrations of commerce and industry. Further, over time, the data show an interaction between the residential location of wealthier suburbanites and the location of taxable business development — that is, wealthy residential development and taxable business development occurred in the same communities. This interaction is similar to that implied by Fischel — both upper class residential development and taxable business growth are fiscally "productive," and suburbs now attempt to attract them both in order to maximize fiscal advantage. The compounding of inequalities is evident over time as rich residential suburbs with commercial development use low tax rates to "import" even better fiscal resources and "export" low income groups and high cost development to other suburbs.

Multi-Region Investigations of Fiscal Zoning

While fiscal motives leading to inequalities is evident in these studies, a more direct examination of fiscal zoning appears in the work of Bruce Hamilton et al. investigating fiscal zoning in a sample of metropolitan areas.[30] Hamilton takes an index of clustering of family income in a set of census tracts as a measure of inequality. In areas with greater income inequalities, the clustering index would be higher — low income families would be clustered together and separate from clusters of high income families. Using a set of 19 metropolitan areas, Hamilton sought to explain variation of this index income clustering and the extent to which fiscal motives affected such inequality.

Fiscal incentives were measured by the degree to which state aid formulae for education, the single largest category for government expenditures, compensated local governments for the tax burdens imposed by concentrations of low income families. Such compensatory aid, it was argued by Hamilton, reduces the incentives for fiscally motivated zoning.

In his study, Hamilton also tried to tap another dimension of the fiscal zoning argument by comparing the degree of income clustering in neighborhoods of the central cities in his sample to the suburban part of the SMSA. In this comparison, Hamilton tried to assess the impact of a larger number of taxing districts as found in the suburbs compared to the existence of a single taxing district as found in the central cities. The argument for fiscal zoning, of course, assumes competition between independent local governments, a condition not existing in the central city.

Hamilton's empirical data tend to support the existence of fiscally motivated zoning. In SMSAs with compensatory state aid, income inequalities were less than in SMSAs without such compensatory aid. Similarly, income inequalities were greater between autonomous suburbs with differing tax rates than between neighborhoods in the central cities. Hamilton's findings on fiscal zoning are supported by a recent study of segregation in 100 large metropolitan areas in the United States conducted by Russel Harrison.[31] While concerned mostly with *racial* segregation, Harrison's findings reflect on fiscal motivations as well. In his study, Harrison relates a variety of social and political measures of the characteristics of these 100 SMSAs to the extent of segregation found in them. He finds that the single most important factor affecting the extent of segregation is the number of local governments found in a metropolitan region. Harrison then goes on to argue that greater government fragmentation creates the incentives for racial *and* fiscally motivated zoning by making local growth control policies less visible and more amenable to control by established local elites who can then manipulate local laws and ordinances to their own advantage.[32] In contrast, Harrison argues that in metropolitan areas with less government fragmentation, such elite control over laws is less possible, but just as important, the motivation for exclusion becomes reduced when suburbs are less autonomous and less reliant on small local property tax bases for the funding of services. In general, Harrison's argument is supportive of the existence of fiscal zoning in metropolitan development.

Building on studies such as these, coupled with the powerful logic of the argument, it is reasonable to assume that fiscal motives are responsible for zoning and growth policy in suburbs, and to a degree help explain the existence of inequalities in suburbia. Following the argument of such works, one could argue that the best means to combat suburban inequalities would be through the manipulation of certain public policies.

In particular, given the findings of these studies of fiscal zoning two approaches to reducing inequalities seem to be indicated. First the incentives for fiscal zoning could be reduced by the manipulation of local tax and fiscal policies. In particular, suburbs could be compensated by state government for the tax and service burdens imposed upon them by the location within their borders of large numbers of poor people. Such compensatory aid would reduce the burden of poor residents on local communities and thus make the poor less undesirable as objects of suburban competition. This might have an impact on reducing inequalities as suggested in Hamilton's study. Related to this, the possibilities of fiscal zoning could be reduced by eliminating or reducing government fragmentation. The existence of large numbers of autonomous local governments has repeatedly been shown to be associated with exclusionary growth patterns. Government policies aimed at reducing such fragmentation might then be expected to ameliorate exclusionary growth patterns.

Yet however compelling these arguments may be, there exists a considerable amount of empirical evidence that indicates that fiscal motives may *not* in fact predominate in determining the growth policies of suburbs. The evidence shows that an alternate explanation for exclusion may exist. Simply put this alternate is that suburbs are not motivated by fiscal motives but rather by concerns for social status and the social class of local residents and by the desire to exclude people who have life styles different from the middle class values structuring suburban life.

Two types of evidence seem to be most important in supporting the "social exclusion" rather than the "fiscal zoning" motive of suburban growth. These are the continued preference of suburbs for single family dwellings, and the related sprawling pattern of metropolitan development. Further, the multi-region investigations such as Hamilton and Harrison are frequently not conclusive in their support of fiscal motives, and at least one multi-region study has shown an absence of fiscal effects.

Social Exclusion in Suburban Growth
The Myopia of Single Family Homes

Zoning ordinances give suburbs power to control the kind of housing that will be built in the community. Several alternate forms of housing construction are possible — the five most common are: single family homes, garden apartments, garden condominiums, townhouses, and high rise apartments. Each form of housing, on the average, attracts a different set of people. Some types of housing attract families with children, others are more fitting for childless couples. Therefore, the number of people demanding local services, and in particular the number of pupils to be serviced by the local school district varies directly with the kinds of housing built in a community.

To be more concrete, of the five forms of housing listed above, single family housing is the most likely to attract families with children. This is a function both of demands for space — families with children need more than childless couples — as well as social values endorsing the single family house surrounded by a yard as the ideal location in which to raise children. On the opposite extreme, suburban high rise apartments would be the least likely to attract families with children, being more suitable instead for single people or childless couples. Table 3.1 shows the number of people and pupils that may be expected, on the average, to occupy each type of housing unit.

If the suburbs were strictly following a fiscal zoning strategy, they would zone their communities to allow only the most profitable development, that is, they would follow a strategy that maximizes taxable resources in relation to service demands. A rough means of estimating the profitability of alternate forms of housing is included in Table 3.1. Let us assume that service demands are roughly proportional to the number of people living in an area. More unassailably, we can argue that education expenses are directly proportional to the number of pupils in a school district. Further, let us reasonably assume that the resources available to pay for these services through the property tax is directly proportional to the assessed valuation of residential property, ignoring here the question of industrial/commercial property. The theory of fiscal zoning would lead one to believe that in zoning for residential growth, fiscally "smart" suburbs would zone to include only the most profitable residential development, and exclude the least profitable.

Two columns in Table 3.1, column 4, value per person, and column 6, value per student, give rough estimates of the fiscal profitability of each type of housing. In terms of assessed value per person, it is clear that high rise apartments and townhouses are the most fiscally productive developments. Further, single family housing is about on par with garden condominiums in terms of fiscal worth, but both are less fiscally productive than apartments and townhouses. However, if we remember that the single largest expenditure of suburban government is the school system, and that the largest single component of property taxes is the school tax, perhaps a more valid estimate of fiscal productivity is not value per person but value per pupil. Inspecting the last column of Table 3.1, it becomes immediately apparent that single family homes, even those with high assessed value, do not seem such a fiscal bargain after all. Because of the number of children living in these units, available fiscal resources decrease to the lowest level of all five types of housing surveyed. In contrast, more dense, smaller housing units present a more attractive fiscal base per student.

Yet despite this data showing a poor fiscal contribution of single family housing,[33] we know that suburbs continue to zone overwhelmingly for just this kind of growth, excluding other, more profitable housing. The continued emphasis on "low profit" single family housing in suburbs leads one to wonder if in fact fiscal zoning is the dominant motive. An alternate explanation is one of social values — suburbanites may value an ideal of their community as a semi-rural retreat, and view high density development and the people who would move into such housing as socially unacceptable even if it would be fiscally attractive.[34]

Thus, it is arguable that suburbs may not zone just on fiscal grounds but rather make community development decisions at least in part on the basis of social values that temper fiscal ones.

Table 3-1 Relationship Between Housing Type and Community and School Fiscal Benefits

Type of Housing	Assessed Value	Expected Number of Persons	Value Per Person	Expected Number of Pupils	Value Per Pupil
Garden Apartments					
1 bedroom	$16,290	1.90	$ 8,895	.046	$ 367,826
2 bedroom	$21,600	2.81	$ 7,701	.344	$ 62,790
Townhouse Apartments					
2 bedroom	$30,000	2.68	$11,205	.220	$ 136,364
3 bedroom	$40,000	3.35	$11,943	.655	$ 61,068
Garden Condominiums					
1 bedroom	$25,000	1.90	$13,144	.046	$ 543,478
2 bedroom	$30,000	2.81	$10,695	.344	$ 87,209
Single Family Housing					
4 bedroom	$50,000	4.50	$11,111	1.63	$ 30,675
5 bedroom	$60,000	5.30	$11,320	2.19	$ 27,397
High Rise Apartments					
Studio	$19,200	1.51	$16,681	0	Undefined
1 bedroom	$28,800	1.82	$15,850	.012	$2,400,000
2 bedroom	$33,600	2.48	$13,527	.181	$ 185,635

Source: Adapted from James W. Hughes, "The Fiscal and Social Impact of Alternate Forms of Housing," in Hughes (ed.), *New Dimensions of Urban Planning: Growth Controls* (New Brunswick, New Jersey: Center for Urban Policy Research, 1974), pages 93, 94.

Service Delivery Styles: Sprawling Away Fiscal Advantage

A second set of data also calls into question the predominance of fiscal motivations in land use and growth policy. Communities can zone land in a variety of ways producing alternate settlement patterns. Land can be zoned for clustered development, or else development can occur in a "sprawling" manner of single family homes spread out on large lots. These alternative patterns of development, sprawling vs. clustered, have different public service costs associated with them. A good illustration of this point comes from a technical report prepared for the Howard County, Maryland, Planning Commission in 1967 evaluating the impact on the county services of alternate forms of development. The impetus for the study was the development in Howard County of the new town of Columbia, an example of a highly planned and tightly clustered balanced suburban development.

The report projected into the future three types of development and associated service costs. The first model of development was that of continued sprawl. The model assumed the non-completion of Columbia, and a continuation of settlement trends evident in the mid-1960s. This model projected that almost 90 percent of housing in Howard County would be built in the low density pattern already evident. In contrast, Model II projected a more balanced growth pattern between clustered development as found in Columbia and the usual pattern of suburban sprawl. About equal shares of development by 1985 in the county were placed in each category of clustered and sprawled development.

On the opposite extreme, Model III projected 90 percent of the growth in the county to be along the clustered and highly density patterns as found in Columbia.

Assuming the same magnitude of growth in the county by 1985, that is a population of 68,276 dwelling units, the Planning Commission presented estimates of costs for each type of settlement pattern.

Table 3.2 presents their estimates. Compare the two extremes, Model I, "continued sprawl," to Model III, "closely clustered." Model I, would consume twice as much land as clustered development at about 60 percent additional cost for land alone.

Table 3-2: Cost of Land and of Public Services
Three Models of Suburban Development By 1985:
Howard County, Maryland

	Model I Sprawl	Model II Partly Sprawled Partly Clustered	Model III Closely Clustered
Area of Land (Acres)	61,150	43,225	29,600
Cost of Land (Thousands of Dollars)	$89,820	$64,211	$50,163
Service Costs (Thousands of Dollars)			
Water Utilities Installations	65,011	47,110	32,068
Sewer Installations	83,941	62,770	38,693
Road Installations	54,745	38,072	25,746
Road Maintenance, 1965-1985	20,548	14,773	10,509
County Land Purchases			
Schools, Open Space	3,946	3,839	3,184
School Bus Operation, 1965-1985	23,968	15,254	9,031
Total Service Costs	254,245	181,925	119,381
Total Costs	337,065	246,136	169,544

Source: Adapted from Marion Clawson: *Suburban Land Conversion in the United States* (Baltimore: The Johns Hopkins Press, 1971), page 155.
Notes: All estimates based on 68,276 dwelling units by 1985, up from 13,600 in 1965, but in different degrees of clustering according to the model under consideration.

But more importantly for the argument concerning fiscal zoning is the estimated cost for government services. In the twenty year period surveyed, local government costs of providing services to sprawling suburbs was estimated at well over twice that associated with clustered development ($254 million compared to $119 million). In short, major improvements in the fiscal strength of local governments can be achieved by allowing and encouraging clustered, rather than sprawling development.[35]

Yet we know that suburbs continue to opt for low density growth and turn down plans for more clustered development. This rejection of clustered development is hardly what we would expect if fiscal zoning was the predominant value in suburban growth. Again, an alternative explanation is one based on social values — suburbs seek to exclude those individuals who would live in clustered housing, preferring to make available widely spaced single family housing for middle and upper class families.

A Multi-Region Investigation of Fiscal Motives

A further challenge to the predominance of fiscal motivation in land use regulation can be found in the work of Eric Branfman and his colleagues.[36] Using a sample of 30 SMSAs, Branfman sought to explain variation in the income clustering between suburbs. In this respect, the goals of the Branfman study were the same as Hamilton's and Harrison's, discussed above. However, the results of Branfman's work are contrary to the others.

Branfman and his colleagues tried to explain the degree of inequality in metropolitan areas using seven variables. Four variables measured "fiscal incentives," and three other variables related to the more general social milieux of metropolitan areas. The authors argued that the theory of fiscal zoning predicts that the extent to which local communities are concerned with having poor residents should vary systematically with the level of importance of the local property tax. The general argument is, of course, now clear — given the importance of the local property tax, the poor represent a fiscal burden, but the degree of the burden would vary directly with the importance of local property taxes. Specifically, Branfman argued that fiscal motivation should be stronger in areas where (1) the local property tax is a larger proportion of local citizen's income; (2) the local property tax is more important in generating local revenues; (3) local schools account for larger fractions of local government expenditures, and (4) state aid formulas are not compensatory and equalizing, thus ignoring the existence of poor people in a community.

In addition to these four fiscal conditions, Branfman's investigation included three other explanatory variables related to the more general conditions of the SMSA. The conditions were racial composition of the SMSA, as measured by the proportion of the population 1960 and 1970 that was either black or of Spanish heritage; the availability of low cost housing; and zoning fragmentation as measured by the number of zoning authorities per million population.

Branfman's analysis provided no evidence linking explicit fiscal conditions to inequality. In contrast to the failure of fiscal effects to appear both racial concentration and zoning fragmentation had significant relationships with income inequality. Branfman's data may indicate that local zoning is really designed to exclude blacks as a *racial* group, not necessarily as an *income* group. In most metropolitan areas, disproportionate shares of the poor are black. In such areas, economic integration would effectively mean racial integration. Yet since suburbs cannot design programs designed to be racially exclusive, land use regulation forcing up the cost of housing to produce economic segregation accomplishes racial segregation which may be the real policy goal. As Branfman puts it: "A *class* policy may be the only effective way to achieve *racial* goals."[37] This speculated use of zoning of course parallels the early attempts to control Orientals in San Francisco, where a land use policy was the only way to achieve racial segregation. But the failure of fiscal variables to specifically explain inequalities in the Branfman study, and the possible alternatives of a social (that is, racial) exclusionary motive become important considerations in the study of suburbia.

If in fact it is the case that fiscal motives inform suburban zoning policies, then state intervention in tax structures, in particular with regard to compensatory aid, would be the indicated solution to exclusionary zoning. However, if it is in fact the case that zoning and community development strategies are racially and socially motivated rather than fiscally informed, intervention along tax lines or through tax policy may not be at all effective. This, however, is an issue that is at present unresolved.

Challenges to Exclusionary Zoning

Even with the paucity of information we have concerning the real motives of exclusionary zoning, we know that such exclusion takes place and is widespread across metropolitan areas. We also know that these practices violate the spirit of equality and equity in the United States. This exclusion also violates many laws. As a result, challenges to exclusionary zoning are now common. In particular, three arenas of challenge to the exclusionary practices of local governments have emerged — the courts, the state governments, and the Federal government.

The Courts and Exclusionary Zoning

The most frequent attacks on the exclusionary impact of suburban zoning have occurred through the court system. Through increasingly frequent court cases, both the constitutionality and the legality of suburban zoning policies have been attacked. Many of these challenges have been based on the argument that suburban zoning has deprived individuals of *constitutionally* guaranteed rights, such as equal protection of the law (as in the case of racial discrimination), the right to travel, or due process of law. Other challenges have been based on the argument that exclusionary zoning contradicts the *statutory* guidelines governing suburban zoning by neglecting such concerns as "regional needs," fair and open housing, the terms of Federal grants for community development, or other legal provisions of state and Federal law governing suburbs.

The most aggressive responses to exclusionary zoning have been found in *state* court systems, and, in particular, the state courts of Pennsylvania and New Jersey. By reviewing briefly several recent decisions in those two states, the extent to which the courts can and do get involved in suburban growth and zoning is made clear.

Pennsylvania's State Supreme Court has been a leader throughout the 1960s and 1970s in judicially regulating the exclusionary impact of suburban zoning. In three important decisions between 1966 and 1970, the willingness of that court to actively intervene into zoning was made clear. In 1966, in the case of *National Land*,[38] and again in 1970, in the case of *Kit Mar Builders*,[39] the Pennsylvania Court subjected minimum lot zoning to intensive review, overturning large lot zoning.

The specific judicial grounds for the rejection of these large minimum lot sizes was the "taking issue" — that is, the Court held that the zoning ordinances under challenge were an unjustifiable regulation of private property. However, in the language of its decisions, the Pennsylvania court clearly showed its real concern for the exclusionary impact of minimum lot size, and made clear its intention of strictly reviewing the actions of suburbs that smacked of exclusion. This is clear in the case of National Land in which the Court held:

> Zoning is a tool in the hands of governmental bodies which enables them to more effectively meet the demands of evolving and growing communities. It must not and cannot be used by those officials as an instrument by which they may shirk their responsibilities. Zoning is a means by which a governmental body can plan for the future — it may not be used as a means to deny the future . . . Zoning provisions may not be used . . . to avoid the increased responsibilities and economic burdens which time and natural growth inevitably bring . . . A zoning ordinance whose primary purpose is to prevent the entrance of newcomers in order to avoid future burdens, economic and otherwise, upon the administration of public services and facilities cannot be held valid . . . The general welfare is not fostered or promoted by a zoning ordinance designed to be exclusive and exclusionary.[40]

In other words, if the legal basis for zoning is the "general welfare" and the police power, then zoning that is exclusionary may automatically violate its own very purpose and rationale.

The willingness of the Pennsylvania Court to get even further involved in local growth policy can be seen by a third decision, *Appeal of Girsh*.[41] In this case, the Pennsylvania Court overturned suburban zoning bans on multi-family housing as being exclusionary and violating the justification for zoning in the police power. The Pennsylvania Courts concern for exclusionary zoning continued to be seen in its 1975 decision, *Township of Williston vs. Chesterdale Farms Inc.*,[42] as well as other recent cases.

But while the Pennsylvania Court has been actively reviewing suburban zoning, the Supreme Court of the State of New Jersey has recently emerged as the leader in the judical fight against exclusionary zoning. This is evident in two related decisions, *Mt. Laurel*[43] and *Madison*.[44]

Mount Laurel was a rural township that in the 1960s began to feel pressure from the continuing deconcentration of the urban population in northern New Jersey. In response, the township enacted strict zoning laws permitting essentially the development of only low density single family housing or of multiple family dwellings designed predominantly for childless couples. When challenged in the courts, Mt. Laurel argued that it was only trying to protect itself from the fiscal and social disruptions of uncontrolled and unregulated growth, and hence, its zoning policy was a legitimate use of the police power. The New Jersey

Supreme Court overturned the Mt. Laurel zoning ordinance. In its decision, the New Jersey Court ruled that while the township's zoning ordinance may have in fact protected the welfare of the *individual* community, it had done so at cost to neighboring suburbs that could not regulate growth as effectively. The New Jersey Court argued that the justification for zoning is the *general welfare* not of the *individual* community but rather of the *region* in which a suburb was located. Therefore, the Court held that competitive suburban growth with a "beggar they neighbor" philosophy was necessarily a violation of the general welfare.[45] Rather than each suburb being in competition to exclude housing suitable for low income residents and seeking only fiscally desirable ones, the New Jersey Court argued that every municipality in a region had an obligation to make available "an appropriate variety and choice of housing" and that in formulating local growth policy, each suburb had to "affirmatively afford that opportunity [for low and moderate incoming housing], at least to the exent of the municipality's fair share of the present and prospective regional need."[46]

This decision began drastically to alter the environment of exclusionary zoning in the state by requiring a new set of *regional* welfare considerations in zoning policy. The New Jersey Court went even further in its later ruling in *Madison Township*, decided in January 1977. In this sweeping decision, the Court stepped beyond a piecemeal concern for the individual exclusionary aspects of zoning ordinances to review in a comprehensive fashion all the "cost generating" features of the zoning practices of Madison Township that drove up the cost of housing and helped exclude low and moderate income families. The Court in its ruling then mandated specific changes in the zoning ordinance to allow the construction of "least cost" housing built within the guidelines of health and safety needs, and, thereby, available to a wider range of income groups.

To allow the construction of "least cost" housing in Madison, the Court ordered, among other things, changes in local zoning ordinances to allow: (1) the construction of more small houses on small lots; (2) the enlargement of the zone of multi-family construction and the reduction on the restrictions on density to allow the construction of larger apartments; (3) the more rapid approval of multiple family construction by the simplification of administrative procedures required by the town before construction begins. Consistent with its *Mount Laurel* decision, in *Madison* the New Jersey Court was once again concerned about the competition between suburbs for exclusive development and the adverse effects this competition has on the *general* welfare, defined not in terms of the individual suburb but in terms of the wider region.

The extent of the judicial intervention included in *Madison* is unprecedented. The Court's action not only overturned suburban zoning ordinances that increased the cost of housing, but imposed on suburbs the obligation to encourage and entice low income residential development, by providing the opportunity for the construction of "least cost" housing.

The decisions in Pennsylvania and New Jersey illustrate how sweeping court intervention can be. But the decisions in these two state court systems are not binding in any manner whatsoever on the actions of other state court systems, or on the actions of the Federal judiciary. In fact, the Pennsylvania and New Jersey Courts have been singled out precisely because they are in front of most other courts, and they illustrate what the courts *can* do, not necessarily what they have done. This is apparent when we contrast the active judicial intervention detailed above with the course of action set by the United States Supreme Court and followed by the Federal judiciary in general.

Zoning and the U.S. Supreme Court

While zoning cases usually constitute a considerable proportion of the case load in state court systems, the U.S. Supreme Court has dealt with only a half-dozen or so zoning cases in its entire history. Moreover, four of those decisions occurred within the space of 3 years in the mid-1970s and even further withdrew the Supreme Court and Federal judiciary from the consideration of zoning on constitutional grounds.

The U.S. Supreme Court's involvement with zoning began with its landmark decision in 1926, *Euclid v. Ambler*,[47] in which the Court endorsed the constitutionality of zoning. Previous to that decision, local governments had been adopting zoning at a rapid rate since its introduction in New York City ten years earlier. But despite this widespread use, zoning was still viewed cautiously by local governments. However, in *Euclid*, not only did the Supreme Court find zoning a constitutionally acceptable use of the police power, but also extended to local government zoning ordinances what is called the "presumption of legality." Under this ruling, the Court held that local zoning ordinances should be presumed valid, and the burden of proving otherwise placed on the person or party who objected to the local zoning law. This "presumption" constitutes strong judicial support. In 1928, in its *Nectow*[48] ruling, the Court reaffirmed its stand in *Euclid*, adding, however, the condition that zoning must be "reasonable" to be considered constitutional. The net impact of these two decisions was to deliver Federal judicial blessing to zoning.

After these cases, the Court literally withdrew from zoning law, refusing to hear any further zoning cases. This withdrawal persisted despite the frequent zoning cases in state courts, and in lower Federal Courts, and despite the accumulating evidence of the exclusionary impact of local zoning. In 1962, after thirty-four years, the Court finally did hear another zoning case, *Goldblatt v. Town of Hempstead*.[49] However, this case did not involve residential development of suburbs, but rather concerned a zoning regulation that prohibited a mining company from digging below the Town of Hempstead's water table, an action the town contended would destroy the suburb's source of water. In this case, the Court held that the town's regulation of the mining property was constitutional since it protected the health and safety of the residents, even if the zoning regulation almost totally destroyed the value of the land to the mining company. In practical terms, the decision signaled the willingness of the Supreme Court to allow extremely stringent zoning regulation of private property when a legitimate health or safety interest was at stake. In general, then, the Court viewed zoning favorably as it had done thirty years earlier.

After *Goldblatt*, it was more than ten years before the Court heard another case explicitly concerned with suburban zoning. The Court then heard several cases in rapid succession. However, the cumulative impact of these decisions seems to assure that future zoning cases will not come its way.

In the first case in this "series," *Belle Terre*,[50] the Court upheld an "anti-grouper" ordinance enacted by an exclusive residential suburb in New York. The zoning ordinance limited development in the village to single family homes and restricted occupancy of these homes to families or to groups of unrelated individuals numbering less than three. The Court's decision showed a general unwillingness on its part to get involved with the local community decision making process, and a willingness to tolerate highly restrictive suburban zoning laws, in the name of the general welfare. Thus, in its decision, the Court held that:

> A quiet place where yards are wide, people few, and motor vehicles restricted are legitimate guidelines in a land use project addressed to family needs. The police power is not confined to elimination of filth, stench, and unhealthy places. It is ample to lay out zones where family values, youth values, and the blessings of quiet seclusion and clean air make the area a sanctuary for people.[51]

In short, while the state courts in New Jersey and Pennsylvania have tried to restrict the use of the general welfare clause in justifying zoning, the U.S. Supreme Court has taken a contrary view. Further, the Supreme Court's essential disposition to endorse local zoning policies was made even more clear in another action by the Court in 1975 in *Warth* v. *Seldin*.[52]

In its decision in *Warth*, the Court severely restricted the kinds of people who could bring suit against zoning cases in the Federal Courts. The Court specifically ruled that the following types of individuals had no "standing" to sue suburbs over zoning: (1) poor individuals who had argued that they would be potential residents of the suburb except for the existence of the exclusionary zoning ordinance; (2) taxpayers in a neighboring jurisdiction who had argued they had to bear the tax burden of successful exclusion redirecting lower income growth into their community; and (3) builders who had not tried to obtain a zoning amendment within the localities administrative and legal mechanisms that would have allowed the construction of multi-family housing they desired to build. In general, the Supreme Court in this ruling severely restricted the introduction of regional considerations into possible Federal judicial review of local zoning;[53] this in direct contrast with the attempt of New Jersey to expand consideration of this direction.

But the intention of the Court to limit Federal Court involvement is even clearer in two more recent cases, that of *Petaluma*[54] and of *Arlington Heights*.[55]

The city of Petaluma is a distant suburb of San Francisco, located in rapidly expanding Marin County. However, Petaluma itself was not subject to suburban expansion until the 1960s. But when suburbanization began, it threatened rapidly and totally to transform the city from a small, mostly rural town into a rapidly growing suburban city. In response to intense growth pressure, the city adopted a series of zoning ordinances restricting the rate of construction of new housing units to about 500 units per year and setting up strict guidelines governing the location of such construction. These types of zoning laws, generally called "development timing ordinances," had been used elsewhere, most notably in the village of Ramapo, New York, where a New York state court had found it a valid tool of growth management.[56] However, when Petaluma tried to impose such restrictions, builders in the area immediately filed suit in Federal District Court. The choice of the Federal court rather than a state court was probably the result of the builder's perception that the California state courts have traditionally shown a willingness to tolerate strict land use management, while the Federal courts have had a different more anti-restriction orientation.[57] The Federal District Court, in fact, ruled in favor of the builders and overturned the city's regulation. The district court ruled that Petaluma's zoning violated the constitutional right to travel. Yet despite this constitutional justification of the District Court's reversal of the zoning law, embodied in the decision was a particular concern for the impact such restrictions would have on lower income groups, whose ability to find housing in the area would be most affected.[58]

However, the U.S. Court of Appeals reversed the lower court's ruling. The Appeals Court did not even discuss the constitutional issue of the right to travel, and instead argued that the zoning ordinances enacted by Petaluma served a legitimate state interest in controlling the disruptions of growth, even though the court conceded exclusion by race and by class would inevitably result. Further, the Appeals Court decision included language that restricted sharply the possibilities of any future judicial intervention into local zoning decisions. Specifically the Appeals Court argued that:

> If the present system of delegated zoning power does not effectively serve the state interest in furthering the general welfare of the region or entire state, it is the state legislature's and not the Federal Court's role to intervene and adjust the system.[59]

The Appeals Court obviously believed that the zoning reform attempted in the courts in New Jersey and Pennsylvania should not be attempted by the Federal courts. Rather than redefining zoning from a local to a regional policy via judicial review, the Appeals Court argued that the redefinition should take place through state legislative action.

The U.S. Supreme Court refused to hear further appeals from this judgment, in effect allowing the Appeals Court ruling to become accepted policy. This signaled a Supreme Court withdrawal from zoning, placing the burden of zoning reform on other branches of government.

The reluctance of the Supreme Court to intervene in local zoning was once again reinforced in the 1977 case of *Arlington Heights*. Arlington Heights, a suburb of Chicago, had refused to rezone a fifteen acre parcel of land from single family to multiple family zoning to allow the construction of subsidized low income housing. The Metropolitan Housing Authority, the sponsor of the proposed construction, filed suit on the grounds of racial exclusion. The Federal District Court upheld the village's right to refuse the rezoning. However, the Court of Appeals for the Seventh Circuit reversed that lower court ruling and held that Arlington Heights was pursuing a racially discriminatory growth policy. While the Appeals Court agreed that the village was trying to follow a long established zoning plan and trying to protect property values, it held that this did not constitute a compelling state interest sufficient to justify racially discriminatory impact. When the case reached the Supreme Court, however, the Court ruled that the village's actions were constitutionally acceptable.

The decision conceded exclusionary *impact* but argued that discriminatory *motives* or *intent* could not be proven. Hence, on constitutional grounds, the Court argued that suburbs can have zoning ordinances that have racially exclusionary impact, so long as it cannot be proven that the zoning was drafted specifically to achieve that goal. But recall Branfman's argument presented above, or the case of California's early attempts to regulate the Chinese community through zoning. In both cases, it was seen that an alternate means of achieving racial segregation through land use was found because racial segregation *per se* was unconstitutional. The Arlington Heights decision may allow suburbs to continue to achieve racial segregation through land use policy.

There is, however, one major caveat that must be introduced. The ruling in Arlington Heights limited judicial review on *constitutional* grounds. It did not disqualify further judicial challenges to zoning on *statutory* grounds. In particular, in its decision, the Supreme Court specifically ruled that the zoning ordinance be reviewed in the lower courts to see whether or not it violated the Fair Housing Act — a review on statutory grounds independent of the constitutional issues rejected by the Court.

From this series of decisions, it seems that the Supreme Court wants to remove the Federal judiciary from active consideration of local zoning on constitutional grounds and leave it to both the state legislatures and the Congress to draft legal constraints and changes in zoning practice. As a result, the active judicial intervention, seen in states such as New Jersey and Pennsylvania is unlikely to be duplicated on the Federal level. Reforms of suburban growth then will come not from Federal court action, but legislative action. Such reforms are now taking place.

Federal Government Responses

During the 1960s, the Federal government involvement in land use and community development in metropolitan areas expanded greatly. One major avenue of Federal government expansion centered on the growing concern in the 1960s and 1970s for environmental pollution and its control. Thus, the Clean Air and

Air Quality Acts of 1970, and their various amendments increased Federal government concern with suburban development through the impact of such development on air quality. Similarly, the Water Pollution Control Act of 1972 vastly increased the Federal government's concern for water management, and expanded the Federal government interest in water supply and sewer systems, both of which have a significant impact on the rate and direction of suburban development. Similarly, the Coastal Zone Management Act of 1972 affects development in 34 states and increased Federal government concern for growth in coastal areas.

While these policies involve Federal regulation of land use and development, attempts to formulate a more explicit national land use policy through a Land Use Policy and Planning Assistance Act were defeated in Congress in both 1973 and again in 1974. This proposed Act would have provided for planning aid to states to assist them in developing state-wide planning and growth controls and forced the states to deal with local development decisions affecting areas of crucial environmental concern. At the same time, the Act would have increased *national* level concern with land use.

However, to the present, the most direct and continual involvement of the Federal Government in community development has been not through the environmental policy arena but through the various housing and development acts that have periodically been passed by Congress. Perhaps the most important means by which the Federal Government has been, and will continue to be involved in regulating suburban growth, and at reducing barriers to exclusionary zoning, is through its policies of subsidized housing. Most attempts at constructing low cost suburban housing run afoul of a basic economic fact — even the cheapest new housing that could possibly be built in suburbs is expensive, usually beyond the purchasing power of most low-income families. Moreover, the reasons for this high cost are frequently beyond the control of local governments. Thus, even if state courts in New Jersey or Pennsylvania order local governments not to impose *additional* costs on new construction, the basic costs of new suburban housing as determined by labor, interest, and material costs would still be prohibitive to lower income families. What is required to ensure a more even class representation in suburbia is not only a dimunition of exclusionary zoning, but the existence of subsidies for the construction and maintenance of low to moderate income housing. By far, the most likely source for such subsidies is the Federal government, although there do exist programs run by some states to subsidize low and moderate income housing construction.

A major response of the Federal Government to the realities of this cost situation was the Housing Act of 1968 through which significant housing subsidies were provided.[60] Two major programs established by the Housing Act accounted for the largest share of subsidies: first, "section 235" of the Housing Act created subsidies for homeownership by low-income families. Similarly, "section 236" of the Act created a program to subsidize rents for new or renovated housing making them available to lower income groups. Through these two programs, the number of housing units constructed or rehabilitated for low income families was considerable — about 540,000 units by 1972. Moreover, these subsidy programs did have an impact on suburban exclusion. Surveys by the Department of Housing and Urban Development showed that subsidized suburban housing was much more integrated than non-subsidized housing and that about 20 percent of blacks moving within SMSAs to subsidized housing represented moves from cities to suburbs. To be sure, the numbers of people involved were small compared to the degree of segregation, but subsidies were, nonetheless, beginning to have an impact on suburban exclusion.[61]

However, these subsidy programs became seriously marred by poor administration and outright corruption. The extent of these problems became so severe that in January 1973 most subsidy programs were frozen by then-President Nixon. After some administrative reforms, and the resignation of Richard Nixon, a new act was passed in 1974 reinstituting Federally subsidized housing programs. This Housing and Community Development Act of 1974 (CDA) included provisions for the continuation of Section 235 homeownership subsidies. Further CDA expanded the rent subsidy program by replacing Section 236 subsidies with what is now known as "Section 8" rent subsidies. CDA further created a new program, "Section 202," to aid in the construction and maintenance of multiple family dwellings for the elderly. Despite the reinstitution of these subsidies through CDA, the level of support for housing remains below the 1968-1972 level and is probably inadequate to meet the housing needs of the moderate and low income families in the United States, including the need for increased access to suburban housing opportunities.

CDA and the "New Federalism"

But perhaps even more important for the development of low income suburban housing than the size of the subsidies available is the change in the guiding philosophy of Federal involvement in suburban growth as seen in the Community Development Act. The Act reflected the concept of the "New Federalism" popular in the Nixon, Ford, and Carter administrations — basically the desire by the Federal government to find ways to make local governments more important in administering public policy. As part of the "New Federalism" local governments now receive Community Development Block Grants (CDBGs) through the Community Development Act. Within very broad guidelines, local governments can use these block grants to fund the local projects they desire, rather than, as in the past, being required to spend Federal money to support specific projects approved by the national government.

However, the Federal government did provide certain restrictions on the use of CBDGs, and in fact significant sections of Title I of CDA seem to clearly indicate a responsibility on the part of local governments, suburban ones in particular, to use these Federal grants to end the spatial concentration of the poor and racial minorities in the central cities.

For example, Section 101 (c) of Title I of the Community Development Act states:

> The primary objective of this title is the development of viable urban communities, by providing decent housing and a suitable living environment and expanding economic opportunities, *principally for persons of low and moderate income.*

In order to make this goal a reality, application guidelines for Community Development money specifically provided that communities seeking block grants must give "maximum feasible priority to activities which will either benefit low or moderate income families, or aid in the prevention and elimination of slums or blight. . ." In addition, communities seeking CDA money were legally required to prepare a "Housing Assistance Plan" (HAP), that would, if successfully done, relate the use of community development grants to available Federal subsidies, especially Section 8 rent monies, to provide expanded housing opportunities for low and moderate income families. Thus, several of the provisions of the CDA seemed to provide the mandate and the means for suburbs to begin to attack suburban exclusion.

However, studies have shown that the shift to increased local discretion in the use of Federal monies, despite the guidelines just mentioned, may make the problem of inequalities in metropolitan areas more severe, and make the satisfaction of the substantive goals of Title I of the CDA aimed at improving the conditions of low and moderate income groups more difficult. Specifically, early studies of the operation of the community development block grant program have criticized its operation on several grounds. First, during the first two years of CDBGs operation, the allocation formula for block grants over-funded the wealthiest suburbs at the expense of both the central cities and of the poorest suburbs.[62]

Second, studies have also shown that during the initial years of operation, block grant monies were *shifted* out of the areas where the poorest residents were located and into wealthier areas of cities and suburbs. According to studies done by the Brookings Institution and by the National Association of Housing Rehabilitation Officers (NAHRO) only about 50 percent of CBDG monies have been targeted on the poorest areas of metropolitan regions. But both studies show that over time, *less* money has been allocated to these poor areas than in year 1 of CDBG's operation. This shifting in funds out of the poorest areas reflects the "closing out" of previous Federal programs, such as Model Cities and Urban Renewal that were specifically targeted at the poorest areas of the metropolitan region and the choice of local governments to shift those monies to other, better off areas. Indeed, one critic of CBDG has gone so far as to argue that CBDG encourages local governments in "triage" — the literal abandonment of the worst off areas in the metropolis.[63]

When these studies have turned their attention specifically to the policy choices made by suburbs, the results are also unencouraging. Evidence suggests that most suburbs are not integrating their community development monies into a coherent attempt at improving the "housing and economic opportunities" of the poor, but that many suburbs have spent their CDBG money on such amenities as parks, improved lighting, and other peripheral services. Furthermore, given the mandate included in CDA for increased citizen participation, the dispersal of funds away from the poorest areas may continue. As local citizen groups begin to participate in the decision process, upper class groups can bring more resources to bear on the allocation process causing the deflection of some of CDBG monies into upper class areas and away from lower class ones. The reduced role of the Federal government, which at one time could have forced the allocation of monies in specific directions, may make it harder for local governments to use their CDA money to ameliorate inequalities.

And finally, HUD has been severely criticized for its lax enforcement of one of the most essential ingredients (the Housing Assistance Plans) that could have integrated the various elements of the Community Development Act into a policy to actually improve the quality and quantity of housing available to low income groups in the suburbs. The provisions of CDA required communities to prepare HAPs including a provision that the number of low income individuals "expected to reside" in the community be estimated and that adequate provision of CDA money be made to meet the needs of these low income individuals. Moreover, the "expected to reside" estimate was supposed to reflect regional needs and a commitment by local governments to provide improved housing opportunities for the low income families in the region, i.e., an end to suburban exclusion. Yet despite the importance of this provision, HUD in the past approved applications that did not provide HAPs or that included only the most perfunctory planning by local governments.[64]

While recent reports by HUD and by the Advisory Commission on Intergovernmental Relations have disputed the findings reported above, in general, it is probably safe to say that during its first 2-3 years of operation, the Community Development Act has not produced any spatial deconcentration of low income families into the suburbs and has probably reduced the level of housing and community development support available to the lowest income families in the metropolitan region.[65]

Recent Changes in CDA: Reforming the Act to Address Suburban Exclusion

While the evidence accumulated to date shows a general failure of CDA to improve the conditions of low and moderate income families, several significant changes in the implementation of CDA seem to be in the offing, changes that might indeed make CDA a more effective tool in expanding housing opportunities for low and moderate income families in the suburbs.

The first change has resulted from the outcome of several court challenges to the use of CDA money by suburbs to continue suburban exclusion. These courts cases have been based on the right of the courts to review the spending choices of suburbs to see if they conform to the statutory requirements and purposes of the Community Development Act. In two recent court cases, the use of community development money by suburbs has been found not to comply with the purposes and intentions of CDA. Fittingly, both cases centered on the issue of Housing Assistance Plans and whether or not suburbs were making full use of their federal money to improve the housing opportunities of lower income groups. The first case, *City of Hartford v. Carla Hills et al.*,[66] involved the city of Hartford, Connecticut which objected to the continued exclusionary policies of its surrounding suburbs receiving Federal CDA monies. The second case involved Brookhaven Township in Long Island, New York[67] which was spending virtually all its CDA monies for amenities for its wealthier citizens without targeting its CDA programs on low and moderate income groups. In both cases, the courts enjoined the continued expenditures of CDA money because of non-compliance with the provisions of the Act.

But at least as important as court review is the change in government policy as articulated by Patricia Harris, the first Secretary of Housing and Urban Development under President Carter. According to Ms. Harris, it is the policy of the Carter Administration to use CDA monies to pressure local governments "to accept a fair share of low and moderate income housing and to promote fair housing vigorously." Further, HUD will now "expect communities to direct development and housing programs toward the benefit of low and moderate income groups."[68]

It is possible that given a concentrated attempt by the Federal Government to insure the proper use of these CDA monies, some change in the behavior of suburbs toward the creation of low and moderate income housing opportunities may come about. However, we know that wealthy suburbs have in the past pursued growth and zoning policies that were not in fact fiscally productive, choosing instead to preserve social values represented by sprawling, single family housing occupied by upper income families. Furthermore, the amounts of monies involved in CDA are frequently not sufficiently large to act as an inducement for changing the pursuit of those values. Indeed, suburbs have already begun to turn down CDA money rather than meet HUD requirements to provide assistance to low and moderate income groups.[69] The resolution of this issue concerning the ability of the Federal government to improve access to suburbia is a process that will unfold over the next few years.

State Responses to Suburban Growth

A theme that frequently appears when discussing the role of the Federal government in regulating suburban growth is the argument that it is the elected branches of *state* government that are the best route to regulating suburban expansion. After all, it is without a doubt these branches of state government that have the most extensive constitutional and legal authority to intervene and regulate suburbia.[70]

Responding to this argument, and to pressures from the Federal government, from the courts, and from local governments themselves, several states have begun actively to formulate plans and policies to intervene in metropolitan development.

The type of responses by the states are wide ranging, and have attempted to control metropolitan development in a variety of ways. On one level, states have begun to change the structural conditions of metropolitan growth that have made suburban exclusion characteristic of today's metropolitan areas. Recall that part of the existence of multiple autonomous suburban governments trace directly back to the actions of state governments in ending central city expansion through the tightening of annexation laws and the relaxation of laws governing incorporation. These actions stopped central city expansion and made the creation of numerous small local suburban governments possible. Several states are now reversing those early decisions, making annexation easy and incorporation more difficult. While this may not reduce the extent of fragmentation presently found in metropolitan regions, it may prevent further fragmentation.[71]

An actual reduction of the extent of fragmentation may be the result of other state policies. State governments have the constitutional power to create metropolitan wide government and to reduce the extent of local autonomy. For example, it was through the actions of state legislation that such metropolitan wide governments as the Miami-Dade County, Nashville-Davidson County and Indianapolis-Marion County consolidations were facilitated. While these will be discussed in more detail in chapter 6, it should be noted that the usual expectation is that metropolitan wide governments have more interest in ending suburban exclusion than do individual suburbs, and that they frequently have the policy means to do so.

States can also ameliorate the need for suburban exclusion through changing fiscal policy. While we have shown that this may not be totally effective since the motives of suburban governments may include a large dose of social exclusion on top of fiscal concerns, active state intervention into local fiscal policy and controlling the adverse effects of the fiscal drag of lower income families is a possible policy choice that states can make to try to reduce suburban exclusion.

Turning more directly to the concerns of this chapter with land use and community development other changes are worth noting. On the most fundamental level, several states, most notably California and New Jersey, have begun to change legislatively the definition of the "public welfare" that is the legal support for zoning. Under present interpretation, the public welfare justification for zoning has been interpreted as referring to the welfare of *each individual suburb*. As a result, suburbs are legally allowed to undertake growth and development policies that have been individually self-serving, while frequently having adverse effects on neighboring suburbs or the entire metropolis. However, by changing state enabling legislation that guiding zoning to include a regional component in the definition of "general welfare," the selfish actions of individual suburbs are now more legally constrained than in the past.

States have also enacted other policies aimed at regulating the social consequences of zoning. A frequently cited example is the Zoning Appeals Law found in Massachusetts. Under the provisions of this law, a public or non-profit private corporation seeking to build low and/or moderate income housing and denied the necessary permits by a suburb, can appeal such local zoning decisions to the Massachusetts State Department of Community Affairs. This state agency is empowered to review the details of the zoning controversy and, if warranted, to grant a development permit that overrides local opposition. This Zoning Appeals Law has withstood court tests, and has been used with some frequency to spread low and moderate income housing throughout metropolitan areas in Massachusetts.[72]

A similar attempt at giving a state agency the power to override local zoning opposition to subsidized housing occurred in the state of New York and involved the state Urban Development Corporation (UDC). Under state legislation, the UDC had the statutory power to begin construction of low and moderate income housing in suburbs, regardless of local approval. Perhaps because of this broad grant of authority, the UDC was viewed suspiciously by suburbs, especially by exclusive suburbs in the New York City metropolitan region. Indeed, once UDC tried to implement its housing plans in wealthy Westchester County, a suburban area just north of New York City, the political reaction in the state legislature was so intense that UDC was effectively stripped of its zoning override power.[73]

Another, but more successful, example of state government intervention into competitive growth between suburbs concerns the Twin Cities in Minnesota. While the laws in Massachusetts and New York, and indeed, the actions of the Federal government through the Community Development Act, are concerned mostly with the location of subsidized housing and lower income people, the Fiscal Disparities Act of 1971 in Minnesota is concerned with the other basic element of suburban competition, the location of business tax base and the impact that such development has on local taxes and local services. Under the provisions of this Minnesota law, 40 percent of added tax revenues that result from business development, tax revenues that would otherwise accrue only to the suburbs in which the development took place, is taken by the Twin Cities Metropolitan Council, a regional level government created by the State. These tax benefits are then placed in a central pool and made available on an equitable basis to all municipalities and school districts in the region. This is a conscious attempt to redistribute fiscal wealth in the region, and to ameliorate the underlying causes for competition between suburbs.

These three examples of state action illustrate the kinds of policies that states may undertake to control social and fiscal competition, and are aimed mostly at the social consequences of suburban growth.

Another type of state intervention into suburban zoning and development is more concerned with the environmental aspects of metropolitan growth. This concern for environmental control can be seen in two types of state activities, the introduction of state-wide land use plans, and the increasingly frequent use by states of "critical areas" legislation, both of which preempt local suburban zoning decisions.

Several states have now enacted state-wide land use plans to which the actions and plans of local governments must comply. Hawaii and Vermont are generally seen as having the most effective land use plans, followed by Oregon, Maine, and Florida.

However, the question of the success of these state land use plans is still being debated, and they have not been in effect long enough to make any clear judgment as to their impact.[74]

More frequent than general state-wide plans is the enactment by state legislatures of "critical areas" legislation. Probably the most sweeping example of this is the regulation of development along the California coast embodied in the California Coastal Zone Conservation Commission. Other states have similarly tried to protect other critical areas from environmental degradation, e.g., park lands (Adirondack Mountains in New York); scenic and valuable mountain areas (Colorado); rural areas (Idaho); or wetlands (Wisconsin). These attempts, however, are only infrequently applied to metropolitan development, and instead tend to concentrate on either rural undeveloped areas, or else the "ex-urban" areas removed from intense current growth pressures. The reasons are obvious: in these undeveloped areas, political organization and local opposition to state intervention are less effective than in the truly suburban areas. Thus, state legislatures get credit for intervening to protect the environment without getting involved in the intense political problems such actions might produce if applied to the suburban areas more in need of state intervention.[75]

Local Reforms in Zoning

If state intervention into suburban growth to create greater equity usually runs into opposition from suburbs, it is possible that the attempts by the state at regulating growth in the name of environmental protection may prove to be more acceptable. This may be seen by the growing number of suburbs that are, on their own initiatives, developing alternative approaches to growth regulation to preserve the quality of the environment.

Many suburbs have experimented with development timing ordinances which try to minimize the impact of growth by tying development closely to the availability of services such as water, sewers, and roads, while other suburbs have gone even further and experimented with growth "caps" — that is, setting a population limit to the size of the community population. Still other suburbs have experimented with new mechanisms of land regulation including the preservation of open space and farm lands, and many have tried to assure that new large-scale developments set aside land for parks, recreation and open space (usually called "developer exactions").[76]

Furthermore, suburbs have frequently changed the rationale for zoning policies, phasing support for new growth strategies in terms of the "carrying capacity" of the local environment. Thus, in the name of watershed management, and the protection of limited water resources, many suburbs now enact large lot zoning.

Yet a real dilemma is posed by this new concern for environmental protection. Almost by definition attempts to limit demands on the environment limit the availability of land for continued growth, or attempt to limit the number of people found in suburbs. Large lot minimum zoning that is enacted on social exclusionary grounds has been challenged and overturned in state courts. Yet large lot zoning based on environmental grounds may find greater support in the courts, even though the impact on racial and class segregation may be identical. As a result of this dilemma, a tension between concerns for social equity and for environmental protection may be common in zoning and growth policy decisions for the foreseeable future.

Summary: Exclusionary Zoning and Suburban Development

Zoning is usually viewed as an important government power available to suburbs to control the fate and composition of community development. Yet zoning's legal and constitutional justification is based on the "police power" of the state — that is, the right of government to protect the "general welfare" of the community rather than on any inherent right of government to regulate and control growth. As a result, through the system of zoning property is left in private hands while the community tells the individual property owner what can or cannot be done with the land. This compares with community development strategies based on outright government purchase of land. And, this characteristic of zoning has an important effect on the ability of a community to control growth and development.

Three additional conditions have also helped structure zoning law and policy. First, is a strong historical antipathy in the United States toward government regulation of private property. Second, is the role of the courts in setting the boundaries in which zoning takes place. And finally, is the United States system of Federalism though which most zoning decisions are made by local governments.

Historically, zoning developed as a reaction to the conditions of rapid urban growth at the turn of the century, including such conditions as heavy immigration and the construction of tenement districts to house these immigrants, the introduction of new technologies that spurred the creation of skyscrapers and congested central business districts, and a general interest in a scientific approach to managing urban affairs.

The first comprehensive zoning law was adopted in New York City in 1916 and zoning rapidly spread to other cities and suburbs. Zoning was found to be a constitutional use of government power in 1926 in the U.S. Supreme Court's ruling in *Euclid vs. Ambler* and its use spread even faster. From its inception, zoning has been criticized as being reactive to political conditions and responsive to the desires of present property owners rather than as a tool for guiding growth.

But perhaps the most persistent criticism of zoning is that it is used for exclusionary purposes — that is, to bar low and moderate income groups from suburban housing opportunities. Both fiscal and social motives are thought to be involved in this exclusion. Fiscally, suburbs may seek to bar individuals who cost more in services than they contribute in taxes. Socially, suburbs may seek to bar individuals and families who have different life styles than those held by community residents. The relative importance of these two motives is really not yet resolved, and each may have different implications for public policies aimed at reducing exclusion.

Regardless of the motives, exclusion does take place. However, exclusionary practices of suburbs have been under attack in recent years. Most notably, courts, especially several state courts, have repeatedly overturned local zoning ordinances as exclusionary. Furthermore, state legislatures have in several cases placed limits on the powers of local governments to exclude low income and racial minority groups. Furthermore, the Federal government has begun to express increased interest and concern for furthering the spatial deconcentration of minority groups out of the central city and into the suburbs.

But the ultimate ability of these higher level governments to limit the exclusionary actions of suburbs is still uncertain. Suburbs have shown a remarkable ability in the past to escape the meaning and intent of restrictive laws and of restrictive judicial review. Furthermore, higher level governments have frequently equivocated in the actual pressure and constraints they place on suburbs.

Notes

1. The work on zoning and land use planning is voluminous. Most studies agree that zoning has an important impact on community development. See for example: James G. Coke and Charles S. Liebman, "Political Values and Population Density Controls," *Land Economics* 37 (November 1961), pp. 347-361; John Delafons, *Land Use Controls in the United States* (Cambridge: The MIT Press, 1969); Fred Bosselman and David Callies, *The Quiet Revolution in Land Use Controls* (Washington, D.C.: Government Printing Office, 1971); or David Listokin, ed., *Land Use Controls: Present Problems and Future Reforms* (New Brunswick, New Jersey: Center for Urban Policy Research, 1974). For a contrary view, see Bernard Siegan's study of "Non-Zoning in Houston," *Journal of Law and Economics* 13 (April 1970), pp. 129-144.

2. Eric J. Branfman, Benjamin I. Cohen and David M. Trubek, "Measuring the Invisible Wall: Land Use Controls and Residential Patterns of the Poor," *Yale Law Review* 82 (January 1973), p. 486.

3. Quoted in Charles M. Haar, *Land Use Planning* (Boston: Little, Brown, 1958), p. vii.

4. See for example, John Delafons, *op. cit.*, or Donald M. McAllister, ed., *Environment: A New Focus for Land Use Planning* (Washington, D.C.: National Science Foundation, 1973).

5. Marion Clawson, "Historical Overview of Land-Use Planning in the United States," in McAllister, *Ibid.*

6. Clawson, *Ibid.*, pp. 25-26.

7. John Reps, "The Future of American Planning — Requiem or Renasance," *Planning 1967* (Chicago: American Society of Planning Officials, 1967).

8. James Sundquist, *Dispersing Population* (Washington, D.C.: The Brookings Institution, 1975).

9. Fred Bosselman and David Callies, *The Taking Issue* (Washington, D.C.: Council on Environmental Quality, 1973).

10. Bosselman and Callies, *op. cit.*

11. Seymour I. Toll, *Zoned America* (New York: Grossman Publishers, 1969).

12. Stanislaw Makielski, Jr., *The Politics of Zoning* (New York: Columbia University Press, 1966). See also Toll, *op. cit.*

13. Indeed, Daniel Mandelker has gone so far as to argue that the rapid spread of zoning based on New York's experience was, in part, a defensive "sales job" undertaken by astute New York lawyers who felt that the widespread use of zoning by other communities would make court challenges to New York's zoning law less likely to succeed — a belief that turned out to be quite correct. ("The Role of Zoning in Housing and Metropolitan Development" in David Listokin, ed., *Land Use Controls* (New Brunswick, N.J.: Center for Urban Policy Research, 1974) pp. 39-54).

14. Malcolm Rivkin, "Growth Controls via Sewer Moratorium," *Urban Land* 33 (March 1974), pp. 10-15.

15. Thomas H. Logen, "The Americanization of German Zoning," *Journal of the American Institude of Planners* 42 (October 1971), p. 393.

16. Lynne B. Sagalyn and George Sternlieb, *Zoning and Housing Costs* (New Brunswick: Center for Urban Policy Research, 1972) ch. 1 and Chester Hartman, *Housing and Social Policy* (Englewood Cliffs, N.J.: Prentice-Hall, 1975), ch. 2, both offer fuller discussions of these issues.

17. Hartman, *op. cit.*, pp. 44-45; also see, Norman Williams, Jr. and Thomas Norman, "Exclusionary Land Use Controls," *Land Use Controls Quarterly* 4 (September 1970), pp. 1-24.

18. Robert Schafer, *The Suburbanization of Multifamily Housing* (Lexington, Mass.: D.C. Heath, 1974).

19. Several court cases have dealt with this issue. In *Dailey* v. *City of Lawton, Oklahoma* (425 f. 2d 1037) 1970, the district court found that the city council's refusal to rezone a tract of land to allow low income housing was racially motivated. A similar finding was presented in *Kennedy Park Homes Association* v. *City of Lakawanna, N.Y.* (436 f. 2d 108) 1971, *cert.* denied (401 U.S. 1010) 1971, in which the court invalidated a rezoning of property to be used for low income housing to a recreation and parks zone. Perhaps the most important case was *Crow* v. *Brown* in which the district court argued that "this nation is committed to a policy of balanced and dispersed public housing. . ." and that "local authorities can no more confine low income blacks to a compacted and concentrated area than they can confine their children to segregated schools. . ." (332 F. Supp. 382) (N.D. Ga., 1971), affirmed (457 f. 2d 124) 1972. The quotation is from 332 F. Supp. 390. Also see *Morales* v. *Haines* (349 F. Supp. 684) 1972, and *Mahaley* v. *Cuyahoga Metropolitan Housing Authority* (355 F. Supp. 1257) 1973, both of which restrict local government's exclusionary behavior. A partial retraction of this stance may be embodied in *James* v. *Valtierra* (403 U.S. 137) 1971, and the general reluctance of the Supreme Court at this time to become involved in local zoning policy, see the section on the courts in this chapter.

20. These cost estimates are from Sagalyn and Sternlieb, *op. cit.*, ch. III.

21. Hartman, *Housing*, p. 42. It should be noted that restrictions on the use of modern and cheaper material and more modern construction methods through building codes are not necessarily a conscious strategy to keep up the cost of housing to exclude low income residents. Indeed, most resistance to modernizing building codes comes from crafts unions which desire to prevent changes that may make their members' skills obsolete. But regardless of the source of opposition, the effect is the same: rigid building codes inflate the cost of new housing and thereby help exclude lower income individuals from suburbia.

22. Anthony Downs, *Opening Up the Suburbs* (New Haven: Yale University Press, 1973).

23. John J. Harrigan, *Political Change in the Metropolis* (Boston: Little, Brown and Company, 1973), p. 205-206. Sagalyn and Sternlieb, *op. cit.*, ch. 1.

24. Dick Netzer, *The Economics of the Property Tax* (Washington, D.C.: The Brookings Institution, 1966), especially pp. 124-135.

25. Netzer, *op. cit.*, p. 125.

26. Norman Williams and Edward Wacks, "Segregation of Residential Areas Along Economic Lines: Lionshead Lake Revisited," *Wisconsin Law Review* 1969, pp. 827-847.

27. William L.C. Wheaton and Merton Schusshen, *The Cost of Municipal Services in Residential Areas* (Washington, D.C.: Government Printing Office, 1965). Also see Julius Margolis, "Municipal Fiscal Structure in a Metropolitan Region," *Journal of Political Economy* 65 (June 1957), pp. 225-236.

28. William A. Fischel, "Fiscal and Environmental Considerations in the Location of Firms in Suburban Communities," in Edwin S. Mills and Wallace E. Oates, eds., *Fiscal Zoning and Land Use Controls* (Lexington: Mass,: D.C. Heath, 1975), pp. 119-174.

29. John R. Logan and Mark Schneider, "The Political Economy of Suburban Growth: A Two Region Comparison," a paper presented to the Annual Meeting of the International Studies Association, Toronto, Canada, February 25-29, 1976. See chapter 2 for more discussion of this issue and more evidence on this point.

30. Bruce W. Hamilton, Edwin S. Mills, and David Puryear, "The Tiebout Hypothesis and Residential Segregation," in Mills and Oates, *op. cit.*, pp. 101-118.

31. Russell Harrison, *Equality in Public School Finance* (Lexington, Mass.: Lexington Books 1975), ch. 5.

32. See Richard C. Hill, "Separate and Unequal: Governmental Inequality in the Metropolis." *American Political Science Review* 68 (December 1974), pp. 1557-1568.

33. Darwin Stuart and Robert Teska, "Who Pays For What: A Cost-Revenue Analysis of Suburban Land Use Alternatives, *Urban Land* 30 (March 1971), pp. 3-16.

34. See Franklin James with Duane Windsor, "Fiscal Zoning, Fiscal Reform and Exclusionary Land Use Controls," *Journal of the American Institute of Planners* 42 (April 1976), pp. 130-141.

35. R.L. Crouch and R.E. Weintraub, "Cost Benefit Analysis of PUD," *Urban Land* 32 (June 1973), pp. 3-13.

36. Branfman *et al.*, *op. cit.*.

37. *Ibid.*, p. 79. Also see Hill, *op. cit.*

38. *National Land and Investment Co.* v. *Kohn*, 419 Pa. 504, 215 A. 2nd 597 (1965).

39. *Appeal of Kit-Mar Builders, Inc.* 439 Pa. 466, 268 A. 2d 765 (1970).

40. 215 A. 2d. 610, 612.

41. *Appeal of Girsh*, 437 Pa. 237, 263 A. 2d 395 (1970).

42. 462 Pa. 445, 341 A. 2d 466.

43. *Southern Burlington County NAACP* v. *Mt. Laurel Township*, 67 N.J. 151 (1975), appeal dismissed 423 U.S. 803, 96 S. Ct. 18, 46 L.Ed. 2d 28 (1975).

44. *Oakwood at Madison, Inc.* v. *The Township of Madison and the State of New Jersey*, decided January 26, 1977, New Jersey Supreme Court.

45. For a similar case in New York see *Barenson* v. *Town of New Castle*, 38 N.Y. 2d 102, 378 N.Y.S. 2d 672.

46. 336 A. 2d at 724.

47. *Village of Euclid* v. *Ambler Realty Co.*, 272 U.S. 365 (1926).

48. *Nectow* v. *City of Cambridge*, 277 U.S. 183 (1928).

49. *Goldblatt* v. *Town of Hempstead*, 369 U.S. 590 (1962).

50. *Borass* v. *Village of Belle Terre* 416 U.S. 1. (1974).

51. 416 U.S. 1 at 9.

52. *Warth* v. *Seldin*, 422 U.S. 490 (1975).

53. David L. Kirp., " 'Growth Management' Zoning, Public Policy and the Courts," *Policy Analysis* (Summer 1976), pp. 431-458.

54. *Construction Industry Association of Sonoma County* v. *City of Petaluma*, 375 F. Supp. 574 (N.D. Cal.); 522 F. 2d 897 (1975), cert. denied 44 USLW 3467 (1976).

55. *Village of Arlington Heights* v. *Metropolitan Housing Development Corporation*, 50 L Ed 450 (1977).

56. *Goulden* v. *Town of Ramapo*, 30 N.Y 2d 359, 334 N.Y.S. 2d 138, 285 N.E. 2d 291 (1972).

57. V. Jeffrey Evans, "Legal Aspects of Migration in the United States," a paper presented to the Annual Meeting of the Population Association of American, April 29, 1976, Montreal, Canada.

58. David Falk and Herbert Franklin, *In-Zoning* (Washington, D.C.: Potomac Institute, 1975), pp. 14-15.

59. 522 F. 2d 847, 908.

60. Of course subsidized housing in the United States traces back further than the Housing Act of 1968. The most common type of subsidized housing is generally known as "public housing" built under programs originating during the New Deal as embodied in the Housing Act of 1937. This housing is built with Federal subsidies but construction and management decisions are made mostly by local housing authorities in the individual communities. The location of these public housing units in central city ghettos has been subject to some judicial consideration and in a recent court case (*Gautreaux* v. *Chicago Housing Authority*), a Federal court ordered the Chicago Housing Authority to consider the regional housing market in making further locational choices. The objective was to achieve a spatial deconcentration of the poor. Part of the intent of the newer housing subsidy programs is to achieve more dispersed housing and to lessen the stigma of receiving housing subsidies. (Also see footnote 19).

61. U.S. Department of Housing and Urban Development, *Housing in the Seventies* (Washington, D.C.: HUD 1974), ch. 4.

62. Bernard J. Frieden and Marshall Kaplan, *Community Development and the Model Cities Legacy*, Working Paper No. 42 (Cambridge, Mass.: Joint Center for Urban Studies, November, 1976), especially pp. 34-36. U.S. House of Representatives, Subcommittee on Housing and Community Development of the Committee on Banking, Finance, and Urban Affairs, *Community Development Block Grant Program*, A Staff Report (Washington, D.C.: Government Printing Office, February, 1977), especially Section II.

63. Victor Bach, Testimony presented before the subcommittee on Housing and Community Development of the House Committee on Banking, Finance and Urban Affairs, 95th Congress, first session, Part I, p. 630.

64. Report of the Comptroller General of the U.S., Meeting Application and Review Requirements for Block Grants Under Title I of the Housing and Community Development Act of 1974 (Washington, D.C.: Government Printing Office 1975).

65. Richard Nathan, Testimony before the subcommittee on Housing and Community Development, pp. 584-585. Also see Carl Van Horn, "Decentralized Policy Delivery: National Objectives and Local Implementors," a paper presented at the Workshop on Policy analysis in State and Local Government, Stony Brook, New York, May 22-24, 1977, p. 24.

66. City of Hartford et al. v. Carla Hills, et al., U.S. District Court of Connecticut, Civil No. H-75-258.

67. Rodriguez et al. v. Carla Hills et al., U.S. District Court, Civ. No. 76-5773.

68. New York Times, March 8, 1977, p. 13.

69. Advisory Commission on Intergovernmental Relations, Community Development: The Workings of a Federal-Local Block Grant (Washington, D.C.: Government Printing Office 1977), p. 46.

70. The support for this line of argument always traces back to "Dillon's Rule" which severely limits the powers of municipalities to those expressly granted by the state making local governments "creatures of the state" and dependent on state laws for their existence and their powers. See the discussion of Dillon's Rule in Thomas P. Murphy and John Rehfuss, Urban Politics in the Suburban Era (Homewood, Illinois: Dorsey Press, 1976), pp. 167-170.

71. Ibid., p. 171.

72. Samuel Schere, "Snob Zoning: Developments in Massachusetts and New Jersey," Harvard Journal of Legislation 7 (January 1970), pp. 246-270. Also see Bosselman and Callies, op. cit., pp. 164-186.

73. Herbert M. Franklin, "Recent Developments: New York Legislature Severely Curbs UDC Power in Suburbs," Metropolitan Clearinghouse Memorandum 73-6 (Washington, D.C.: Metropolitan Clearinghouse Program, Potomac Institute, 1973).

74. R. Robert Linowes and Don. T. Allensworth, The States and Land-Use Controls (New York: Praeger Publishers, 1975), chs. 3 and 4.

75. Linowes and Allensworth, op. cit., ch. 4; Earl Finkler and David L. Peterson, Nongrowth Planning Strategies (New York: Praeger Publishers, 1974), ch. 1.

76. On nongrowth planning strategies see Finkler and Peterson, op. cit..

Chapter 4

Education Services
in Suburban Areas

While zoning and community development are services provided by local governments, they are different than the ones to which we turn in the next two chapters. Zoning is essentially a regulatory activity through which the use of private property is controlled. As a result, while zoning has an important impact on the shape of suburban growth, and while it excites attention on the part of local area residents, it is a relatively simple and inexpensive service for local governments to provide. No large and expensive bureaucracy exists to administer zoning laws. Instead zoning decisions are frequently made by the existing local government town or village council and the expense of maintaining a local planning board (where they exist) to assist in preparing a master plan and associated zoning maps is relatively low. In contrast, the services which we investigate in the next two chapters entail considerable monetary costs to local governments. This is especially true of education, the single most expensive service offered by local governments in the United States. In addition, many of the other services to which we now turn have a major impact on the shape of suburban growth.

In this chapter we look at education services in metropolitan areas. In the following chapter we look at service delivery in several other important policy areas: public safety, solid waste management, and public investment in sewers and transportation, two essential "infrastructural" investments necessary to sustain growth and development. Taken together these chapters illustrate the impact that the form of suburban government and service delivery can have on the lives of people and on their settlement patterns. The examination of service delivery systems in these policy areas also serves to highlight some of the major issues facing suburban government. Such issues include, among others, the conflict between cities and suburbs over present patterns of metropolitan development and service delivery; the choices made by suburbs in the quality and quantity of services provided and the adequacy of such policies; and, the pressure on local governments to transfer many of the services for which they have traditionally been responsible to higher level governments.

While most of the services examined illustrate these issues, the educational policy system in metropolitan areas is the most reasonable place with which to begin. There are several reasons for this choice. Most important is the expense of schools to suburban governments. On the average about 60 percent of total government expenditures in suburbia are devoted to local school systems. Therefore, tax burdens in local communities are directly related to the costs of schools. In addition, schools are almost universal throughout suburban communities. Many suburbs which are only minimally involved in other local public services are invariably involved in educating children and running local schools. Furthermore, public involvement in schools is high. While people may only infrequently require the use of local police or fire service and may take the supply of water or the removal of their waste products for granted, citizen involvement with the schools through their children and their tax bills is usually at a higher level. Indeed, since the search for quality schools is often thought of as a reason for suburban migration and is a concern of most people when choosing between houses in different suburban communities, local interest and involvement in the schools is often higher than found for other services. Further, other basic issues that are generally important to the study of suburban government and policy, concerns such as the preservation of local autonomy, the effects of government fragmentation, and the impact of racial and fiscal imbalances between communities in the metropolitan region, are all repeated, sometimes with a vengeance, in school systems in metropolitan areas.

A Brief Historical Overview

It is useful to begin the investigation of local schools with a brief historical overview of the development of the educational policy system at the local level. Two particularly important characteristics of education in the United States are evident in such an overview. First, it is important to note the traditional isolation of local school policy formation from the practices and demands of the normal political system of local communities. During the last 50 years or so, one operating principle of local education policy in many communities is that schools and politics do not mix. As two leading scholars of the governance of American schools have recently noted: "By a mutual but unspoken long-standing agreement, American citizens and scholars have contended for many years that the world of education is and should be kept separate from the world of politics."[1]

Related to this traditional isolation of schools from community politics, and just as important, is the fact that educational policy making has historically been overwhelmingly rooted in the local community. Education has not usually been viewed as a national right nor even as an especially important national policy concern. Instead, educating the population and governing the schools, including raising the money necessary to run them, has been almost totally a state and local government function — with a strong tradition of deference to local school district control. While this is changing, and federal funding and involvement has increased, and while the states have also expanded their role in setting education policy over the past decades, much of school policy is still determined locally and almost 50 percent of the money for schools is raised through local school district taxes. In turn, this pattern of local finance has created considerable differences in the amount of money available to schools in different communities. These fiscal imbalances between local school districts have become the source of substantial policy debate in suburban areas of late.

Thus, in contrast to many other services delivered by local governments, where higher level governments have long constrained the actions of local communities, education policy making is in fact still heavily rooted in the 19,000 or so local school districts spread throughout the country. As a result of this system of local schools, considerable variation exists concerning the issues and needs of different school systems and concerning their mode of governance. In the next few pages only the most common characteristics of governing the schools are discussed. But it should be kept in mind that there are sometimes large differences between school districts and that only some of the "central tendencies" of local school systems are highlighted.

It should also be noted that while school board elections are among the most commonly held elections in the United States and that school boards are charged with making important policy decisions affecting the lives of large numbers of people, not much is really known about them. This is due largely to the long standing historical belief that schools were run in a non-political fashion and hence, to the belief that there was very little to study in school governance. Recent research has proven this not to be the case and has shown that school politics do exist. This research has also shown that two basic issues facing local schools portend a further politicization of local school systems, threatening to end the isolation of schools from local politics and threatening to force the centralization of school policy into the hands of higher level governments. These two issues concern the funding of schools through local property taxes and the racial integration of schools in metropolitan areas.

In short, four basic considerations at present define education policy in local communities: the use of local school districts historically with relative autonomy from state and federal governments; the isolation of school policies from normal community politics; the problem of financing the schools from local tax sources; and the need for desegregating local school systems. The first issue need not concern us further. We look at the other three in greater detail in the following pages.

The Isolation of Schools from Politics

In examining the governance of education at the local level, we begin by noting the isolation of schools from the normal electoral and partisan political activity found in most communities. The standard argument presented by educational policy elites, and incorporated in the practices of most local communities, is that education and politics do not mix, and that school policy should be made by trained educational experts and not by lay people. This position is directly contrary to patterns of education and schools in earlier times, when virtually all school policy was expected to be determined by the active participation of the local citizenry. The isolation of the schools from politics resulted largely from the excesses of political party leaders in large urban centers during the late 1800s and early 1900s. At the turn of the century, educational policy and the everyday operation of the schools were highly politicized. In most large cities, schools did not operate through a single large city-wide school district. Instead, several smaller school districts dividing the city was the normal means of running the school — a pattern resulting from the desire to root schools closely in community life. These smaller school districts within the cities were not run by professional administrators; rather they were the province of local political party leaders. Jobs, contracts, and the other "goodies" associated with running the schools were awarded on a partisan political basis by party leaders. In other words, the schools were treated in the same manner as many other public services provided by city governments at the turn of the century — as a potentially lucrative source of political favors and rewards. Partisan involvement persisted for some time. However, by the early 1910s, the power of party leaders in many cities began to erode as good government and progressive reform groups began to argue for the "scientific management" of urban government based on the "efficient" and apolitical provision of urban services. The effects of the good government reform movement were felt throughout most cities and across most urban services, but the impact on education was particularly pronounced. In part, this was due to the nature of the clientele — everyone wanted the best education possible for the children in the schools. But just as important was the fact that education was such an expensive service for local governments, and good government reformers thought that a more efficiently run school system would be a potential source of savings for city government.[2].

As a result of the importance of education, a wave of reform swept school systems during the 1910s and 1920s. Most of these reforms were designed to increase the efficiency of school administration and to remove from the schools the "subversive" and expensive influence of partisan political activity. While the exact nature of these reforms is beyond the scope of this discussion, we can say that their general impact was to create a drive for more efficient centralized schools run by a new class of educational administrators. The beliefs and intentions of reformers can be summarized along several dimensions: centralization of the schools, the use of expert and professional standards, the isolation of the schools from partisan political control, and the achievement of efficiency through these other reforms.[3]

This new class of educational administrators was not subservient to the political party structure as had been their predecessors. But, these new administrators sought not only to keep their autonomy relative to party leaders, they also sought to protect their positions relative to other "outside" groups. By the 1920s, the widespread success of the ideology and methods of Progressive Education gave educational administrators a body of "expert" knowledge they claimed to be beyond the understanding of the lay public. Based on this body of knowledge and supported by other business and professional elites who also believed in expertise and efficiency, school administrators began successfully to press for the further isolation of school policy processes from the normal political decision making processes of local governments. As a result of their success, from the early 1920s to the present time, schools have usually been considered beyond the legitimate reach of local political systems.[4]

This drive for isolation is often embodied in the desire for professional autonomy inculcated in most school superintendents through their professional training and orientation.

Superintendents are trained to emphasize their professional expertise in setting educational policy for their school districts and they often view policy demands coming from the general environment as unwarranted interference into a policy decision process in which only they, the superintendents, have the requisite expertise. This relative imbalance between the general public and professional autonomy is also reflected in the relationship between school superintendents and the members of local school board who are supposed to be the representatives of the public in setting school policy. Legally, school boards have ultimate policy authority. And ultimately, superintendents serve at the pleasure of the local school board, hired by the board and removable by it. However, in actuality, the claim of expertise and the unwillingness or inability of school board members to challenge that claim has relegated most school boards to the role of ineffective decision makers who spend most of their time on relatively trivial administrative matters, leaving most important decisions to the superintendent.[5]

The process by which school boards are selected further isolates the school policy process from local politics. About 85 percent of the seats on school boards are elected positions. This would seemingly make the school board closely tied to the local political environment. But the election process for school board members is usually conducted in an apolitical manner: virtually all school board elections are held at different times than elections for other political offices and virtually all school board elections are nonpartisan affairs. This helps insure the isolation of school boards from the general politics of an area. Furthermore, most school board members are elected on an at-large basis across the entire school district rather than standing for election as the representative of a ward of a definable geographic subarea of the district. Research exploring the effects of electoral formats on politics has documented that the nonpartisan and at-large elections by which school board members are chosen mute conflict, blur issues, and, in general, excite less interest and attention than partisan elections using ward representation.[6] In other words, the very process by which school members are elected is designed to reduce the input of the mass public.

Furthermore, while the election process itself is already isolated from the general public by its very format, the choice of candidates presented to the public may have already been preselected, further limiting public input. While the vast majority of school board members are elected, there is evidence that a conscious screening process operates preceding school board elections. In a survey of school board membership across the nation, it was found that over half the members questioned had either been appointed to the school board or had been asked to stand for office by other members of the board. As a result, many districts, even if they have public elections, seem to be characterized by a conscious "self-perpetuating" educational elite that is removed from the general political world of the local district.[7] The groups that are most likely to be part of this self-perpetuating elite are civic and service groups such as the PTA, the Kiwanis, Jaycees, etc. Members of these groups tend to be of high social status and are usually supportive of ongoing school policies and administration. These high status individuals also are likely to believe in the value of expertise and hence are willing to defer to the knowledge represented by the school superintendent. In short, the process by which the public participates in the governing of the schools is designed to limit their input into school policy.

Politics in School Districts

These general patterns describe in broad terms the operation of most school boards in the United States and their isolation from usual political practices. Yet, there are significant departures from these norms. Some school districts, especially districts in lower status communities, never seem to have operated within this apolitical framework. In other districts, political controversies spring to life with a frequency far greater than would be expected from the description of normal school policy processes. It is also the case that, across all school districts, the relative ability of school to maintain their apolitical posture is declining. School districts have been racked by intense policy conflicts in the past decade involving such issues as desegregation, rising costs, taxpayer revolts, teacher unionization, and the general decay of belief in the ability of the schools to accomplish their mission of educating children. Issues such as these are making the schools a focal point of much greater and more intense public attention, often politicizing school policy and limiting, if not totally eroding, the ability of school superintendents to operate as independent experts with a secure body of knowledge to guide their actions.

As this politicization occurs, the strong support among the public for schools turns out to be much weaker than often thought. Thus, while the public seems to have been acquiescent to the system of school isolation, this acquiescence was passive and perhaps not deeply felt.[8] As a result, when important issues do emerge in school policy making, seemingly high levels of public support may rapidly evaporate. In fact, we know that school board elections, district support for superintendents, and changes in school policy are often characterized by episodic "flash flood" involvement of the public, frequently overwhelming the existing school establishment. A school district will seem to be operating on a level of low attention from the public, with an apparently high level of support. An issue will intrude that disturbs that equilibrium. And once a "politicizing" issue appears, public support evaporates, conflict increases, partisan activity grows taking the place of the nonpartisan civic group activity that usually defines school politics, incumbent school board members are turned out of office, and finally, the school district superintendent is fired or resigns.[9] This sequence of events illustrates the vested interest school superintendents have in keeping school policy out of the general political arena. To the extent that school policies become the subject of political debate, the autonomy and independence of the school superintendent declines. His claims of educational expertise will become challenged by the school board and the general public, and ultimately the superintendent's job itself may be in jeopardy.

If the episodic "flash flood" politicization of the schools is now found in a variety of districts at one time relatively immune to such phenomena, it is also true that some districts never developed the apolitical isolation often put forward as the typical pattern of school policy making. Early research in the 1960s tried to tie patterns of school expenditures and policy to the existence of a "power elite" in school districts.[10] But this research has proven less than conclusive. More convincing is the research conducted in the Chicago area investigating patterns of school expenditures and school politics. David Minar's work was among the first such pieces of research.[11] Minar compared the patterns of school politics in 24 high status suburban school districts to those in 24 low status districts. He concluded that in the high status districts there was less conflict, more support for the schools and a higher deference to the expertise of school administrators. This was explained in two ways. First, the residents of the high status school districts were themselves more likely to be experts in their own occupations, and hence a tendency to rely on expertise was more likely part of their everyday behavior. Second, Minar argued that the high status boards were more likely to be skilled in "crises management" skills enabling them to avoid conflict. Part of this crises management skill consisted of the ability to control the nomination process to the school board. In low status districts, conflict was more contentious and the school board was more willing to question the superintendent's expertise. This research indicates that the norm of apolitical school policy may be more widespread in upper-class homogeneous suburban school districts than in lower class and heterogeneous ones.[12]

Building on these findings, a recent study has tried to relate local suburban politics to patterns of educational policy making in a more comprehensive manner than previously attempted. William L. Boyd uses the concept of "political culture" — the systematic differences in underlying orientations toward politics of different groups in a community — to explain school politics in suburban Chicago.[13] According to Boyd's study, high status groups are marked by a political culture supportive of non-partisan politics emphasizing expert solutions to policy problems. High status individuals also are more likely to believe in the existence of an overriding public interest and the existence of an objective way of achieving this interest. As a result of this "cultural" orientation, contested school board elections are viewed as potentially disastrous deviations from the pursuit of the common good. In contrast, in lower class districts with different cultural orientations, contested school board elections are enjoyed by the citizens.[14] Further, while demands on the school board in upper class districts are found to be phrased in terms of the needs of the district as a whole, demands in lower class districts seem to emanate more from conflicts between definable subsets of the community rather than being couched in terms of the general welfare. In short, in many school districts, especially lower class ones, the wall between politics and the schools has never been as completely realized as in upper class suburban districts. This same study also showed that the level of conflict and the intensity with which political controversies intrude into expected patterns of school administration were highly dependent on the quality of leadership found in a district. In districts with higher than expected levels of conflict, local school leadership on the board or by the superintendent was invariably naive or inept, while in districts with lower levels of conflict, leadership was better than average. Hence, the continuance of "apolitical" educational policy making may be dependent on the *political* abilities of the educational policy elite.

Another recent study of suburban school districts in the Chicago area shows further the intrusion of politics on school policy. Noting that in most school districts educational expenditures are largely determined by school district wealth (rich districts spend more on schools than poor ones), some suburban school districts were found to vary considerably from their "expected" level of expenditures as predicted by their community wealth. The level of political intervention into school policy was more intense in deviant school districts than in nondeviant ones.[16] In particular, in deviant school districts, interest groups were found to be operating that not only placed their policy demands before the school board, but also actively put forward their own candidates for positions on the board and actively campaigned during any referenda dealing with school policies, taxing, bonds or budgets. These groups, either pro-school or anti-school, were successful enough to cause school expenditures in the district to deviate from what otherwise would have been expected. In nondeviant districts, such "partisan" groups did not appear and most issues were defined internally by the existing educational elite, usually by the school superintendent. But in a considerable number of districts, "politics" were of importance in defining school policy.

Unfortunately, studies such as these may not be generalizable to other suburban areas across the country. The studies are overwhelmingly based in Chicago suburbs, where a history of political partisan activity is exceptionally strong. There also exists in the Chicago metropolitan area a large number of older suburban communities that were originally satellite cities. These communities often have lower class populations. Hence the diversity and the high level of political activity found in the suburban school districts surrounding Chicago may not be widespread in other metropolitan areas. Yet despite this limitation, research has shown that the norm of apolitical schools is often violated and that political activity centered on the schools is the usual pattern in many communities. However, exactly how many such communities exist and the extent of political activity associated with school policy is still unknown at present.

But if politics in the schools has been common in certain suburban school districts, many conditions may be developing that will further break down the nonpolitical milieux in which other schools have operated. Nonpolitical schools seem to require homogeneous populations. To the extent that suburban development produces more variety in the suburban population than in the past, nonpolitical school policy processes may become increasingly untenable. In particular, the isolation of schools from politics seems most likely to be found in homogeneous upper class districts. The development of working class and lower middle class suburbs may create political controversies in a larger number of suburban school districts.

The outmovement of blacks into suburbia may further reduce the ability of school districts to remain seemingly above politics. Desegregation of schools is an issue that almost always excites political activity and transcends the ability of a superintendent to impose an "impartial" expert solution. One study has also shown that suburban blacks tend to be more resistant to tax increases than their white counterparts.[17] Growing black suburbanization in some communities may portend more fractious school politics as the issue of tax increases to support quality schools splits racially heterogeneous suburban districts.

Yet, as politics intrudes more frequently into the operation of local school districts, it may be that regardless of the community and the intensity of local conflict over schools, school district politics can no longer amount to more than a "tempest in a teapot." More and more issues and the solutions to the problems facing schools emanate from levels of government higher than the local community. For example, the issue of school desegregation is often imposed upon metropolitan area school districts by the courts and by the federal government. Similarly, inequalities in school finance between suburban school districts first became an issue of major importance because of court cases and the investigations into school finances initiated by governors in several states. The solutions to desegregation may ultimately require the elimination of autonomous suburban school districts through the use of cross-district metropolitan-wide busing. The reduction of unequal school fiscal resources will inevitably require greater state intervention into local school board taxing and expenditure decisions. Other important issues regarding personnel, teaching practices, curriculum, and citizen input may all eventually be determined by levels of government higher than the local school district. And while research has shown how fiercely suburbanites will defend the autonomy of their schools,[18] the forces of change may be too strong for them to resist. With the growing intrusion of federal, state and regional concerns into educational policy making, the autonomy of local school boards and the "apolitical politics" associated with it may be totally transformed.

The Changing Environment of School Policy

If a range of issues is acting to reduce the autonomy of local schools while at the same time making local school politics more contentious, two issues stand out as particularly severe challenges to the normal environment of suburban schools. Not surprisingly these issues focus on money and race. In particular, they are concerned with the desegregation of schools and with the continued use of the local property tax as the prevalent means of raising money to support the schools. These two issues, both with the potential to radically transform the present environment of local school policy making, deserve further investigation.

Fiscal Inequalities in Metropolitan Education Systems

The tradition of local autonomy has had a major impact on the financing of local schools and has given rise to great inequalities between the resources available to local communities to pay for quality education. The tradition of local autonomy in the schools can be traced back to the colonial settlement of the United States, where the organization of school districts and the running of local schools was almost totally dependent on local initiative, and state or federal government intervention ran from minimal to nonexistent. As a result of this historical tradition of local control, the educational system throughout the country became the function of a large number of small, locally organized school districts. As late as the 1940s, there were well over 100,000 local school districts. Moreover, the funding of education became heavily dependent on the one tax to which these local school districts had easy access — the property tax. Yet the differences in the level of community wealthy, the autonomy of local school districts, and the heavy use of local property taxes inevitably meant that inequalities in the financing of local schools resulted: wealthy communities had rich school districts and well supported schools, poor communities had poor schools.

This variation in the quality and cost of schools between different districts subsequently has had an effect on the shape of suburban growth. People shopping for new housing find the cost of maintaining a house (and their ability and desire to purchase a particular house) directly dependent on the rate of local property taxation. Since in many suburban areas the local property tax is mostly determined by school taxes, differences in school district wealth and tax rates will have an effect on housing choices and on the nature of community development. In addition to this financial aspect, people may choose different housing locations depending on the reputation of the local school system — i.e., they may be willing to pay a higher price for housing in a school district with a good reputation than for similar housing in a less well regarded school district. Intuitively then, we expect a relationship to exist between school quality, school costs and suburban development. However, the independent effects of the quality of schools on the location of individual housing choices between city and suburbs and between different suburbs empirically is hard to isolate. People who are moving usually have a variety of motives inspiring the move and it may not be possible to say exactly how important the concern for schools is compared to other motives. Nonetheless, the fact that variation exists between school districts in both the quality and the expense of educational services has most likely had an effect on the shape of suburban development.

Despite the magnitude of differences between suburban school districts and the impact on metropolitan development, as in most educational policy questions, the federal government has maintained a strict hands-off policy with regard to inequalities of school finance, viewing education constitutionally as a state responsibility. The reticence of state governments to intervene to redress fiscal imbalances is somewhat more difficult to understand — states clearly had the authority to intervene, but they probably lacked the political will. In fact, state government intervention into most aspects of local educational policy making was minimal in the 1700s and through the mid-1800s. By the time of the Civil War, however, state involvement in the affairs of local school districts did begin to increase. This intervention usually took the form of the state setting minimal educational requirements in areas such as school calendars, teacher certification, and curriculum to which local schools had to conform. But the fundamental question of inequalities in the wealth of school districts and the use of state aid to reduce such inequalities was not addressed. In short, through the turn of the century, education continued in a historical mode of small local school districts marked by considerable inequalities in the money available to pay for education.[19]

This situation began to change in the 1920s and 1930s. Under the guidance of educational policy specialists such as George D. Strayer, Robert M. Haig and Paul Mort, the need for state intervention to redress fiscal imbalances in local schools began to be recognized as a legitimate policy concern of state governments.

The most important document in this effort was probably the report in 1923 of the Education Finance Inquiry Commission investigating educational funding in the State of New York. This report laid the conceptual framework for the most frequently found mode of state intervention into local school finance — "foundation programs."[20]

Through foundation programs, states allocate money to school districts to provide a basic minimum level of education, regardless of the wealth of the local district and its ability to finance these state requirements. Foundation programs require local school districts to maintain a certain minimal tax effort. Poor districts, in which the revenue from this tax rate is lower than the "foundation" guaranteed by the state, receive state aid to bring their educational funding up to the required level. Thus, the state guaranteed a minimal level of educational expenditures for all students, even those in the poorest districts. Rich districts, on the other hand, usually receive some state aid, but it is less than the aid to poor districts. But rich districts can easily build on the state "foundation" by supplementing state money with local tax revenue.

Clearly, foundation programs tend to be more important to poor districts than to rich ones and help bring poor districts up to minimal levels of education they might otherwise not be capable of supporting. In turn, since the 1930s, the involvement of the states in local educational finance has increased dramatically. In the 1930s, local revenues accounted for about 85 percent of educational expenditures as a national average. The remaining 15 percent came almost entirely from the states, while federal support for education was almost nonexistent. However, with the adoption of state foundation programs, the fiscal mix has changed. Overall, at present, local governments still account for the majority of expenditures, contributing about 52 percent of educational monies. Across the nation about 40 percent of money for education comes from the states.[21] There is a continuing tendency for the states to contribute increasing amounts of educational funds relative to local governments. Federal contributions are also increasing, although still minor compared to local and state responsibilities. At present, Federal funds account for about 8 percent of education monies.

State and Federal contributions to educational finance are usually aimed at poorer districts and tend to balance off the inequities resulting from the reliance on local property taxes. But despite the equalization inherent in higher level government intervention, inequities still abound in metropolitan school financing. These inequalities take the form of differences between city schools and suburban schools and differences between suburban schools themselves.

City Schools/Suburban Schools: Fiscal Imbalances

To understand the present fiscal imbalances between central city schools and their surrounding suburban ones, a historical perspective is helpful. Seymour Sacks, in his work *City Schools/Suburban Schools: A History of Fiscal Conflict*,[22] argues that the development of fiscal conflict in metropolitan education systems has passed through four distinct historical periods, reflecting the general overall balance between cities and suburbs.

The first period identified by Sacks encompasses the years immediately before 1900. This period was marked by the intense concentration of wealth and population in the nation's central cities. According to Sacks, the evolution of central city school systems paralleled the development of the cities themselves — that is, both cities and their schools were built, grew rapidly, and were relatively prosperous compared to outlying areas.

In the second historical period, 1900-1930, the consolidation of wealth in the central cities continued and intensified. Indeed, during this time period, central city schools were undoubtedly at their peak of performance and excellence relative to other school systems in the country. The wealth of the central cities allowed their school systems to expand to service a growing urban population, to increase their coverage to more and more students, and to implement educational innovations such as comprehensive high schools and vocational schools which were too expensive for other school districts outside the central cities even to consider. Moreover, because schools were financed by local property taxes, given the concentration of business and industry in the central cities, central cities were often so "property rich" that they could produce expensive educational services without high tax rates.

However, even while central city schools were experiencing this boom, certain changes were taking place that would eventually create fiscal problems for them. First, there were the beginnings of outmigration of wealthy individuals and high profit businesses to the suburbs. Indeed, during this time period some of the very wealthiest suburbs, for example, Oak Park outside of Chicago, Scarsdale outside of New York City, and Shaker Heights outside of Cleveland, began to spend more on their students than their central city counterparts. Thus, there were the beginnings of central city erosion relative to the suburbs. But this was only a minor phenomenon at the time: the wealth of central cities was still overwhelming and their school systems far superior to surrounding ones. But perhaps more important, the end of this time period saw the beginnings of increased state intervention into the financing of local schools and saw the increased interest of the states in reducing the level of inequalities between school districts. Given the concentration of wealth in the central cities, any decrease in inequalities inevitably meant that central cities had to pay for the development of higher quality education in outlying areas. State funding formulas adopted during the 1920s and 1930s had the effect of "pumping" money out of the cities and into the suburbs.

Yet despite these early attempts of the states to reduce inequalities between city and suburban school districts, the next period, between 1930 and 1950, was still one of stability for central city schools relative to their suburbs. The Depression and World War II kept the demands for new school buildings and for salaries low, and the development and concentration of wealth in the central cities was maintained. However, the "modern" period beginning in 1950 marked a severe change in the relative position of central city schools. The rapid suburbanization of population and industry began to deplete the central cities of their wealth. The demands of suburbs for state help in constructing schools to help service a growing population led to state aid policies that focused even more heavily on the suburbs while neglecting central city needs.[23] Indeed, it may have been the case that given the strong fiscal wealth of the central cities until the 1950s, state policy makers simply assumed that these school systems had the continued ability to finance their own educational programs without increases in state aid. But whatever the motivation, in general, through the 1950s and 1960s, states neglected the growing fiscal needs of central city schools and concentrated aid on their suburban ones.

Of course this neglect could not continue indefinitely without cost to the central city. Declining wealth and the continuing exodus of middle class people and industry to the suburbs began to erode severely central city fiscal capacity. The outmigrating middle class population was replaced by a younger lower class population with large numbers of school age children. This contributed to a growing demand of school services while a declining tax base was also evident. In addition, many central cities have functional responsibility for services that suburbs often avoid (e.g., hospitals, museums, welfare) and central city tax revenues have to be spread across a wide range of services. In contrast, suburban communities can usually more easily focus their expenditures on schools. As a result of all these conditions, we know that central city schools have suffered severe decline, and that they are no longer viewed as competitive in quality with their surrounding suburban school systems.

Yet, the worst imbalances in educational expenditures probably do not involve the comparison of central city and suburban schools. While it is true that central city school systems must be funded from a stagnant or declining property tax base, central cities still are endowed with expensive real estate in their central business districts that can be taxed to pay for schools. Because of this wealth, many central cities can impose lower property tax rates than their surrounding suburban districts lacking such property wealth.

Furthermore central city schools still spend more on their students, on the average, than many suburban school districts. In a study of educational expenditures, the Urban Institute found that in eight large states surveyed, central city educational expenditures were about 25 percent higher per student than in the surrounding suburbs.[24] While it is likely that the educational needs of students in central cities, especially those coming from minority groups and from lower class backgrounds, may be greater than the needs of many suburban students, central cities still can raise more money per pupil than can their surrounding suburbs.

Finally, while state aid formulae still tend to benefit suburban schools over central city schools, that pattern is slowly changing and more state aid and attention are now being given to the highly visible problems of central city schools.[25] But this may mean that poor suburban schools will be neglected.

In short, while central city/suburban school inequalities are pronounced, the greatest disparities in educational finance probably involve the comparison not of central city and suburban schools but of the schools in poor suburbs to those in rich ones.[26] As noted in the report prepared for the President's Commission on School Finance, "disparities by type of district . . . are greatest among suburban districts."[27]

Fiscal Inequalities in Suburban Schools

The inequalities between suburban school districts have been documented in a variety of places. Typical of the pattern is that situation reported by the Fleischmann Commission investigating school finances in New York State. Table 4-1, drawn from that report, comparing two suburban school districts in Long Island, illustrates the magnitude of the inequalities. The two districts, Levittown and Great Neck, are in the same suburban region. Great Neck is one of the richest suburbs in the entire country, while Levittown is a middle class suburb developed immediately after World War II. The disparities in the local property tax base are marked — at the time of the study, Great Neck had a market valuation of more than $64,000 per pupil, almost 4 times greater than Levittown.

Because Great Neck is so rich, it has the luxury of choosing whatever level of educational expenditure it desires. It can choose a high level of education without overburdening itself with an excessively high tax rate. In contrast, the educational policy choices of Levittown are restricted — it must tax itself heavily to provide a much lower level of education. Consider that both communities have imposed an identical tax rate of $2.72 per $100 of assessed property valuation. Yet because the property tax *base* in Great Neck is so much higher than in Levittown, the tax *yield* in Great Neck far surpasses that of Levittown. The richer community gets by far higher educational expenditures at an equal tax effort.

Close inspection of Table 4-1 will also alert us to some other factors concerning the funding of education in the suburbs. Most important is the role of state aid in financing suburban schools. Reliance on local property taxes is the obvious source of inequities in educational financing. However, state aid can reduce those inequities by disproportionately benefiting the poorest community. Federal aid can also act as an equalizing force, since it too tends to flow to the poorest districts and away from the richest. But the impact of Federal and state aid is minimized by the importance of local property taxes to educational funding. Thus, it is obvious that the reduction of inequalities in local school finance requires involvement of higher level governments, and in particular the states. Indeed, much attention has been focused on the role of the state in equalizing educational expenditures between school districts.

The Courts and School Financing

While inequalities between school districts were of some concern on an intermittent basis over the past, a concerted interest in reducing inequalities in school financing became important only in the 1960s. Moreover, while some legislative and gubernatorial action in the states was apparent, the arena in which most debate and decisions took place was the courts.

In 1968 a suit was brought in Illinois[28] followed by a 1969 case in Virginia[29] in which the validity of local school finance laws producing inequalities was challenged. The argument put forward by the plaintiffs was that under the present system of state aid, money was distributed to local schools with no consideration of educational needs, and that the states helped support a system "providing some students with a good education and depriving others who have equal or greater educational need."[30] The argument was appealing, yet plaintiffs in neither case were able to

Table 4-1   Fiscal Inequalities Between School Districts

	Per Pupil Enrolled	Percent of Total
Great Neck: (Student Enrollment: 9,869)		
Revenue from Local Property Tax	$1,684.07	81.1%
Revenue from State Sources	364.16	17.5
Revenue from Tuition and Other Local Sources	29.29	1.4
Revenue from Federal Sources	0	0.0
Total Expenditure	$2,077.52	100.0
True Value Assessed Property: $64,400 per pupil		
Tax Rate: $2.72 per $100		
Levittown: (Student Enrollment: 17,280)		
Revenue from Local Property Tax	$ 410.31	34.5%
Revenue from State Sources	764.48	64.3
Revenue from Tuition and Other Local Sources	13.87	1.2
Revenue from Federal Sources	.71	0.1
Total Expenditure	$1,189.37	100.0
True Value Assessed Property: $16,200 per pupil		
Tax Rate: $2.72 per $100		

Source: The Fleischmann Report on the Quality, Cost, and Financing of Elementary and Secondary Education in New York State. Data are from 1969.

present a clear definition of education needs, nor a method of assessing it. As a result, the courts felt that they had no clear means by which to intervene. Both the McInnis and Buruss cases were dismissed by the U.S. District Courts, and appeal to the U.S. Supreme Court was denied. But then in 1971, a landmark case was heard in California that radically transformed the debates concerning educational financing. Rather than argue the case against state aid on the basis of educational need, the plaintiffs in *Serrano* v. *Priest*[31] argued that educational finance formulas violated a more measurable standard of "fiscal neutrality," that is, under present educational finance laws the education one received was determined mostly by the fiscal capacity of the local school district. The resulting imbalances, it was argued, violated the rights of individuals to "equal protection of the laws."

The California Supreme Court, after inspecting empirical data documenting the wide variation in tax rates and yields, agreed with the plaintiffs and held that the system financing education in the State of California, based overwhelmingly on local property taxes, was unconstitutional. Immediately following the ruling in *Serrano*, seven other cases concerning inequalities in educational finance were filed in either state or Federal courts.[32] These cases, in one form or another, claimed that the system of local property taxes supporting schools violated the right to equal protection under the law. The cases were argued either on national constitutional grounds, in particular the 14th Amendment's requirement of "equal protection," or on individual state constitutional or legal grounds. The national constitutional issue was settled for the present by the U.S. Supreme Court in its ruling in *Rodriguez* v. *Independent School District of San Antonio*.[33] In this 1973 ruling, the Court held that education was *not* a national right, and therefore Federal constitutional guarantees were not violated by the present inequities in local school systems. But this ruling did not foreclose the possibility that the inequities in school finance violated individual state constitutional and legal requirements. Indeed after the *Rodriguez* decision, several state courts have found such violations of state law. In effect, the Supreme Court's position, while removing Federal intervention, has turned the issue back to the states for consideration and resolution. State courts have often responded forcefully to the challenge.

The judicial process continues to put pressure on state governments to reform present systems of school financing. But just as important is the changing political environment. Taxpayer revolts (such as Proposition 13 in California) against the high property tax burden necessary to support schools are common, putting pressure on the continued use of that tax system. These revolts are often fueled not only by a concern for high tax rates but also by a growing citizen awareness of the inequities in tax burdens between neighboring communities. As both judicial and political pressures on the present system of school finance mount, school fiscal reform has become an item on many state policy agendas. In fact, about half of the states have, in one form or another, responded to these judicial and political pressures by considering or actually adopting some increased level of state involvement in local school financing practices. But while it is clear that to achieve equalization state school aid will have to increase, the extent and form to which the present system of school finance will change is at present unclear. In particular, there are several major alternatives to existing systems of local financing and state aid that are currently considered viable.

Foundation Programs: Why They Fail

At present, most state aid programs are tied to the foundation programs developed in the 1920s and 1930s. These foundation programs can reduce inequalities by bringing up poor districts to a minimal level of education and increasing the spending capabilities of poor districts relative to rich ones. As Table 4-1 shows, state aid did in part offset the advantage the wealthy suburb enjoyed by virtue of its high property tax base. In general, studies have shown that the greater the state aid, the less the inequalities found between school districts.[34]

However, despite recent reforms in foundation programs and interest in equalizing educational expenditures, existing foundation programs tend to provide only minimal relief to inequalities. First, foundation programs require that local school districts tax themselves at a minimum rate or higher. State aid goes mostly to communities that tax themselves at the minimum rate but do not produce revenues sufficient to provide the educational "foundation" mandated by the state. But wealthy districts can tax themselves at any rate they want higher than the minimum mandated by the state and use the additional tax revenues to improve their schools. State foundation programs therefore provide a "floor" for the poor districts but put no limit on the ceiling for rich ones.

Further, the minimum aid levels set in state foundation programs tend to be fixed in legislation that does not change over time. As inflation pushes up the cost of education, the minimal level guaranteed by law becomes a smaller percentage of actual educational expenditures, and the equalizing effect of state aid decreases. Moreover, because of political pressures in state legislatures, it is not uncommon for a minimal flat grant of state aid to be guaranteed to every school district in a state regardless of its wealth. To the extent that rich districts then participate in the flow of state aid, the equalizing potential of this aid is decreased.

In short, while we know that state aid *can* decrease district inequalities, present state foundation programs, the most common approach to state aid, empirically do not do so.

Full State Assumption

Perhaps the most radical solution to this problem of unequal school district wealth would be for the states to assume full responsibility for financing schools. The state could then institute a state-wide property tax for education, replacing existing local ones. Additional taxes such as a state-wide sales tax or an income tax could be instituted to relieve property tax pressures. The centrally collected educational monies could then be distributed by the state according to the norm of "fiscal neutrality" — equal money would be spent on similar students. Rather than students in rich school districts getting the most educational support, the state could decide which *types of students*, regardless of geographic location, should receive greater aid. Aid could be targeted on students, such as the physically or emotionally handicapped, with the greatest educational needs, regardless of the local wealth of their school district.

Possibly the strongest fear limiting the appeal of this alternative is the deeply held belief that education should be a local policy, controlled by community school boards. The argument against full state funding assumes that with the centralization of school financing, power to make all types of educational policy decisions would also be centralized in the hands of the state, and local control over the schools would decrease or disappear. While empirical data suggest that state control over greater proportions of school financing does *not* increase state control over local policy,[35] people's viceral feelings with regard to local control of the schools may be unswayable by social scientific evidence.

Increased State Involvement: Power Equalization

Perhaps the most viable alternatives to full state assumption lie in approaches to achieving equalization through greater, but not total state involvement in educational finance.

The most common alternatives proposed to equalize school financing through state intervention short of full state assumption revolve around schemes known generally as "power equalization." Conceptually, these reforms seek to achieve fiscal neutrality by guaranteeing that every local school district taxing itself at the same rate as any other district will receive equal revenue.

In "power equalizing" reforms, the state first determines the "base level" that should be guaranteed as every community's minimal property tax wealth. As a matter of practice, most states guarantee approximately a property tax base equal to a school district with average property wealth per student. Once this base level is determined, the state then guarantees the yield for each tax rate as applied to that base.

An example of the approach can clarify the concept. If a state sets the guaranteed base for every local school district at $50,000 per student, then a 1 percent property tax is guaranteed to yield $500, a 1½ percent tax $750, a 2 percent tax $1000, etc. Any school district choosing a given tax rate will then receive the return set by the state. If a community is below the guaranteed base, and applying a given tax rate yields less than the specified minimum, state aid makes up the differences. To use the example in Table 4-1, Levittown chose a 2.7 percent tax but produced local revenues of only $410. If the state guarantees a $50,000 base, the set yield of a 2.7 percent tax would be $1350 per student. State aid would then make up the $940 difference between the guaranteed yield and the actual yield in Levittown. Great Neck in contrast would receive no state aid, and in the extreme form of power equalization would actually lose to the state all revenues above the set yield of $1350.

Power equalization has appeal because it allows the local community to retain control of the decision determining tax effort, while achieving fiscal neutrality through the guarantee of equal educational funds for equal tax effort.

Table 4-2 illustrates some other dimensions of power equalization and, in general, shows some of the possible effects of state power equalization for a district above and a district below the base level set by the state. The table also shows the effect of a

Table 4-2 Power Equalization: A Hypothetical Example

Tax Base Per Pupil	Tax Rate	State Guaranteed Base Per Pupil	Tax Collection Per Pupil	State Aid Per Pupil	Revenue Per Pupil
$40,000	1.10%	$50,000	$440	$110	$550
	1.10	55,000	440	165	605
	1.65%	$50,000	$660	$165	$825
	1.65	55,000	660	248	908
$60,000	1.10%	$50,000	$660	-$110	$550
	1.10	55,000	660	- 55	605
	1.65%	$50,000	$990	-$165	$825
	1.65	55,000	990	- 82	908

Source: Adapted from Betsy Levin *et al.*, *Public School Finance* (Washington, D.C.: The Urban Institute, 1972), Tables III-14, III-15.

changing state guaranteed base and different tax rates on state aid to local districts.

From Table 4-2, it is clear that the level of aid given by the state to its districts is a function of both the guaranteed base set by the state and the tax rate chosen by the district. The higher the base, the greater are state costs. First, a higher base means there will be more districts under the guaranteed base eligible to receive state aid. Second, as more clearly seen in the table, the amount of aid given to poor communities increases with the distance they are below the base. The hypothetical community shown in Table 4-2 with an average tax base of $40,000 per pupil receives $110 per pupil when the state guarantees a $50,000 tax base, but would receive $165 per pupil state aid when the guarantee is $55,000. Similarly, the choice of tax rates also affects state aid. If the below average wealth community chooses higher tax rates (in our example, 1.65 percent compared to 1.1 percent), the amount of state obligation increases. Critics of power equalization argue that this may increase the incentives for poorer suburbs to choose higher tax rates since they can increase the amount of money given them from the state. If all or most poor communities adopt this strategy, state education aid would escalate beyond reasonable bounds.

Viewed from the perspective of above average school district, the power equalization scheme is not as attractive as it is for below average districts. This table presents an extreme form of power equalization. The example shown assumes that the state will actually transfer money out of the richest school districts to poorer ones. From the perspective of a richer district, the higher the guaranteed base the better. At equal tax rates, the higher the base (e.g., $55,000 compared to $50,000), the lower the penalties assessed by the state. This gives very real incentives to wealthier districts to fight for the highest guaranteed base possible. But as the guaranteed base increases, so do state costs — presenting a real possibility for political conflict between state budget officials and local governments. But perhaps as important is the possible effects of higher tax rates on the pattern of school spending in rich districts. Note that as the tax rate increases, the amount of money siphoned off by the state likewise increases. At the higher tax rate, the rich school district is still able to spend more than at a lower tax rate, but there are severe penalties to rich districts for assessing higher taxes — the state gets more money at their expense. Critics of this approach to equalizing school funding argue that given these penalties, most wealthy school districts would choose the lowest tax rate permissible by law and establish private schools in which to educate their children.

Conflicts between rich districts and poor districts have led to modification of true power equalization schemes. Our example is extreme in that it assumes a penalty to rich districts, that is, money would actually be taken out of the district. This penalty to rich districts helps supply the transfer to below average districts. As a result, the net level of educational expenditures may not increase dramatically, and mostly the distribution between districts changes. This option is usually referred to as "levelling down," i.e., certain rich districts are brought down to the level of others. Obviously the political battles involved in this redistribution would be severe, and powerful wealthy suburban areas would fight such a scheme with whatever resources they had available.

An obvious alternative is "levelling up," in which the poorer school districts are brought up to the expenditure levels of the wealthiest school districts. While this might minimize conflict among school districts, it would increase educational expenditures beyond acceptable levels.

One solution for this dilemma is that put forth by the Fleischmann Commission in New York. The Commission suggested that the present levels of expenditures of above average districts be *frozen* and that the state not take money away from them. Instead, new state educational aid would be directed at the poorest districts, slowly raising their level of educational expenditures. Given increasing expenditures because of inflation, and with the help of state aid, more and more districts would increase their expenditures relative to the above average districts locked into a fixed level. Over time, districts would converge. This is a levelling down process in that the real expenditures of the above average school districts would decline, although the state has not actually taken money away. It is also a levelling up process in that new state aid is targeted on the poorest school districts raising their expenditures relative to the rest of the school districts.[36]

The future of power equalization is not clear although variants of it are always discussed with regard to equalizing educational expenditures. One apparent lesson, however, is that given the political resistance to "levelling down," any equalization process will necessarily increase the need for educational expenditures on the part of the state. If a state has the extra funds available, then the possibilities of educational reform are improved. If new or increased taxes are required, then the possibilities of educational equalization are subsequently reduced.[37] Indeed, given the severe fiscal constraints facing states in recent years, substantial educational financial reform has bogged down. Essentially state action falls into three categories at present: no interest in reform, examination of the need for fiscal reform with no concrete action, or adoption of new equalization measures without the funding necessary to achieve desired goals.[38] Reform that is actually implemented is now a rarity.

Given these limitations, comprehensive equalization is not likely in the foreseeable future. To be sure, state courts will prod action in some states, as has happened in New Jersey. Just as importantly, to the extent that educational finance reforms are sold as property tax relief and limitations on educational spending they may prove to have intrinsic political appeal.[39] In addition, some more incremental reforms to present state school aid are already apparent. Rather than state aid being tied strictly to property tax base as in the past, more basic state goals in educational policy are being served by new state aid formulas that include: greater recognition of the need of central city students; targeting aid to poor populations in cities, suburbs and rural areas; increasing aid to the emotionally or physically handicapped; etc.

But given the limitations on state fiscal wealth and the strong political base of wealthy suburbs threatened by true equalization, inequalities in education finance may be expected to continue for some time.

Metropolitan Schools and Blacks: Integration, School Busing and White Flight

The division of metropolitan area school systems between city schools and suburban ones, and the division of suburban schools into small autonomous districts also has had a major effect on the nature of racial segregation, the need for school busing, and the reaction of whites to "forced" school integration. In particular, the fragmentation of metropolitan schools of northern areas has presented dilemmas to those seeking integrated school systems.

Since 1954 the courts, in particular the U.S. Supreme Court, have led the push for school desegregation. This effort was originally focused on the southern states where a system of dual schools embodied in state law had existed. In the 1950s, but especially in the late 1960s, the Supreme Court pushed for effective school desegregation in the South. This line of decisions peaked in 1971, when the Supreme Court was faced with a major decision involving integrating the schools in Charlotte and Mecklenberg County, North Carolina.[40] Building on a set of precedents, the Supreme Court addressed the question of *how* desegregation could be achieved. In its opinion, the Court held that *busing* was one acceptable means of achieving school desegregation. In addition, the Court, noting that whites lived disproportionately in the outlying areas of the city and county while blacks were confined more to the central areas, ordered extensive county-wide busing to achieve school desegregation.

Neighborhood schools were to be sacrificed in order to achieve the competing social good of racially integrated schools.

The decision in Charlotte opened up a wide range of questions for metropolitan school systems throughout the United States. First, while the Court's decision referred to a Southern area where legal segregation had existed in the past, and hence in the type of area where the Court had always maintained stricter scrutiny, northern and western cities began to wonder about their continued ability to escape court investigation. After all, segregation in northern schools was as extensive as in the South, only that such segregation was never formally enforced by state legislation.[41]

But just as important was the question of the sanctity of neighborhood schools. In the Charlotte decision, the Court had ordered the elimination of many neighborhood schools and ordered the use of county-wide busing to create racially balanced schools. But in the Charlotte region, as in much of the South, counties were the unit through which schools were organized. Thus, the city and the suburban schools in the county were legally part of the same school district. Therefore the Charlotte decision did not require the elimination of local school districts nor the crossing of local school district lines to achieve desegregation. In short, no "cross-district" busing was required. But metropolitan areas outside the South, especially in the northeast and midwest, did not have such comprehensive metropolitan-wide school districts — just the opposite condition existed in most northern areas. In the north, a central city school district was usually surrounded by a large number of legally autonomous suburban school districts. Given the racial imbalances between cities and suburbs, any attempt to achieve school integration in these northern metropolitan areas would necessarily involve the use of city/suburban cross-district busing that would have to ignore the sanctity of local school district lines.

Racial Imbalances Between City and Suburban Schools

The severity of this problem in the larger metropolitan areas of the country, and the dilemma it poses for the achievement of integrated schools in the north, can be seen in the data reflecting

**Table 4-3   Blacks as Proportion of Total Public School
Enrollment, Cities and Suburbs 1970s
15 Large Metropolitan Areas**

SMSA	% Black Central City		% Black Suburb		Ratio City/Suburb	
	1960	1970	1960	1970	1960	1970
New York	26	40	6	6	4.33	6.66
Los Angeles	19	24	5	7	3.80	3.43
Chicago	43	55	5	5	8.60	11.00
Philadelphia	50	61	10	11	5.00	5.55
Detroit	46	64	6	5	7.67	12.80
San Francisco	39	40	10	8	3.90	5.00
Boston	19	32	1	1	19.00	32.00
Washington, D.C.	80	93	6	10	13.33	9.30
Cleveland	48	57	2	5	24.00	11.40
St. Louis	51	65	13	14	3.92	4.64
Pittsburgh	36	42	6	6	6.00	7.00
Minneapolis	5	8	0	6	Undef.	Undef.
Houston	27	32	12	7	2.25	4.57
Baltimore	53	67	6	4	8.83	16.75
Dallas	22	34	3	2	7.33	17.00
Average	37.6	47.6	6.1	6.1	6.16	7.80

Source: Adapted from Reynolds Farley, "Residential Segregation and Its Implications
for School Integration," *Law and Contemporary Problems*, 39 (Winter 1975), figure 3,
pp. 172-173.

black student concentrations in 15 large metropolitan areas.
Table 4-3 shows empirically what should be evident to most
readers — there is a huge disparity in the concentrations of blacks
in city and suburban schools. Overall, of the fifteen large
metropolitan areas shown, in 1960 about 38 percent of the student
body in the central cities were black. This increased to 48 percent
over the course of the following decade. In contrast, the suburban
school surrounding these cities averaged only 6 percent black in
1960 and remained constant in that percentage over the next ten
years.

Further, in 1960, only 4 of the largest central city school
districts were majority black (Philadelphia, Washington, D.C.,
St. Louis, Baltimore). By 1970, there were seven (now including
Chicago, Detroit and Cleveland). In contrast, the average percent
black in the suburbs surrounding these cities never exceeded 15
percent, and in the overwhelming number of suburbs, barely

exceeded 5 percent. Moreover, while the percent black increased in every central city school district, the percent black in the surrounding suburbs increased in only 5 areas and always by a miniscule amount compared to the increase in the central city schools. Furthermore, the concentration of black students actually declined in 5 suburban areas, and stayed the same in the remaining suburbs.

In short, there are enduring differences in the racial distribution of students in city and suburban school districts. The ratios presented in the last two columns of Table 4-3 translate these differences into a single rough measure of city/suburban disparities.

Within this pattern of central city/suburban differences, some regional differences occur, ones not unlike those portrayed in Chapter 2 comparing cities and suburbs on a variety of socio-economic measures. Note that the most glaring racial imbalances between cities and suburbs are in the northeastern metropolitan areas, such as Baltimore, Detroit and Cleveland, while the lowest disparities seem to be found in western metropolitan areas, such as Los Angeles, San Francisco and Houston. There are some exceptions to this trend, but in general racial differences between cities and suburbs in the northeast are greater than in other regions of the country.

This regional pattern is explicable by several conditions. First, of course, is the fact that racial imbalances in general residential settlement patterns are greater in the northeast than elsewhere. But this demographic fact is compounded by the system of governing education. In the northeast there is a greater number of independent suburban school districts surrounding the central city than in the South. Northern metropolitan areas may have on the average 5 times the number of school districts as southern metropolitan areas.[42] Thus, in the South, central city schools with large numbers of blacks are more likely to be combined in the same school district with suburban schools having a lower proportion of blacks. In contrast, the greater fragmentation of school districts in the north helps ensure school segregation by separating whites in suburban schools from blacks in central city ones.

Furthermore, the blacks that do reside in northern suburbs tend to be highly segregated in school systems isolated from neighboring systems with more whites. For example, in Chicago in 1972, of 204 suburban school districts surrounding the central city, 53 were found to have no black students at all, 93 were less than 1 percent blacks, while at least 4 districts were majority black. Similarly, in Detroit in the same year, of 78 suburban school districts, 11 had no blacks, 27 were less than 1 percent black, and 2 were majority black. Yet at the same time, the student populations in both central cities were more than 55 percent black. It is obvious then that central city/suburban racial differences are found, and that considerable differences between suburban schools also exist. In the north, where the education system is divided up into small independent and autonomous school districts these racial differences are the most evident.[43]

Cross-District Busing and School Desegregation

Faced with this demographic pattern reinforced by a strong political tradition involving local control of schools, the courts have been reluctant to order effective metropolitan-wide desegregation in the north, preferring instead to maintain the sanctity of local school districts. This is not to say that where suburban school systems have engaged in blatantly racist activity, the courts will not intervene to correct the situation. For example, in both Wilmington, Delaware and Louisville, Kentucky it was found that city and suburban school officials had engaged in collusion to create and maintain segregated schools.[44] This action was sufficiently repugnant to the courts to order cross-district busing to achieve better racial balance. Similarly, in St. Louis County, three suburban school districts were found by a lower Federal court to have collaborated to maintain school segregation.[45] Of the three districts, the student population in one was almost all black, in another 35 percent black, and the third about 3 percent. Apparently, these three districts had cooperated to maintain this racial imbalance, and in particular, the all-white district had consistently attempted to avoid contact with either of the other two school districts. In its decision, a lower Federal court ruled that all three districts had to consolidate to achieve racial balance.

In specific cases, the use of cross-district busing and the willingness to ignore the sanctity of local school district lines is apparent. Yet the general willingness of the courts to undertake such radical remedies is limited. The governing precedent in most metropolitan wide school busing cases in the north is not the Louisville, Wilmington or St. Louis cases, but the 1974 decision of the U.S. Supreme Court concerning the City of Detroit and its surrounding suburban schools.[46] In its ruling, the Court refused to order the combination of suburban and central city school districts to achieve racial balance. Among the reasons cited in the decision was the value of local autonomy and local control of the schools as legitimate values balancing the need for school desegregation. But if at present the issue of court-ordered cross district busing in the north seems to have been settled in favor of continued separation of city and suburban schools, the issue is by no means dead. The Supreme Court decision in the Detroit case was close, and it is possible that future cases may be decided differently.[47]

White Flight and School Desegregation

If cross-district busing has had limited applications in desegregating schools, the integration of schools *within* individual school districts especially in central cities is proceeding rapidly. The pattern of neighborhood schools reflecting racial segregation in housing and residential development within cities is giving way to extensive school busing to achieve desegregation. But in recent years there has been concern that the destruction of neighborhood white-dominated schools has accelerated the exodus of white families from the central cities to the suburbs — a phenomenon generally referred to as "white flight."

The interest in white flight from desegregation intensified around 1974 with the conversion of a leading sociologist, James Coleman, from a strong proponent of school busing and desegregation to a leading questioner of the long run gains to be achieved by school busing.

Based on his empirical research, Coleman began to express fears that forced desegregation and school busing would only encourage "white flight" to the suburbs, resulting in a higher level of racial segregation than would exist in the absence of school desegregation:

> The extremely strong reactions of individual whites in moving their children out of large districts engaged in massive and rapid desegregation suggest that in the long run the policies that have been pursued will defeat the purpose of increasing overall contact among the races in schools.[48]

This position advocating a slowing of school desegregation to avoid white flight has been strongly attacked by proponents of school desegregation. Subsequent research has shown that white flight to the suburbs in reaction to school desegregation does exist, but on a much more limited scale than suggested first by Coleman.

White flight seems to be particularly prevalent in large cities rather than in small ones. This is related to the fact that large cities tend to be surrounded by independent suburban school districts that remain legally separate from central city schools. The racial composition of these suburban districts tends to be more white dominated, and hence, white flight to the suburbs is "rewarding" — whites can move to a suburban area and go to local schools that are majority white. On the other hand, in areas where county-wide schools exist, places such as Jacksonville, Tampa, Miami, Nashville, Charlotte, etc., and where desegregation of city and suburban schools occurs together, the "rewards" for white flight are much more limited, and the phenomenon is less prevalent. (But even within these county-wide systems, "fleeing" whites will try to move into areas least affected by busing.)[49]

White flight also seems to be more frequent in metropolitan areas where there are larger concentrations of minority students in the central city. This may be related to the "tipping" phenomenon noted by several researchers. Individual schools seem to be racially stable below black student concentrations of 30-35 percent. However, once this threshold is passed, schools "tip" rapidly to majority and then to almost exclusively black. As black concentrations in central cities increase, and as desegregation spreads black student populations over more schools, the increased number of schools "tipping" to black may lead whites to seek escape to the suburbs.

Finally, it must be noted that the movement of white families, and white students to the suburbs, predates by far the current controversies over school desegregation. School desegregation may have only a minor impact on this continuing outward movement. In particular, it seems as though school desegregation has a one year/one time effect in that a number of white families that were probably considering moving to the suburbs may find that desegregation only reaffirms their predispositions and their move comes sooner rather than later. Thus, white flight to the suburbs does exist, but it may be insignificant in the long run, and will most likely be found where suburban districts can maintain their separate identities from central city schools and from other suburban schools more subject to black in-migration.

Other Educational Policy Concerns

If money and race are the major issues around which much of the policy issues facing the schools revolve, other issues are also important. For example, in the past 15 years or so, the unionization of school teachers in metropolitan school districts has been of major concern. Unionization has several impacts on local schools. First, unionization can increase the bargaining power of local teachers, increasing their salaries and forcing up local taxes necessary to pay these higher costs. Perhaps equally important is the fact that union contracts frequently spell out in detail limitations on the actions of local school boards in issues over which at one time they had greater control. Powerful unions may be able to specify class size, work load, scheduling, and other administrative and educational policy concerns limiting the freedom of the school board and the district superintendent. The impact of teacher's unions has been most studied in large central cities where they have had the most visible impact, but unionization of suburban schools has taken place.

But perhaps more important than the issue of unionization is the changing demographic composition of the American population and its impact on schools. Demographers have for several years been calling attention to what they call the "graying of America." Americans are having fewer children than in the past. This is the result of changing family patterns (more single person households, higher divorce rates, later marriages) as well as the choices of married couples to have fewer (or no) children. Anyway, there are about 1 million fewer children being born every year in the mid-1970s than was the case 10 to 20 years ago. As a result of this declining number of children, schools are becoming a "surplus" commodity: there are fewer children to fill schools built to accommodate a larger school population.

In many suburban areas this problem of declining number of school age children is compounded by the limited size of school districts and the continuing deconcentration of population to further out suburbs. Thus, many older suburban areas are heavily populated by the first "wave" of post-World War II suburbanites, people now in their 40s, 50s or 60s. These people are past their child rearing stage of life and thus the number of school age children living in these houses is very small. In addition, younger suburban families with school age children are more likely to be found in newer suburban communities than in these older ones. As a result, many older suburban school districts are faced with a surplus of school capacity. School buildings must be closed, sold for or converted to other uses (e.g., office space). But while some suburban districts are faced with surplus schools, other newer communities are still faced with growing school enrollments. Present trends in the birth rate and the experience of older suburban communities indicate that newer suburbs should proceed with caution before expanding their school facilities. If they will do so is an important question worth watching in the future.

One final developing policy question concerning local education practices deserves notice, and this concerns the growing importance of the federal and state governments in defining local education policy. Most important is the growing federal presence in the funding of local schools through the Elementary and Secondary Education Act (ESEA) of 1965. Since ESEA went into effect, federal support of local schools has increased considerably. However, even at present, federal support still represents less than 10 percent of the monies spent on local schools. Given the extent of fiscal pressures on local governments and school districts this federal support becomes extremely important — local schools may find themselves unable to forego the support and federal "leverage" over local school policies may be greater than the extent of support itself may indicate. Thus the role of the federal government in defining local school practices has already grown in the years since 1965 and will undoubtedly increase in the future. If federal intervention and policy guidance through the manipulation of its aid increases, if the states continue to increase their supervision of local school policies, and if state and federal courts define the major problems and corrective procedures for local school districts, what happens to the deeply held value of local schools locally run that has been part of the history of school in America since its settling?

Issues such as these will continue to face metropolitan school systems in the foreseeable future.

Summary: Education in Metropolitan Areas

Schools and the delivery of educational services are overwhelmingly based in a tradition of local control and local financing. Virtually all suburban communities run schools and, on the average, the associated costs of education consume well over half of local government expenditures in suburban areas. Given the expense of schools, their ubiquitious presence, and the importance of the clientele (that is, children), concern for schools often is intense in many suburban areas. Traditionally, however, schools have been held to be separate from the normal political and policy processes of local government. Thus, schools are most often organized into largely independent school districts that are legally separate from the general governance of the community. School districts are governed by school boards that are elected separately from mayors or village council members. Moreover, school boards appoint district superintendents who have been trained to believe in the need to rule districts according to expert norms to which only trained professionals have access.

The isolation of school policy making from normal political processes grew out of the corruption of local schools by machine politics at the turn of the century. However, in the last 15 years or more, the isolation of schools has been eroded. Schools have become expensive to run and local residents often resent the property taxes necessary to pay for educational expenses.

Taxpayer revolts and closer monitoring of school expenditures had reduced the isolation of school districts from normal politics.

One variant of school financial problems is the growing concern for the inequalities in the fiscal resources of local areas necessary to support schools. Rich school districts have low taxes and high revenues, poor school districts have just the opposite — high tax rates and low revenues. Such fiscal inequalities have become increasingly important policy concerns since the landmark case in California in 1971, *Serrano* v. *Priest*. In the years since then, a number of state courts and state legislatures have sought means of achieving "fiscal neutrality" in the financing of local schools. This state involvement has taken a variety of forms, many of which have constrained the autonomy of local school districts.

Racial issues have also become important in the governance of local schools in metropolitan areas. Most often the issue of race intrudes *within* school districts, mostly central city ones, when racial segregation has been found by the courts. However, inter-district segregation — usually whites in suburban districts and blacks in central city ones — has so far been relatively immune to court intervention and court ordered desegregation. But there have been instances (e.g., St. Louis County, Wilmington) where courts have ordered cross-district busing to achieve desegregation of schools. To what extent such remedies that may affect more directly suburban school districts will appear in the future is unknown. At present, the most important case, *Milliken* v. *Bradley* concerning the Detroit metropolitan area, has preserved the sanctity of suburban white school districts from central city black ones. However, in this volatile issue area, change can always occur.

But until metropolitan-wide desegregation becomes accepted policy, perhaps the most important impact of school desegregation concerns the extent to which large scale desegregation in central city school districts causes increased "white flight" to the suburbs. At present the evidence linking school desegregation and white residential movement to the suburbs is less than conclusive and a "battle of sociologists" concerning the phenomenon is waged in academic circles, in the press, in the courts and in government agencies. While the evidence is less than conclusive, it appears that white flight is a short-lived phenomenon most often found in large metropolitan areas in the northeast and midwest — the regions where movement from a black dominated central city school district to a separate and autonomous white suburban one is most likely successfully to avoid racial integration. Further research on "white flight" will be required before the issue can be resolved. In the meantime, however, concern for racial integration, and the impact that local autonomous school districts have on such segregation will call added attention to schools, reducing further their traditional political isolation.

Other issues have intruded into the normal "apolitical" world of school policy making, continually reducing the traditional isolation of schools from local politics. But as school policy making at the local level becomes more intense and conflictual, the most important decisions may no longer be controllable by local communities and school boards at all. The solution to many of the major issues now facing schools are issues that require state and often federal money and intervention. As higher level government intervention and guidelines increase in frequency and specificity, the autonomy and policy leeway of local school governance will necessarily decrease. Ironically, then, at the same time that community involvement in local school policy debates may be expected to increase in frequency and intensity, the policy arena in which the issues will be resolved has shifted out of the local community to higher level governments.

Notes

1. Frederick M. Wirt and Michael W. Kirst, *The Political Web of American Schools* (Boston: Little, Brown and Co., 1972), p. 5.

2. Raymond E. Callahan, *Education and the Cult of Efficiency* (Chicago: University of Chicago Press, 1962).

3. Wirt and Kirst, *op. cit.*, p. 7.

4. See Callahan, *op. cit.*, and David Swift, *Ideology and Change in Public Schools: The Latent Functions of Progressive Education* (Columbus, Ohio: Charles E. Merrill, 1970).

5. L. Harmon Zeigler and M. Kent Jennings, *Governing American Schools* (North Scituate, Mass.: Duxbury Press, 1974), especially Part III.

6. On the effects of nonpartisan at-large elections in reducing the salience of

politics see, e.g., Robert R. Alford and Eugene C. Lee, "Voting Turnout in American Cities," *American Political Science Review* 62 (September, 1968), pp. 1192-1206; Robert L. Lineberry and Edmund P. Fowler, "Reformism and Public Policies in American Cities," *American Political Science Review* 61 (September, 1967), pp. 601-716; and, Mark Schneider, "Urban Political Parties: Electoral Reform and Campaign Work," *Polity*, 10 (Fall 1977), pp. 130-142.

7. Zeigler and Jennings, *op. cit.*, p. 51.

8. Norman R. Luttbeg and Richard W. Griffin, "Tying Elite and Public Opinion Difference to Levels of Public Support," *American Politics Quarterly* 3 (April, 1975), pp. 107-129.

9. See, for example, Robert L. Crain, *Politics of School Desegregation* (Chicago: Aldine Publishing, 1968); David Minar, *Decision Making in Suburban Schools* (Evanston, Illinois: Northwestern University Press, 1966); John C. Walden, "School Board Changes and Superintendent Turnover," *Administrator's Notebook* XV (January 1967).

10. Ralph Kimbrough, *Political Power and Educational Decision Making* (Chicago: Rand McNally, 1964); Warner Bloomberg and Morris Sunshine, *Suburban Power Structures and Public Education* (Syracuse, N.Y.: Syracuse University Press, 1963).

11. David W. Minar, "The Community Basis of Conflict in School System Politics," *American Sociological Review* 31 (December 1966), pp. 822-835.

12. This finding is supported by the extensive investigation of school politics reported in Zeigler and Jennings, *op. cit.*

13. William L. Boyd, "Community Status and Conflict in Suburban School Politics," *Sage Professional Papers in American Politics* 1, 04-001 (Beverly Hills, Calif.: Sage Publication, 1973).

14. *Ibid.*, p. 22.

15. On the relationship between SES and educational expenditures see, for example, H. Thomas James, *Wealth, Expenditures and Decision Making for Education* (Stanford, Calif.: Stanford University Press, 1963) or Seymour Sacks and David Ranney, "Suburban Education: A Fiscal Analysis," *Urban Affairs Quarterly* 2 (January, 1966), pp. 103-119.

16. David O'Shea, "Suburban School District Governance," *Education and Urban Society* 5 (August 1973), pp. 405-436.

17. John N. Collins and Bryan T. Downes, "Support for Public Education in a Racially Changing Suburb," *Urban Education* 10 (October 1975), pp. 221-244.

18. See, for example, Louis Masotti, *Education and Politics in Suburbia: The New Trier Experience* (Cleveland: Case Western Reserve University Press, 1967).

19. Marian Lief Palley and Howard A. Palley, *Urban America and Public Policies* (Lexington, Mass.: D.C. Heath, 1977), p. 80.

20. Charles S. Benson, *The Economics of Public Education*, 2nd edition (Boston: Houghton Mifflin, 1968), p. 160.

21. Within this national average there is considerable variation between the states. Hawaii stands out as a true exception to the tradition of local funding: 89 percent of school money comes from the state and only 3 percent from local government. Of the continental states, the state of Delaware contributes the most to education (about 69 percent) and New Hampshire contributes the least (about 5 percent). In general, there is a tendency for southern states to contribute larger proportions of school money, while New England states contribute the least.

22. (Syracuse, N.Y.: Syracuse University Press, 1972).

23. Sacks, *op. cit.*, p. 170.

24. Betsy Levin, Thomas Muller and William J. Scanlon, *Public School Finance*, Volume II (Washington, D.C.: The Urban Institute, 1972), pp. 41-42.

25. Donna Shalala and Mary Frase Williams, "Political Perspectives on Efforts to Reform School Finance," *Policy Studies Journal* 4 (Summer 1976), p. 370.

26. Robert D. Reischauer and Robert W. Hartman, *Reforming School Finance* (Washington, D.C.: Brookings Institution, 1972), p. 32.

27. Levin *et al.*, *Public School Finance*, Volume I (Washington, D.C.: The Urban Institute, 1972), pp. 47-49.

28. *McInnis* v. *Shapiro*, 293 F. Supp. 327 (N.D. Ill., 1968).

29. *Burruss* v. *Wilkerson*, 310 F. Supp. 572 (W.D. Va., 1969).

30. *McInnis* v. *Shapiro*, p. 329.

31. *Serrano* v. *Priest*, California Supreme Court 938254, L.A. 29820 (1971).

32. *Van Dusartz* v. *Hatfield* in U.S. District Court in Minnesota (1971); *Rodriguez* v. *San Antonio Independent School District* in U.S. District Court in Texas (1971); *Robinson* v. *Cahill* in New Jersey state courts (1972); *Hollins* v. *Shofstall* in Arizona courts (1972); *Sweetwater Planning Committee* v. *Hinkle* in Wyoming (1971), *Caldwell* v. *Kansas* (1972) and *Milliken* v. *Green* in Michigan (1972).

33. *San Antonio School District* v. *Rodriguez*, 411 U.S. 1 (1973).

34. Russell S. Harrison, *Equality in Public School Finance* (Lexington, Mass.: Lexington Books, 1976), chap. 2.

35. Levin *et al.*, *Public School Finance*, vol. 1, chap. 2.

36. *Report of the New York State Commission on the Quality, Cost, and Financing of Elementary and Secondary Education*, vol. 1 (N.Y.: The Commission, 1972), chap. 2.

37. Shalala and Williams, *op. cit.*, pp. 371-372.

38. *Ibid.*, p. 373.

39. Joel Berke, "Comment," *Policy Studies Journal* 4 (Summer, 1976), pp. 378-379.

40. *Swann* v. *Charlotte-Mecklenburg Board of Education*, 403 U.S. 912 (1972).

41. This is the distinction between *de jure* segregation created by state law and *de facto* segregation resulting from such things as residential housing patterns but where dual school systems were not mandated by law.

42. Reynolds Farley and Clarence Wurdock, "Integrating Schools in the Nation's Largest Cities" (Ann Arbor: University of Michigan Population Studies Center, January, 1977).

43. *Ibid.*, also see the same authors' paper "Can Governmental Policies Integrate Public Schools," (Population Studies Center, March, 1977); also Gary Orfield's comment in *Social Policy* 6 (January/February 1976), pp. 24-29.

44. Mary von Euler, "Meeting the Courts' New Research Needs," *Education and Urban Society* IX (May, 1977), pp. 277-302.

45. *U.S.* v. *Missouri* 363 F. Supp. 739 (E.D. Mo., 1973).

46. *Milliken* v. *Bradley* 418 U.S. 717 (1974).

47. See von Euler's discussion of the vote in "Meeting the Courts' New Research Needs."

48. James S. Coleman, Sara D. Kelly and John A. Moore, *Trends in School Segregation: 1968-1973* (Washington, D.C.: Urban Institute, 1975), pp. 21-22. Also see his article "Liberty and Equality in School Desegregation," *Social Policy* 6 (January/February, 1976), pp. 9-13. Rebuttals to Coleman include Thomas F. Pettigrew and Robert L. Green, "School Desegregation in Large Cities," *Harvard Education Review* 46 (February, 1976), pp. 1-53; Christine H. Rossell, "School Desegregation and White Flight," *Political Science Quarterly* 90 (Winter, 1975-1976), pp. 675-695; Farley and Wurdock, "Integrating Schools" and "Governmental Policies."

49. J. Dennis Lord and John C. Catau, "School Desegregation Policy and Intra-School District Migration," *Social Science Quarterly* 57 (March, 1977), pp. 784-796.

Chapter 5

The Delivery of Other Selected Services in Suburban Regions

If education is the most expensive service provided by local governments in metropolitan areas, other activities also demand their time and resources. It is an investigation of several of these additional services to which we now turn. We begin with two services, police and fire, concerned with the public safety of residents of local communities. Similar to education, these services historically have been provided mostly by local governments and have resisted pressure for higher level government involvement. Solid waste management practices in metropolitan areas are then examined. This service, too, has been overwhelmingly provided by local governments. However, in the past ten years, the problem of disposing of solid wastes has grown to such proportions that the conventional arrangements have been discarded and higher level governments are increasingly involved in the management of such solid waste products.

The management of wastewater through sewering and other treatment systems is also investigated, as is the provision of transportation services in metropolitan areas. These last two services, especially transportation, long have required the cooperation of governments beyond those at the local level.

Together then, these policy areas provide a description of a range of important services provided by local governments, document the ways in which the delivery of these services has been organized, and illustrate both the pressure for higher level government involvement in the affairs of local governments, as well as some of the existing cooperative (and sometimes conflictual) multi-government service arrangements found in metropolitan areas. This theme of multi-government cooperation concerning specific services is returned to in a more general fashion in the next and final chapter investigating reform of suburban and metropolitan government.

The Police: A Historical Overview

Historically, two basic characteristics of policing in the United States are evident. First, police work in the United States is overwhelmingly a function of local government. Given the fear of authoritarian rule that marked early settlers in colonial United States, the creation of any centralized police force was strongly opposed. Within these beliefs, the system of federalism placed the provision of police services in the hands of state governments, which in turn further delegated the responsibilities for policing to local communities. As a result, police departments in the United States are numerous (there may be over 30,000 police agencies in the country), they are overwhelmingly local in character (85 percent of these police departments are strictly local agencies, most run by municipal governments), and they are small (almost 90 percent of these police departments have fewer than 10 full time sworn police officers). The effects on public safety of fragmentation and the existence of small local police agencies, usually called "Lilliputs," is one of the major research questions facing analysts of police services in suburban areas.[1]

A second general concern in the study of policing also grows out of historical developments. In the United States, the traditional "policing" of urban areas was accomplished by two separate forces. The first force consisted of constables who were legal officers of the court and assigned the function of enforcing the law. Constables delivered warrants and carried out court orders. Most constables were unpaid, and it was regarded a civic duty to perform this police function. Supplementing this constabulary was the nightwatch concerned with keeping order in the community. Watchmen walked the streets doing such odd jobs as removing obstacles to the flow of traffic, catching stray animals, breaking up fights, and quelling riots. These watchmen were *not* officers of the law. They were providing a public service by maintaining order, but they had no responsibilities for enforcing court directives.

As urban areas grew, the influx of immigrants created a more diverse population and made law and order more difficult to maintain. Demands on police increased. Indeed, it was the urban unrest of the 1830s and 1840s that first led to the creation of full time police departments. As the pressures from urban unrest continued to force changes in police practices, both the constabulary and the nightwatch were usually combined into a single force. By this historical accident, even today police are expected both to enforce the law and to deliver many non-legal public services to the community they serve.

Yet the way in which the two traditions of law enforcement and public service combine may differ significantly between departments. This creates differences in the "style" of policing found in local communities.

Police Styles and the "Varieties of Police Behavior"

James Q. Wilson, a leading student of police in urban areas, believes that three distinct patterns of police behavior are presently evident in local communities.[2] These "varieties of police behavior" show different mixtures of the nightwatch and service function, on one hand, with law enforcement and the constabulary function, on the other. While Wilson draws his conclusion specifically from an analysis of 5 cities and 3 suburbs, he argues that generally there exist the following three types of police behaviors:

The Watchman Style: Police departments characterized by this style of behavior are more concerned with the maintenance of order than with the strict enforcement of the law. As a result, minor infractions of the law are tolerated so long as they do not seriously violate community norms. There is also an emphasis on the "informal" settlement of minor crime. For example, juveniles committing crimes may be punished in a "familial" manner with a swift kick or with a "heart-to-heart" talk. Similarly, minor adult infractions are also dealt with outside the formal law enforcement mechanisms.

In general, Wilson found that three of the eight communities in his sample shared this watchman style. Not coincidently, all three were lower class/blue collar cities (Albany, Amsterdam, and Newburgh, New York). Further, in these cities, the police were low paid and had low levels of education. Most officers had been born and raised in the city and the atmosphere of the police station and police work was more like a fraternity than a profession.

The Legalistic Style: As might be expected in a department characterized by this type of police work, the majority of infractions detected by the police are judged against the standard of the law, rather than against the more flexible morality of the street. As a result, communities with this type of police department characteristically show high arrest rates, especially for minor crimes that in the "nightwatch" style would be dealt with on the street. For example, in contrast to a "familial" approach to juveniles, legalistic departments show a reliance on court ordered punishment and a heavy use of institutional and specialized professional responses to juvenile crime. In general, compared to the "fraternity" and familial atmosphere of watchman style departments, police work in legalistic departments was professionally oriented.

In terms of the administration of legalistic departments, Wilson notes that they are usually created in reaction to some major scandal involving inordinate amounts of police corruption. Evidence of this reaction was found in the three communities described as legalistic: Oakland, California; Syracuse, New York; and Highland Park, a suburb of Chicago.

The Service Style: The final style of police work was found in the two relatively homogeneous, middle class suburbs in Wilson's sample: Nassau County, New York and Brighton, a suburb of Rochester, New York. Wilson believes that these middle class suburbs have a high degree of consensus on the type of police work they want. These communities share a desire for public order, but show no demand for strict legal formalism. As a result, illegal activity is suppressed because there is community demand for its suppression, but the arrest rates for minor crimes are relatively low. Juvenile crimes, for example, are not overlooked as they might be in a "watchman" style, but only infrequently are juveniles formally charged for minor crimes — in contrast to the "legalistic" approach.

As the name implies, service-oriented departments are very much concerned with performing noncriminal-related activities for the community. Indeed, Wilson notes that fully 47 percent of the requests for service to Brighton police were for clearly noncriminal matters,[3] and in general this type of more leisurely, noncrime related activities characterize much of the police work in these middle class suburbs.

The service orientation of these departments also led to an emphasis on a good physical appearance of policemen with a special concern for an outwardly friendly personality.

Implications of the Varieties of Police Behavior

To be sure, Wilson's work is based on a small and unrepresentative sample of cities and suburbs from which to generalize to other communities with any degree of confidence. But the logic of his argument is persuasive. To the extent that Wilson is correct, we would expect different police styles to be found in certain types of suburbs. Industrial suburbs, especially those surrounding older central cities in the northeast and the midwest, might most likely be characterized by the watchman style. This might be especially true in inner suburbs where black population growth is occurring. Wilson found that in four of the five watchman cities a growing black population was evident and the concern for the maintenance of order may have resulted, in part, from racial conflict disguised in other forms.

But the other two styles of police work are more likely to be widespread in suburban areas. Indeed, all three of the suburbs included in Wilson's analysis were either "service-oriented" or "legalistic." Middle class, homogeneous suburbs might be expected to be service-oriented, while the type of community that can be expected to be legalistic is somewhat more difficult to identify. Certainly reaction to historical events, such as police scandal, is involved in the creation of legalistic departments — but so is a commitment to a "professional" style of government. It is probably not coincidence that the two communities in Wilson's sample with professional city managers both had legalistic police departments. But the actual distribution of "styles" of police work is at present unknown, and all we can do is speculate.

Size of Police Departments in the Metropolis

While not much has been done to trace out the distribution of police styles in the metropolis, the past several years has witnessed a virtual explosion in arguments concerning the "proper" size of police departments. As noted earlier, police work has been a local community-based service throughout American history. As a result, law enforcement is divided into about 30,000 police departments, most of which are agencies of local government. In recent years, there has been pressure to shift police work to higher levels of government, such as counties or states. This shift is justified by its proponents as a means to equalize police services to disparate and separate political jurisdictions, especially in suburban areas, and to increase the level of police professionalism.

The "upward drift" of police work poses a fundamental dilemma to those who are concerned with local control over police, and to those who do not believe that centralization of police work will produce any significant improvements in police services.

Among those urging the upward transfer of police work into more consolidated regional police agencies and away from the small "Lilliputs" of metropolitan policing was the Presidential Commission on Law Enforcement and Administration of Justice. Specifically, in 1968, the Commission found that:

> The machinery of law enforcement in this country is fragmented, complicated and frequently overlapping. America is essentially a nation of small police forces, each operating independently within the limits of its jurisdiction. The boundaries that define and limit police operations do not hinder the movement of criminals, of course. They can and do take advantage of ancient political and geographic boundaries, which often give them the sanctity from effective police activities.

. . . coordination of activity among police agencies, even where the areas they work in are contiguous or overlapping tends to be sporadic and informal, to the extent that it exists at all.[4]

As a result of this finding, the Commission went on to recommend that:

Each metropolitan area and county should take action directed toward the pooling, or consolidation, of services through the particular technique that will provide the most satisfactory law enforcement service and protection at the lowest cost.[5]

This critical view of small departments was echoed by the prestigious Committee for Economic Development in its investigation of *Reducing Crime and Assuring Justice* in which they argued that Lilliputian police forces lack "anything resembling modern professional police protection."[6] In reaction to these critical reports, state laws or state commissions in several states, e.g., Michigan, Maryland, Vermont, and Nebraska, have recommended the phasing out of small police departments.

The arguments in favor of consolidating the Lilliputs of metropolitan policing can be summarized into several major points. As opposed to small departments, larger, consolidated police departments would, supposedly:

1. eliminate the lack of coordination criticized in the Presidential Commission Report. One large department with jurisdiction over an entire metropolitan area would be able to respond more effectively to the behavior of criminals who easily cross jurisdictional boundaries.

2. achieve "economies of scale," that is, larger departments would be more economical and efficient to run because they would be large enough to purchase more expensive and more effective anti-crime devices, and would avoid the duplication of services and machinery maintained by numerous small departments.

3. increase the level of specialization and professionalization in police work, so that the quality of police service would improve. And, finally, because of all these improvements, larger departments would

4. produce higher levels of citizen satisfaction with police work.

While many of these arguments were routinely accepted in the 1960s and early 1970s, criticisms of centralizing reforms recently have been mounting. For each of the benefits supposedly achieved by consolidation of police departments, opponents of centralization list a corresponding drawback or else question the validity of each statement. For example, to the argument that jurisdictional boundaries inhibit police response, critics note that most police departments have the right to cross jurisdictional boundaries when in "hot pursuit" of criminals. Critics of consolidation argue that the other advantages of consolidation are likewise overdrawn. Yet despite a growing body of research, this conflict between proponents and critics of consolidation remains unresolved as seen in following issues concerning police services.

Satisfaction with Police as a Function of Size

Proponents of consolidation believe that larger more professional police departments would elicit higher levels of satisfaction with police work since the police would be more efficient and more professional. Yet, critics of consolidation argue that the effects of size would be just the opposite: smaller departments are "closer" to the people they serve and, therefore, are more responsive. Many suburban communities specifically form small local police departments rather than rely on larger county ones specifically because they want this "local touch."[7] As a result, the effects of size can be hypothesized to go in either direction: larger departments produce more satisfaction or smaller departments do so.

Empirical evidence is necessary to resolve this conflict. A recent analysis of the relationship between size of metropolitan community (unfortunately not of the size of the police force) and citizen satisfaction provides some data relevant to the argument.[8] As Table 5-1 shows, size *is* negatively related to the level of citizen satisfaction with police work: the larger the community, the lower the satisfaction. Thus, these initial data give some support to the anti-consolidation argument — people in smaller communities seem to be more satisfied with their police departments than people in larger metropolitan communities. However, it is known

**Table 5-1   Citizen Satisfaction with Police Work
and Size of Community**
(Percent of Communities by Size by Level of Satisfaction)

Citizen Satisfaction Level	Central City	Large Suburb (over 25,000)	Small Suburb (10-25,000)
Low	26.7%	3.8%	0.0%
Medium	53.4	15.4	12.5
High	20.0	80.8	87.5
	(n = 15)	(n = 26)	(n = 16)

Adapted from: Harry P. Pachon and Nicholas P. Lovrich, Jr., "The Consolidation of Urban Public Services: A Focus on Police," *Public Administration Review*, 37 (January/February 1977), page 41.

that important community characteristics such as racial and class composition vary systematically with size of community, as does the need for police as measured by crime rates. It is possible, therefore, that variation in the level of satisfaction found in different sized communities may not be a function of size itself, but of these other community characteristics. Indeed, it turns out that once the community characteristics of different sized communities are held constant, the independent effects of size disappear almost entirely.[9] Future investigations will inevitably cast further light on this important relationship. Yet at present, debate continues, and the policy question concerning the "best" sized police department must be argued on grounds other than the effect of size on citizen satisfaction.

Service Efficiency and Size

Compared to the effects of size on citizen satisfaction, the question of the efficiency and quality of police work in metropolitan areas has been more intensively investigated. Again, it is often assumed that small police departments and fragmented police services in metropolitan areas produce uncoordinated, and low level services. The major "assault" on this belief has come from a group of analysts led by a political scientist, Elinor Ostrom. For example, Ostrom asserts that the "common picture of metropolitan police agencies [as] . . . too numerous and diverse to work together . . . is largely inaccurate."[10] In contrast to this picture, she argues that the numerous police agencies in metropolitan areas have usually reached a satisfactory degree of coordination and cooperation among themselves, and as a result the "police industry" in a given metropolitan area is *informally* coordinated, even if not legally consolidated into one metropolitan police force.

The major evidence supporting the existence of informal coordination comes from a study of policing in 80 metropolitan areas in the United States.[11] Within this sample were included more than 1400 police agencies. About 70 percent were municipal police departments, the remainder were sheriff departments, or State or Federal law enforcement agencies, such as the highway patrol, campus police or military police.

In the study, the services provided by police agencies were divided into two major categories: (1) "direct services" such as patrol, traffic control, criminal investigation of residential burglary and homicide; and (2) "auxiliary services," such as radio communication, adult pretrial detention, entry level training, and crime laboratory analysis.

Inspecting the distribution of these services among the agencies surveyed, the data show a surprising lack of duplication of services and a high degree of coordination of activity. For example, small police agencies overwhelmingly devote their resources to patrol work, leaving more specialized and technical work to larger agencies, such as county or state police. Moreover, even while concentrating on this particular direct patrol function, small local police agencies have frequently worked out cooperative arrangements with larger police agencies to avoid duplication and overlap. The most common means by which duplication of patrol is avoided is by an alternation of patrol work between the small local police agency and other larger police agencies with competing interests. This alternation may be arranged by time, some small municipal police departments are daytime patrols only, leaving post-midnight patrols to the sheriff's office; or it may be by space, campus or park police do not overlap with municipal or county police; or it may be by clientele, military police may patrol an entire area with concern only for military personnel.

Furthermore, coordination also exists by the level of severity of crime problem. Little or no coordination exists, because it may not be necessary, for traffic patrol or accident investigation. But explicit and frequent coordination exists for more serious crimes, such as homicide. Similarly, more expensive auxiliary services such as pretrial detention or entry level training are highly coordinated. Smaller police agencies rely on the larger departments more able to support the specialized services.[12]

Moreover, since these small police departments choose to specialize in patrol, they seem to do it more efficiently than larger police departments. Thus, smaller police departments have a higher proportion of their police force on actual patrol than larger agencies: small suburban departments (those with less than 10 officers) assign, on the average, 90 percent of their men to police patrol. On the other hand, the largest police departments (those with more than 150 officers), assign less than 60 percent of their officers to patrol work, the rest being absorbed by the greater needs for administration, auxiliary services, or other police services.

Finally, in these 80 metropolitan areas, smaller municipal police departments also provided a higher "density" of patrol: at 10 p.m. smaller municipal departments had deployed one officer for every 2,400 citizens while larger municipal agencies had deployed only one officer per every 4,200 persons.[13]

From data such as these, Ostrom and her supporters have argued that, if anything, efficiency of police service, especially for patrol work, declines as size of police department increases, weakening the consolidationist argument. However, it should be noted that there is a serious flaw in this line of argument. It is true that small suburban police devote more of their resources to patrol, while larger municipal agencies devote more of their resources to other services. Yet the small suburban police departments are direct beneficiaries of the concentration of resources and special services in larger departments. And these benefits are often at no cost to the small suburb. This may mean that central city police departments which make services available to suburbs, or that larger suburban police departments which make resources available to smaller neighboring departments, have higher costs than they should, while the smaller departments may have artificially lower costs.[14] Thus, arguments that increasing size is associated with higher police costs may be overstated.

The Limits of Policing

One final point should be noted with regard to cost of police work. Not much is really known about the effectiveness of police work in preventing crime or solving crimes once committed. Most crimes simply are not reported — as much as 50-70 percent of crimes in many categories never come to the attention of police. Even if reported, the police frequently fail to record the crime.[15] Moreover, even when police do respond to calls for help, crimes may be difficult to solve. With most property crimes, no clues are left behind for police to follow. Crimes against the person committed by unknown assailants may be equally difficult to solve. Consequently, there is little evidence that police patrol or most other forms of police work really have an impact on reducing crime.[16]

As a result, it is now popular to argue that the most effective way of protecting a population against crime may not be to rely on professional police forces at all, but to reinvigorate neighborhood life to provide a form of "natural" surveillance and protection. Thus, at present, the safest places to live in the metropolis are probably small homogeneous suburbs with a well-ordered social life. These communities are able to police themselves with only limited backup by the police. On the other hand, in larger metropolitan communities, the anonymity of individuals and the absence of community structure may leave neighborhoods and their residents more vulnerable to crime. As a result, several new programs of crime prevention are aimed not at bolstering police forces themselves, but at strengthening neighborhoods in the metropolitan community to increase their natural role in crime prevention.[17]

Police Work in Different Suburbs: Some Speculations

While policy debate continues concerning the proper size of a police force for metropolitan areas, residents in small, homogeneous wealthy suburbs seem to have the best of worlds concerning police services. They are most likely to have a "service-oriented" department that lends a helping hand to citizens in need of legal or non-legal assistance. Given the nature of the community, crime rates are likely to be low. Furthermore, satisfaction with police coverage is likely to be high. In addition, these communities are also able to afford more intensive police patrol through an independent local community police department, even if their crime rates would be "naturally" lower than other communities that cannot afford the more intensive coverage.

In contrast, larger more heterogeneous suburbs are likely to have police departments characterized by different, less service-oriented types of behavior than found in smaller suburbs. Satisfaction with police coverage may be lower, but that may be a function of community characteristics, rather than of the size of the department itself.

Yet while the debate about the size of police forces and the styles of police behavior continue, only limited data to answer the questions posed in these debates actually exist. Future research on policing suburban areas will surely be forthcoming.

Fire Services

Besides police work, fire departments constitute the other major component of public safety in metropolitan areas. But despite the importance of fire protection, studies of this service are few in number. Indeed, it is only within the past few years that attempts at even the simple cataloguing and description of various forms of fire service delivery in suburban and metropolitan areas have been attempted. More intense analysis is, of course, also in short supply.

Existing research has been interested in several types of questions: cataloguing the modes of service delivery, identifying the determinants of different levels of spending of fire agencies, and identifying the components affecting the efficiency of fire departments.

The Two Roles of Fire Safety: Prevention and Suppression

In general, fire services can be viewed in two dimensions. First, fire services can be preventive in nature. Through fire safety regulations, building inspections and the enforcement of a variety of fire and building codes, local fire departments can attempt to minimize the incidence of fire. Most of this preventive work is handled through the private market, that is, the individual owner of a building or house is responsible for keeping the structure safe. The public fire department provides oversight and regulation, furthering or enforcing private actions. Fire departments also can provide educational activities, giving lectures to school and civic groups on how to minimize the risk of fire.

The other aspect of fire services is fire control — the detection of fires, the organized response to such fires, and finally the control and ultimate suppression of a fire once ignited, minimizing loss of life and property. In general, fire services have been aimed at this control and ,suppression activity rather than prevention. This emphasis on control is at least in part because of the importance of a private agency, the Insurance Service Organization, in shaping fire services. The ISO is concerned with inspecting and evaluating municipalities and parts of municipalities to determine their fire insurance rates. Their grading system measures the availability of resources to suppress fires once they start — water pressure, response time, availability of fire fighting apparatus, personnel. Residents of cities low on the ISO ratings must pay higher insurance rates, and vice-versa. This produces incentives to maximize suppression services, and most municipalities seem to emphasize fire control rather than prevention.[18]

Staffing Local Fire Departments

Another consequence of the emphasis on control and suppression, rather than on prevention, is evident in the staffing patterns of metropolitan fire departments (Table 5-2), and in the data reflecting the relative efficiency of different sized fire departments (Table 5-3). Fires by their very nature are episodic and often unpredictable events. In most communities, especially in suburban areas, fires are relatively rare. Moreover, when housing and population density are low, and when no large commercial establishments representing high concentrations of property value are present, the danger of loss from fires may be

Table 5-2 Distribution of Fire Department Types In Metropolitan Areas

| | Urban Fringe[1] | | | Urban Ring | | Central City | |
	less than 5,000	5,000-25,000	less than 5,000	5,000-25,000	more than 25,000	less than 10,000	more than 100,000
Fully Voluntary	86.5% (141)	37.7% (29)	66.7% (32)	31.5% (40)	0.0%	0.0%	0.0%
Mostly Voluntary*	13.5 (22)	45.5 (35)	33.3 (16)	36.2 (46)	19.7 (12)	0.0	0.0
Mostly Paid	0.0	16.9 (13)	0.0	15.0 (19)	21.3 (13)	0.0	0.0
Fully Paid	0.0	0.0	0.0	17.3 (22)	59.0 (36)	100 (14)	100 (13)

Source: Adapted from Research Triangle Institute et al., *Municipal Fire Service Workbook*, (Washington, D.C.: Government Printing Office, 1977), Chart 1.

*Most voluntary is less than 50 percent of department is full-time professional.
Mostly is defined as 50-99 percent full-time professional.

[1]Urban fringe is defined as the outer most part of the metropolitan area, that is, beyond the urbanized section, which includes the inner suburbs of the ring, and the central city.

Table 5-3 Effectiveness and Performance of Metropolitan Fire Departments

Community Size Less Than 5,000

	Ring		Fringe	
	Fully Voluntary	Mostly Voluntary	Fully Voluntary	Mostly Voluntary
Median Number Fires per 1,000 Protected	9.20	9.49	10.77	25.61
Median Dollar Property Loss per Fire	$ 7.62	$13.03	$13.80	$30.18
Total Organization Performance[1]	$18.69	$84.35	$26.37	$97.31

Community Size 5,000-25,000

	Ring				Fringe		
	Fully Voluntary	Mostly Voluntary	Mostly Paid	Fully Paid	Fully Voluntary	Mostly Voluntary	Mostly Paid
Median Number Fires per 1,000 Protected	5.94	9.43	9.75	10.37	3.90	10.87	9.19
Median Dollar Property Loss per Fire	$ 8.06	$ 7.69	$ 7.85	$ 6.68	$4.17	$ 9.72	$11.40
Total Organization Performance[1]	$15.58	$28.75	$22.92	$35.92	$6.54	$24.99	$32.14

Community Size 25,000-100,000

	Ring			Central City	
	Mostly Voluntary	Mostly Paid	Fully Paid	less than 100,000 Fully Paid	more than 100,000 Fully Paid
Median Number Fires	7.44	9.32	10.25	12.78	11.80
Median Dollar Loss	$10.35	$ 7.05	$ 7.28	$10.40	$12.29
Total Organization Performance[1]	$27.03	$33.05	$33.27	$33.10	$36.74

Source: Adapted from Municipal Fire Service Workbook, Charts 1, 1a, 3.

[1]Total Organization Performance is a measure of the relationship between effort and efficiency of the total department. Its numerator is the total property loss per capita plus fire department expenses per capita.

relatively low. As a result, in many local communities, a reliance on volunteer fire fighters rather than paid professionals is evident. As seen in Table 5-2, the smallest suburbs, those with populations less than 5,000, have an overwhelming reliance on volunteer forces. Thus, in these small communities fully 87 percent of fire departments in those suburbs on the urban "fringe" and two-thirds of departments in more close-in suburbs are all volunteer. The other departments in these communities are classified as "mostly" volunteer. However, larger communities, those in the 5,000-25,000 population range, show a somewhat greater use of professionals. In further contrast, in the very largest suburbs, almost 60 percent of departments have fully paid professional staff. Thus, there exists a clear pattern of reliance on volunteers in the smaller and outer suburbs, and a growing reliance on paid fire fighting professionals as suburbs increase in size and as one approaches the central city.

As currently organized, volunteer forces respond to fire alarms by leaving their businesses or homes and reporting to the fire house to man the equipment and to respond to the fire. For many suburbanites, the volunteer fire department serves as a civic obligation that is fun and exciting, and an esprit de corps is certainly evident at Fourth of July picnics and parades when volunteers don their uniforms and march through the main street of town to cheers and applause. Volunteer forces thus serve many functions, only one of which is the suppression of fires. And, on one level, these volunteer departments are inexpensive to operate. Being volunteer forces, the labor costs of the local suburban fire department are minimized. But this strategy of relying on a local volunteer force can apparently be used only in the smaller suburbs in the metropolitan area, and larger communities invariably require more expensive professional forces to fight fires. In many communities this is especially true as high rise buildings and commercial establishments frequently require the maintenance of specialized equipment and skills to fight possible fires.

Efficiency in Fire Departments

Besides questions of staffing fire departments, researchers have begun to examine the questions of the costs and efficiency of fire services. In examining questions of costs, a usual starting point is the question of economies of scale — do large fire departments operate more inexpensively than smaller ones? Similar to the pattern of police departments, there exist a large number of very small fire departments in metropolitan areas. Again, similar to police departments, there also exist a relatively small number of very large fire departments that often service the majority of the population in metropolitan areas. For example, only one fire department will usually be found in the central city where a plurality of metropolitan citizens may live. By comparing the costs of operating the small departments to the larger ones in the metropolis, economies of scale may be identifiable, as may be other components of efficient fire services.

Table 5-3 presents some data on that question. Three measures of efficiency are presented for the types of departments found in the metropolis. These measures are (1) median number of fires per 1,000 population protected, (2) median dollar property loss, and (3) median total cost per capita. This latter measure tries to assess "Total Organizational Performance," since it combines the per capita costs of fire loss with the per capita cost of operating the fire department in the community — that is, an approximation of all fire related costs in a community.

The issue of economies of scale and efficiency most easily can be addressed by looking at the total organizational performance measure, median fire cost per capita. The data show that despite low personnel costs, the smallest departments in *total* costs are expensive to their community. For example, fully voluntary departments in the smallest fringe suburbs cost about $26 per person every year. In contrast, departments in larger suburbs in the urban fringe cost less than $7.00 per person per year. Even more striking is the cost to fringe communities with "mostly voluntary" forces, that is communities where some full time professional fire fighters are employed. The smallest fringe communities with mostly voluntary forces spend almost $100 per person every year on fire services. This is almost 3 times the cost of any other type of fire department in the metropolitan areas surveyed. The smallest communities in more densely populated "ring" sections of metropolitan areas also spend disproportionately more on fire services than other larger suburbs.

As a result, it is now believed that significant economies of scale are being lost by the maintenance of these very small suburban fire departments. Economies of scale are believed to be achievable in departments servicing populations of up to 25,000, after which, as Table 5-3 shows, department operating costs level off and no economies in the largest departments are evident. Therefore, while small suburbs might get some form of civic enjoyment out of local volunteer forces, and might in fact feel that they are minimizing costs by retaining a small local force that is volunteer, the total fire related costs to the community are in fact quite high. Part of the explanation for the high costs is the incidence of fire in such small communities. This high incidence probably results from the fact that these smaller non-professional forces usually engage in no preventive work and have no enforcement procedures for code violations.

Other facts concerning the level and types of fire service in suburbs are evident in the data presented. In general, within any type of community classified by size and by location in the metropolitan area, costs rise with an increase in the use of paid rather than volunteer forces. This is obviously because labor costs are so large a part of total fire fighting costs. But for many types of communities, in particular larger suburbs in the metropolitan ring, a reliance on more professional departments decreases property loss per fire. This results from the shorter response times to alarms characteristic of professional forces. In such departments, personnel are already in the fire house and do not have to get there from other locations. In turn, shorter response time reduces the spread of fire and thereby minimizes loss. These departments also invest more in preventive services and code enforcement. Surprisingly, this pattern is not evident in the fringe suburbs, nor in the smallest suburbs (less than 5,000 population) regardless of location. This may suggest that the fire departments in these areas are not properly using their personnel. Indeed, such communities frequently require little or no training for their fire fighters and most do not use their personnel for preventive work. Again, the choice of small suburbs for non-professional fire services may be more expensive than they think.

Environmental Factors and Fire Service Costs

Some other factors have been found to relate to fire department costs and efficiency, but most of these are not controllable by local communities.[19] Thus fire fighting costs are higher in colder climates and in areas that experience more inclement weather. Costs are higher where buildings are older and deteriorating and where the residents served are poor and densely settled. Residential instability tends to be strongly associated with costs — high turnover inevitably means the need for a professional force, rather than a voluntary force, with an increase in costs. In general, most of these environmental characteristics combine to increase the cost of fire service in central cities relative to suburbs. But these costs are not easily subject to control by local governments. However, we have seen that certain decisions that can be made by suburban decision makers to reduce total fire costs are not being taken. As a result, by choosing volunteer forces, many of the smallest suburbs are subject to far higher total fire costs than they need be. This situation may in part result from the desire of suburbanites to have a local fire department in which residents can participate openly and fully and communities may be willing to pay the costs associated with that participation.

Police and fire services, along with education and schools, consume the lion's share of local government budgets. These services are labor intensive and, despite the use of volunteers in many fire departments, are therefore expensive to local governments in metropolitan areas. In addition, all three services historically have been rooted in local communities and attempts at consolidation of these services to achieve economies of scale in their provision have been hotly contested, largely because of the possible impact on local control.

In contrast to these services, solid waste disposal, wastewater management, and the organization of transportation services in metropolitan areas are much less labor intensive — fewer people are involved in delivering the service. In addition, while in the not-so-distant past, local government control over such services was significant, the involvement of higher level governments in these service delivery systems recently has increased dramatically. This is most clearly seen in the field of transportation, where federal involvement is particularly intense. But given the continuing growth of suburbs, and the concomitant demands placed on the environment, waste disposal by local governments has necessitated the involvement of higher level governments in what was once almost strictly local government policy domains.

Hence, a comparison of the service delivery systems found for police, fire and education on the one hand, with those for solid and water waste disposal and transportation, on the other, provide illustrations of the wide range of service mechanisms found in metropolitan areas. Such comparison also illustrates the evolution of higher level involvement in a growing number of services once provided strictly by local governments.

Solid Waste Management

Suburbs are the product of affluence. After World War II, a large proportion of the American population desired the life style associated with suburbia. The increasing number of suburban residents soon presented significant problems to suburban governments faced with managing the waste products of an affluent community.

American society is, in general, a high consumption society that generates large quantities of waste products. This is true of business and industry, but is also true of residential living. For example, food products come heavily packaged, and once the contents are used, the boxes and wrappings have to be disposed of as do discarded household appliances, furniture, and automobiles. A simple item such as disposable diapers which have widely replaced cloth diapers will also increase significantly the bulk of waste generated in many younger suburban communities. In short, a typical suburban community will generate a large mass of solid wastes. Some of these solid waste products may be recycled through now popular garage or yard sales and others may simply find their way into basements, attics, or garages. But most waste products sooner or later must be moved away from the community and placed "out of sight and out of mind." As the affluence of society continues to grow, the actual number, weight, and bulk of objects disposed increases. At the same time, suburban sprawl reduces the number of places in which to dispose of these wastes.

Moreover, our society rightfully desires to protect the environment from pollution. But this desire usually places further restrictions on the ability of communities to dispose of their waste products. As a result, in the relatively recent past, problems related to solid waste management have become increasingly severe.[20]

The History of Solid Waste Management

In earlier times, solid waste disposal was a simpler, if perhaps unhealthier matter.[21] The usual "system" for managing residential waste in urban areas was easy — residents threw their trash and garbage into the streets. New "deposits" were mixed with already existing dirt on the street and the weight of street traffic eventually would trod this dirt down to form new layers of street surfacing. Regardless of the merits of this system, one obvious by-product (besides disease and horrible odors) was rising street levels. Since garbage was never removed, street levels would rise as garbage accumulated. Eventually doors and windows of houses would be blocked by the rising street level and new openings at higher levels would have to be cut. In its most extreme form, the problem of rising street levels sometimes required that new floors be added to a building while the original ground floor gradually converted to the status of an underground basement.

While this simple "on-street' disposal system was common in Europe through the middle ages, other disposal systems had been tried earlier. The most notable success in solid waste management in earlier times was probably the Greek system of collection and removal of wastes to city dumps outside of city limits. The Greeks organized this waste removal system as early as 500 B.C. Greek cities used scavengers, paid for and supervised by local government officials, to keep streets and bridges clean, and to cart collected wastes to city dumps. This reasonably effective system broke down with the decline of Greece, and their successors, the Romans, never were able to duplicate the efficiency of the Greeks. As a result, the city of Rome was a relatively dirty and unhealthy place to live. With the decline of the

Roman Empire, the filth of city life in European cities in the Middle Ages made urban living virtually impossible. Plagues and disease, resulting at least in part from poor sanitation, decimated the urban population and cities went into a period of decline.

But as in many other services, it was likely the experience of London that affected the United States the most. In London, a system of "laystalls" was established as central collection places for waste. Street debris was collected by "rakers" who would deposit waste in laystalls for central collection. Scavengers supervised the collection process and would then supervise the removal of wastes to dumps outside the city. The charges for street cleaning were levied against property owners, and eventually rakers became city employees. This system had a telling effect on American practices. Through a gradual process of municipal involvement, street cleaning and solid waste collection controlled by city government became a common arrangement in most larger American cities, especially those cities on the eastern coast settled by the English.

However, if municipally owned and operated solid waste collection systems are common in large cities, their use in suburbs is far less common. Residential solid waste in most suburbs is collected by private firms that are either on contract to the local municipal government, or are franchised by that locality.[22] The difference in these two arrangements is that fees for contracted services are usually paid for directly by the local government, while franchise operators usually bill the property owner from whom waste is collected. But the bulk of solid waste generated by households in suburban areas is collected by fleets of trucks owned and operated by private firms that are regulated by the village, town, or county in which they operate.

This system of waste collection seems to be in a fairly steady state. Conversion of municipal systems to private ones are unlikely, and most suburbs do not seem interested in assuming the responsibilities for a municipally owned waste collection system. Furthermore, the technology by which waste is collected also seems relatively stable, and not much change is foreseen.

Essentially trucks that are capable of compacting residential waste and delivering it to some disposal site is the way waste has been collected in the recent past and will continue to be the way it is collected in the foreseeable future. Alternate technologies such as widespread use of garbage disposals attached to a sink that grind up garbage into a slurry to be carried away through the sewer system, or fancier vacuum systems such as found on Roosevelt Island in New York City are unlikely to make a dent in old fashioned waste collection by truck in the near future.

Disposing of Collected Solid Waste

However, if waste *collection* is in a steady state, the question of the *disposal* of municipal solid waste, once collected, is highly explosive. The overwhelming pattern of waste disposal has been and still is for local governments to operate small disposal sites used exclusively by residents of that local jurisdiction. These disposal sites are either "dumps" — where wastes are deposited and forgotten, or else they are operated as "sanitary landfills" — where the wastes are compacted down and covered by a layer of dirt at the end of every day. But regardless of the type of site, local disposal areas have tended to be small and operated by individual local government.[23] For a long time, this system of waste disposal appeared to be relatively successful. In 1963, the Advisory Commission on Intergovernmental Relations concluded that solid waste management was clearly a local function without any obvious need for regional cooperation and the involvement of the Federal or even state governments. But that conclusion was soon put aside. Just two years later, Congress passed the Solid Waste Disposal Act of 1965 establishing a national concern for the disposal of waste. Federal involvement was further intensified by the Resources Recovery Act of 1970 in which a national policy of recycling and reclaiming the resources contained in municipal solid wastes was clearly evident. But it was not only the federal government that put pressure on local waste management practices. Since 1965, more and more states have adopted regulations governing solid waste disposal. The time honored and unsanitary practices of locally run dumps and less than perfect sanitary landfills have been subject to intense scrutiny by state governments.[24]

Higher level governments began to intervene in local

government disposal practices for several reasons. First, and perhaps most important, was the fact that the problem of solid waste disposal simply broke through local governmental jurisdictional lines as suburban expansion made land for disposal sites scarce and often nonexistent in some communities.[25]

Further, present practices of municipal waste disposal were found to have severe effects on environmental quality — most notably through air and water pollution. One common way to reduce the bulk of solid waste was for local governments to incinerate it. Effective incineration can reduce the bulk of solid waste by 80-85 percent and reduce its weight by about 65 percent. However, most incinerators, especially older ones, produce enormous amounts of air pollution and cannot meet present environmental standards. As a result, older incinerators are frequently closed down. New ones are not built to replace them. Furthermore, incineration destroys the possibility of resource recycling, further reducing interest in the construction of new incinerators. But as a consequence, local governments that at one time might have incinerated their waste and then landfilled the smaller remaining bulk, are now faced with the problem of a much larger quantity of waste to be landfilled, and increasingly limited space in which to dispose of it.[26]

Existing disposal practices of local governments are also criticized because of the effects on water quality. Dumps and poorly managed sanitary landfills produce a substance called "leachate" that can severely pollute existing water supplies. Leachate results as rain water percolates through collected solid waste. It is a liquid solution containing suspended particles of solid wastes and microbial waste products generated as a product of the deterioration of the organic materials in the solid waste. Leachate may be relatively more contaminated than raw sewage and can easily run off into streams and lakes or seep into ground water causing severe pollution.[27]

Improperly operated landfills also produce other noxious side effects — highly volatile and poisonous methane gas, carbon dioxide, rats, flies, and insects. A fire hazard can also be created.

Given these environmental problems, state governments, under the prodding of federal agencies, have begun to close down local disposal sites and demand that existing ones be upgraded, or that new ones meeting rigorous engineering and environmental standards be constructed. However, local disposal sites often cannot meet these tough new standards — the costs are too high for the limited resources of small local governments. As a result, regional or multisuburban government collaboration on solid waste disposal should be expected to increase in the future. However, since no one really wants to have a dump or landfill in their backyard and most new sites can be criticized on some form of environmental, economic, or engineering grounds, the question of siting municipal solid waste disposal sites should long be with us.[28]

Resource Recovery as a Solution to Solid Waste

There is one promising solution to these disposal problems that is only now being seriously addressed — the growing pressure for recycling and resource recovery. In fact, at present, arrangements to recycle municipal solid wastes are increasingly common. While many recycling efforts are located in central cities, multi-jurisdictional arrangements between suburbs are possible. One such example is now found in the Town of Saugus outside of Boston. In this multi-government arrangement, 10 suburban towns have leased a central collection site to a private company that will accept all their municipal refuse, at a fee. The Refuse Energy Systems Company (RESCO) that operates the collection site uses available technology to separate resalable materials such as aluminum and ferrous metal from the municipal waste. The non-reclaimable waste is then burned to produce steam sold on a contractual basis to the General Electric Company. Early indications are that this venture in recycling is successful and profitable for all parties involved.

Resource recovery technologies, such as that used by RESCO, usually combine a method of reclaiming reusable metals from municipal waste. Other recycling technologies include the reclaiming of paper products and newsprint for cleaning and reuse. Most technologies include the use of remaining materials directly as a dry fuel or for the conversion of the waste through "pyrolysis" into a low grade fuel used to supplement fuel oil in the generation of energy. However, some of the most successful recycling technologies require "at source" separation of solid waste — that is, households must separate newspapers, aluminum cans, glass, and other categories of materials. Introduction of such recycling systems will necessarily cause changes in solid waste collection procedures. But, many of the existing recycling technologies can operate with unsorted waste but usually at a higher cost and lower efficiency.

In general, most present resource recovery technologies require a larger input of waste than can be generated by small individual suburbs. As the nation moves toward the use of recycled material, and as existing landfills disappear and new ones cannot be found, more and more regional arrangements for the disposal and reuse of suburban solid waste can be expected.

However, if solid waste disposal systems are only now in the process of shifting from a strictly local policy arena to one requiring the cooperation of several suburban governments and/or higher level government involvement, the management of wastewater is further along in that transition. In part, this is because sewering necessary to treat wastewater is more expensive than any of the systems that historically have been used for solid waste disposal. In addition, wastewater disposal has usually required the use of waterways which flow through several local jurisdictions, requiring greater coordination than the traditional methods of solid waste disposal which used sites located mostly within the boundaries of a single jurisdiction.

It is useful to think of the provision of sewers and wastewater treatment plants as "infrastructural" investments by governments, that is, the government is investing its resources in providing an expensive service that is essential to support suburban life. Since suburban life would be impossible to sustain without certain basic infrastructural investments in necessry services, governments can manipulate the rate and shape of growth through the provision or non-provision of such infrastructural investments. While the other services discussed so far, to one degree or another, help form the suburban infrastructure, sewering is perhaps more important, given the concern with growth and development. According to the Council on Environmental Quality, sewering along with highways and mass transit are government policies that are "The Growth Shapers."[29]

Sewers and Wastewater Management

If suburbs are faced with the problem of managing their solid waste products, the problem of managing wastewater is also one of growing importance. All suburban communities must in one way or another, provide the means for residents and businesses to dispose of the large quantities of wastewater they generate. Suburban communities cannot exist without this capability.

Suburbia must deal with three basic sources of wastewater.[30] First, and perhaps most important, is the problem of dealing with domestic human waste products, usually referred to as "sanitary sewage." Second, communities must face the task of treating wastewater generated by business or industry. Depending on the nature of the industrial processes involved, special treatment may be required to deal with industrial chemicals or pollutants resulting from manufacturing processes. Finally, there is the problem of "surface run-off." This is the result of excess storm water from rains or heavy snows running across impervious surfaces such as roads, streets, parking lots, or buildings. Prior to the construction of these surfaces, most water would seep into the ground on which it fell. With development, the amount of water that can do so is reduced and as the excess unabsorbed water "runs-off" impervious surfaces, it collects sediment, chemicals, and other contaminants that eventually find their way into rivers, lakes, or groundwater.

As with most other suburban services, the management of wastewater was a more simple matter in the not-so-distant past. Smaller suburban populations and lower density development reduced the amount of wastewater produced and allowed natural environmental processes more easily to absorb whatever wastewater was generated. These conditions have, of course, changed with suburban population growth. In turn, the management of wastewater is now a policy concern of most suburban governments.

While any of the three sources of wastewater can be a legitimate focus of investigation, the provision of sanitary sewers and the impact that government policies on sewering has on suburban growth will be investigated here.

The Historical Development of Sewering

The need for sewers is relatively recent. Before the invention of flush toilets, the bulk of domestic waste generated by households was disposed of with minimal water use. Domestic waste was placed into dry outhouses or transferred to vacant fields to decompose through natural processes. Practices associated with the disposal of domestic waste generated the genteel term "night soil" — referring to the not-so-genteel but common habit of individuals dumping their own waste on another's property under cover of darkness.[31] Despite the seeming unpleasantness of these disposal practices, human domestic waste was kept in relatively small bulk that was easy to manage. The use of water in waste disposal was minimal. Indeed, the treatment of human waste without use of water was almost universal by the late 1800s. A common approach to waste treatment was "sewage farming," in which human wastes were composted into fertilizer and humus used in conditioning soil for agricultural production. Sewage farming had been familiar to the Japanese and Chinese for centuries. It was introduced to Europe in the 1500s, and spread rapidly throughout Europe and, eventually, to the United States.[32]

However, rapid urbanization and population growth reduced the availability and increased the cost of land for such sewage farming. As a result, the introduction of water removal of wastes, as compared to land treatment, became common by 1900 and is now almost universal.

Human waste removal based on water starts, of course, with the flush toilet. Each flush of the average toilet uses more than 5 gallons of water, and more than 10 flushes per day per person in any household is not unusual. As a result, what starts off as a small volume of human waste is carried off by a large volume of contaminated water.[33]

The least expensive and most common early form of managing this domestic wastewater was the installation of individual septic systems or cesspools for each household to replace dry outhouse pits. Cesspools collect wastewater and through various physical and biological reactions reduce the volume of the solids it carries. The remaining liquid wastes percolate into the soil, are filtered by this percolation, and eventually dissipate into the ground. For low density population, this is an effective system of wastewater management.

However, the ability of the soil to absorb liquids from cesspools is limited. Higher population concentrations cannot effectively use them. Thus, in many areas, as population growth continued and density increased, individual septic systems eventually failed. The overflow from backed-up systems was often simply dumped into open street and storm drains. But the exposure of the population to the bacteria and virus contained in human sewage led to high rates of disease, especially from typhoid and hepatitis. The frequent failures of individual cesspools and the resulting exposure to disease produced an early recognition in most urban areas of the need for sanitary sewers.

At first, the installation of these sewers consisted of the construction of conduits to carry wastes from individual homes to a stream or waterway where the "raw" untreated sewage was discharged. Running water can be a good treatment system — but only if the volume of sewage is not great and if sufficient time is available for the river to clean itself through natural processes before some downstream community needs the water. However, with a growing urban population leading both to an increased volume of sewage discharged into waterways and to an increased need for clean water, the system of dumping raw sewage into waterways became untenable. Treatment of sewage on basic health grounds alone was necessary. Furthermore, in more recent years the growing concern for environmental protection has increased the demand for treatment of sewage before discharge into waterways.

Levels of Sewage Treatment

As presently defined, three levels of treatment are available to process municipal sewage before its discharge. These are called primary, secondary, and tertiary treatment, referring more to the *means* of treatment, rather than to the end quality of the treated water.[34]

Primary treatment is essentially a mechanical process designed to remove large particles and floating matter from wastewater. Essentially, primary treatment involves a settling process in which wastewater sits in large collection tanks for several hours. The resulting "treated" water with large solid removed is then heavily chlorinated to kill bacteria and virus, and the effluent of primary treatment discharged into a nearby waterway. This effluent is obviously heavily contaminated and unfit for immediate use. But given sufficient time, once discharged into a waterway, natural processes can clean the water and return it to a more usable state.

Secondary treatment takes the effluent from primary treatment and carries the cleansing process one step further by the application of biological methods. Most commonly, water from primary treatment is passed through a filtration process using a biologically active agent that reduces the amount of waste carried in the water. Secondary treatment also attempts to simulate the cleansing action of a waterway by exposing wastewater to a large number of "good" bacteria in a high oxygen environment. The bacterial action reduces the volume of waste and changes the water's composition to a cleaner state. The effluent from secondary treatment is then heavily chlorinated and discharged into a river or other body of water. This effluent is *not* fit for immediate consumption and further cleaning by the natural action of a waterway is also necessary.

Tertiary treatment is usually designed specifically to meet the needs of a particular community or a particular polluter, such as a large industrial firm. Tertiary treatment is possible for domestic waste and usually relies on further filtration to purify wastewater.[35]

The construction of sewer systems is extremely expensive, regardless of the level of treatment involved. Capital costs for sewer plants are high, and as the demand for secondary or tertiary treatment increases, costs grow further. In addition to treatment plant costs, the laying of pipes connecting households to sewer plants is also a major construction project. These high costs have produced an emphasis on construction subsidies from higher level governments, and an emphasis on the construction of regional sewer systems usually located at downstream points in river basins. Such a downstream location allows a large regional plant more efficiently to gather through natural drainage and water flows the sewage from an entire area, hopefully minimizing costs.

Regional sewer systems are often termed "structural" alternatives to wastewater management in that they involve large scale engineering projects. Yet because the provision of these sewers affects suburban growth, infrastructural investments in sewers based on engineering considerations may have significant social consequences for the shape of the metropolis.

How Sewers Affect Growth: The Availability and Profitability of Development

In many suburban regions, soil or other environmental conditions prevent the use of individual household septic systems. In areas such as these, development simply cannot take place in the absence of sewering. Suburban development often is wholly contingent on the laying of sewer lines and the construction of sewer plants. In other areas, high density development may mean that individual septic systems are failing and that sewering is a service necessary to sustain present development and is certainly necessary before any new development can proceed. In turn, through the manipulation of the availability of sewers, governments can affect the form of suburban growth in such areas: growth can only occur where sewers are built.[36]

But the provision of sewers also can affect the timing of growth through changes in the profitability of development. When sewers must be provided, suburban developers are faced with two means by which to do so. First, there exist "packaged" sewer treatment plants that are designed specifically for individual residential developments. These packaged plants are constructed by a developer to service the houses in his development. The costs for the construction of packaged plants must be included in the cost of each house in the development and housing prices necessarily will be higher. Alternately, a sewer system can be constructed by local government. This means that the costs of the sewer service are spread over a larger population, and the direct costs to a developer are significantly lower. To the extent that a local government picks up the bill for sewers, housing costs become lower, development becomes more profitable, and in response rapid growth may result.[37]

Several examples illustrate the point. Perhaps most dramatic is the case of Fairfax County, a suburb of Washington subject to intense development pressure in the past two decades. Between 1963 and 1969, Fairfax County was trying unsuccessfully to control suburban sprawl and to impose a system of more orderly development in the county. In 1969, the County Planning Commission argued for a system of phased growth through the establishment of "holding zones" in rural undeveloped areas. Designated holding zones were to be off-limits to construction for five or more years. By removing this land from development, county planners hoped to channel growth into already developing areas and preserve open space. The first major test of this concept occurred in 1969 when 2500 acres in a rural section of the county were designated as being "held" for at least 6 years. Despite this planning decision, a sewer line extension into the area was approved at virtually the same time. Given the existence of this sewer facility, development pressure on the area increased dramatically. Furthermore, the courts refused to deny access to the sewers, which they conceived of as an expensive and valuable public health facility. Zoning controls and planning decisions designed to limit development were overturned in the courts. The construction of the sewer system had effectively negated attempts to control development. According to an investigation by the Council on Environmental Quality, the entire episode in Fairfax shows that "in areas with heavy growth potential, local zoning and planning processes often cannot control the development pressures which sewers release."[38]

A similar case of residential growth responding to sewering occurred in the Tulsa region. Broken Arrow, a suburb of Tulsa, was tied to the city by a new expressway. While the entire metropolitan area was subject to intense population growth and economic expansion, Broken Arrow, despite its easy access to Tulsa, did not grow. The reason was environmental — general soil conditions precluded development without the installation of a sewer system. Throughout the 1960s, the money for this construction project could not be raised and suburban growth in Broken Arrow failed to materialize. However, federal funds for the construction of sewers became available in the early 1970s. In turn, rapid residential development in Broken Arrow resulted.[39]

Sewering has obvious strong impacts on residential growth. The absence of government investment in sewers can prevent growth or can certainly limit the intensity and size of development. On the other hand, providing sewers can mean rapid development in previously unsettled areas. Through the manipulation of subsidies necessary to the construction of sewer systems, some control of suburban growth should be possible. The provision of federal and state grants to local governments for the construction of sewers has *not* been tied to orderly physical development. In addition, once sewers are built, local governments often cannot withstand the demands of builders for rezoning to allow rapid development. Furthermore, the very engineering nature of sewer systems may make it difficult to use them to regulate growth.

Sewer systems are major capital investment projects involving considerable construction. Local governments building sewer systems receive high construction subsidies from state and federal government agencies. This makes it reasonable from a local government perspective to build the largest sewer system possible — that is, to construct a system with capacity in excess of present demands. Such construction is "cheap" for the local government — up to 90 percent of costs are paid by state and federal governments. The project provides work for local firms. Furthermore, building excess capacity minimizes possible disruptions from future expansion. Yet by definition, the resulting excess capacity means that an existing sewer system can service more housing. Since costs for sewering have already been paid by government, developers see a means of reaping higher profits. As a result, large sewer systems, justified on cost-efficiency grounds, frequently produce demands for rapid development despite social or environmental consequences.

The failure of federal grants for sewer construction projects to serve social goals is evident in other ways. In 1968, the Douglas

Commission on suburban growth recommended that federal government programs providing subsidies for the provision of water and sewage facilities be tied to the existence of state and local commitments to the creation of open housing in suburbia, including the construction of subsidized low and moderate income housing. However, no sustained policy commitment tying sewer grants to opening up the suburbs was ever forthcoming. The limited role of federal government subsidies for sewers on exclusionary growth was recognized by the Seventies.[40] About the same time, environmental rather than social policy considerations in the provision of federal wastewater subsidies became dominant. This is seen in recent major federal legislation.

The Federal Water Pollution Control Act Amendments of 1972

Federal government involvement in sewering local areas took a quantum leap in 1972 with the passage of the Federal Water Pollution Control Act Amendments (FWPCA). Prior to 1972 the federal government had been involved in wastewater management but on a limited scale. Recent federal concerns for water pollution date back to at least 1948 with the passage of the original Water Pollution Control Act. This 1948 Act gave primary responsibility for setting and enforcing water quality standards to the states, limiting direct participation by the federal government — a pattern of divided responsibility that was to last 25 years.

In 1956, the law was amended to provide federal subsidies for the construction of wastewater treatment facilities. In 1965, further amendments providing financial incentives for the construction of regional wastewater treatment systems were incorporated into the law. Throughout this period, however, emphasis remained on the states as the implementors of wastewater treatment. Despite federal incentives, the states were slow in responding to the need for wastewater management. The Amendments of 1972 dramatically increased the direct federal pressure on state governments to clean-up waterways and to regulate the flow of waste.

Specifically, the 1972 FWPCA set up a timetable with 1983 as the deadline for the elimination of major sources of water contamination. The Amendments rely heavily on the construction of sewer facilities, and require that at least secondary treatment of sewage be adopted by all municipal wastewater treatment plants. In addition, the Amendments specify that by 1983 the best technology "economically available" be adopted, perhaps suggesting tertiary treatment be introduced. In response to the FWPCA, regional solutions to wastewater management are common. For example, the Municipality of Metropolitan Seattle was established as a regional sewage agency designed to clean up Lake Washington and to prevent the pollution of Puget Sound. Similarly, in the Central Valley-San Francisco Bay Area a combined regional solution to the pollution of San Francisco Bay had been sought. These examples suggest that in response to the 1972 provisions, the approach to water pollution problems has been a continued reliance on "structural" engineering solutions emphasizing the placement and construction of regional sewer systems.

Yet within the provisions of the 1972 Amendments lies an alternative approach to the problem of wastewater management that may have significant implications for future patterns of suburban growth. In the past, engineers have dominated the planning of sewer facilities. As a result of engineering considerations, local governments were frequently overwhelmed by resulting development pressure, and planned growth related to sewering was not easily accomplished.

However, Section 208 of the FWPCA, by reducing the emphasis on strictly engineering considerations, may have a significant long run effect on the provision of sewer facilities in suburban regions and the nature of growth. Essentially, Section 208 requires that states identify areas with significant water pollution control problems and designate a regional agency to formulate comprehensive regional plans for dealing with that problem. Many suburban areas fall into the appropriate category, and eventually most should be covered by Section 208. The provisions require that a "multi-modal" planning perspective be adopted in considering problems of wastewater management. In particular, Section 208 requires that demographic, land use, legal, fiscal, and institutional considerations be included in any regional wastewater management plan seeking federal support through the FWPCA. Simple engineering data and solutions will no longer be sufficient.[41]

As a result, regional planners are becoming more important and the comprehensive study of the interaction between development patterns and wastewater management is now more common. Section 208 also mandates that non-structural solutions to wastewater management be considered. These alternatives include regulating the density of communities to allow the continued use of individual household septic systems, a return to land disposal of wastewater, plus the retention of green belts and open space to maximize the flow of clean water in a watershed.

The full implications of Section 208 have not yet been realized. Structural solutions involving large-scale sewer systems dominated by engineering decisions still predominate. To the extent that regional planners can increase their influence over engineers in wastewater treatment plans and in provision of sewer systems, regional growth patterns more closely tied to and regulated by the provision of sewers may result, and the future of suburban growth will be altered.

Transportation Policy

Because of the expense of major transportation systems and because they cut across local government boundaries, transportation policy in metropolitan areas has largely been made by higher level governments, especially by the federal government. Throughout this century federal policy has been tied almost exclusively to subsidizing the construction of highways. Such federal subsidies have often led local communities to build roads and highways they may not have otherwise built, and have caused them to neglect other components of a balanced transportation system on which they might otherwise have concentrated.[42] Furthermore, federal subsidies have helped create a powerful political lobby — although signs of weakening have occurred — supporting the continuation of highway building even when the need for more alternative transportation systems balancing highways with other forms of transportation became apparent.

Federal Aid to Transportation

Present federal policy toward transportation can be traced back at least to the original Federal Highways Act of 1916. Three key provisions in that law have had a continuing impact on federal transportation policy. First, the original highways act had a strong rural bias. Second, there was a "highways only" emphasis on federal transportation aid, excluding aid to other forms of transportation such as buses or subways. Third, there was a lack of concern for coordinated planning and integration of highways with patterns of metropolitan development.[43]

The Historical Evolution of Federal Aid

The Highways Act of 1916 was passed in response to a strong coalition of rural interests, not urban ones. In particular, the Act responded to the demand by farmers for federal aid in the construction of farm-to-market roads.[44] Farmers, a powerful and well-organized force in American politics in the early 1900s, were supported by the burgeoning automobile industry, which immediately recognized that improved roads would increase the demands for and use of their products. Somewhat surprisingly, given the long term disastrous impacts of highways on their fortunes, the 1916 Highways Act was also supported strongly by railroads. Their interest was in the construction of good rural roads to allow farmers to deliver their products more quickly to rail stations. This rurally oriented "highways coalition" proved successful. The 1916 Highways Act established a Federal Bureau of Public Roads in the Department of Agriculture to supervise the flow of federal subsidies for the construction of highways, but only in rural areas less than 2,500 in population.

The 1916 Highways Act, of course, proved to be only the opening wedge for greater federal involvement. The federal role increased markedly during the Depression, when interest grew in road construction conceived as public works projects to fight unemployment and to stimulate the economy. The focus of federal aid also changed somewhat under the public works approach. Urban streets and roads received some federal attention and aid was not as narrowly focused on rural needs as in the past.

But continuing with tradition, no interest was shown in supporting the construction and maintenance of urban mass transportation systems — even as the stress of the Depression led to the deterioration and failure of large numbers of companies delivering this essential urban service. Similarly, continuing with tradition the need for comprehensive integrated transportation, land use, and community development, planning was neglected in favor of the single-minded emphasis on highway construction.

The federal government further expanded its intervention into transportation policy with the Federal Aid Highways Act of 1944. A "highways only" orientation was again apparent in the legislation. No funds for urban mass transit systems were included. The 1944 Act was supported by a greatly expanded automobile industry, while a declining railroad industry, realizing that it was being adversely affected by the growth of highways and trucking, dropped its support. But to replace the rail component of the highway lobby, tire, rubber and gasoline companies, and truckers and their unions were more than willing participants. Yet, one of the strongest advocates of more federal money for highways was a government agency itself, the Bureau of Public Roads, which coordinated lobbying efforts and provided some of the strongest evidence for the need for more highway subsidies.[45]

The 1944 Highways program continued to change the rural focus of the past toward more support for urban highways. While the 1916 Highways Act barred support for road building in communities greater than 2,500 population, the 1944 Federal Aid legislation provided 25 percent federal funding for roads in cities greater than 5,000 population. One consequence of this wider federal support was that suburbanization became evident as former central city residents now had better roads to commute from suburban homes to central city employment. Government policy-makers were willing to accede to this trend, and the perhaps irreversible move toward suburban sprawl supported by federal highway money began.[46]

While the 1944 Act did not include requirements for the integrated planning of highways and other transportation networks, by the mid-1950s the recognition of the need for coordination and planning was emerging. The first attempt at regional planning supported by the federal government was embodied in the Housing Act of 1954 which established "Section 701" grants to local governments to aid in comprehensive planning.

While funded at only a modest level, Section 701 nonetheless represented a federal concern for balancing highway construction with other suburban development needs. But this tentative effort at balanced planning was soon totally overpowered by a renewed emphasis on a "highways only" approach embodied in the 1956 Federal Aid Highways Act creating the Interstate Highway System.

Perhaps the most significant characteristic of the 1956 Act that cemented the highways orientation of federal aid was the creation of a Highway Trust Fund supported by excise taxes on gasoline. Revenues from the Trust Fund, under the terms of its creation, could be used solely for the construction of highways. Moreover, while previous federal highway programs had limited federal subsidies to 25 or 50 percent, depending on the type of road being constructed, the 1956 Interstate Highway System authorized 90 percent federal subsidies. This high level of support, plus huge sums of money accumulated in the Trust Fund, presented an irresistible temptation to local governments to build highways, regardless of the long range implications of such construction on metropolitan transportation practices. As a result of the massive highway building undertaken since 1956, the preeminence of automobile transportation patterns and suburban sprawl created on roads built with massive federal subsidies was guaranteed. Further, under the terms of the 1956 Act, functional engineers concerned with the construction of highways dominated transportation planning, over-riding the concerns of more "generalist" urban and regional planners concerned with the more difficult job of integrating highways with other forms of transportation to promote orderly growth and development.[47]

In short, while the ability of the federal government to control suburban growth through infrastructural investments in transportation existed in theory, emphasis on highway construction and the lack of concern for integrating highway building with community development created not balanced and planned suburban development but sprawling growth overwhelmingly dependent upon the automobile.

Balancing the "Highways Only" Policy

After 50 years of an almost exclusive emphasis on highway construction, and after a decade of large-scale development authorized under the Interstate Highways System, the federal government began to show a commitment to the support of transportation networks other than those based on highways and autos. A significant early attempt occurred in the 1960s when the Bureau of Public Roads and the Housing and Home Finance Agency (now the Department of Housing and Urban Development) cooperated to develop Areawide Transportation Studies integrating highways, other forms of transportation, and general planning considerations. However, these areawide plans failed because highway planners were still unable or unwilling to cooperate with "generalist" regional planners concerned with less well-defined policy questions than the simple engineering questions most highway planners had long mastered.[48]

Despite the failure of this effort, other attempts at modifying a "highways only" approach continue. Perhaps the most significant action was the creation of a Federal Department of Transportation (DOT) in 1966 and the subsequent creation of similar departments in many states following the federal lead. DOTs by their very nature mix highway and other transportation planning concerns into a single bureaucratic agency, increasing the possibilities of more balanced planning. On the state level in particular, the undisputed power of state highway departments in defining transportation plans may in the long run be mitigated by their incorporation into a larger DOT.[49]

Legislation supporting more balanced transportation networks also include the Urban Mass Transportation Assistance Program, begun on a small scale in 1961 and expanded by the Urban Mass Transportation Act of 1964. The Urban Mass Transportation Assistance Act of 1970 put some of this funding on a long term basis. More importantly, the 1973 Federal Aid Highways Act contained a significant departure from previous "highways only" legislation. In effect, the 1973 Act "breaks" the Highway Trust

Fund by making money from the fund spendable by local governments (in limited amounts) on transit programs rather than just on highway construction. While the funds transferrable are still limited, and the overwhelming bulk of funds are still available only for highways, continuing federal support or urban mass transit is now available. This support was also reinforced by the National Transportation Act of 1974 which calls for multi-modal comprehensive planning for the development of transportation systems in metropolitan areas.[50] But while such changes are now just beginning after 50 years of federal aid to highways, the dominance of the automobile in local transportation systems is entrenched and may be irrevocable.

Transit Versus Highways

But why is there concern for the development of alternate transportation networks? Why can't we just continue to rely on the automobile and highway construction?

These questions are particularly pointed since there can be no doubt that mass transit has failed the "market test" of consumer choice over the past half century — fewer and fewer people choose to use buses and trains, preferring to use automobiles. This choice is not recent — the transit industry has been in decline since the 1920s, and has experienced a literal hemorrhage of customers since 1945.[51] In part, passenger loss is due to problems within the industry. In particular, critics cite the poor management of most transit firms and their inability or unwillingness to introduce innovations and reforms in transit practices. These management failures result largely from the small size of many older transit companies plus a rather unappealing image that failed to attract new and aggressive talent into the field. Lackluster industry leadership also face declining competition from other transit firms because local and state governments heavily regulate and subsidize most transit companies. Given these forces, a general deterioration of the industry may have been expected in the face of the development of the appealing competitive form of transportation represented by the automobile.[52]

Yet such failures by themselves do not "justify" government intervention into the transit field. If people do not want the services offered by transit companies, why should the government pay to have them supplied? However, several considerations enter the policy process that have made government willing to support mass transit.

First, the recognition that government policies in the past fostered the growth of automobiles and highways at the expense of transit facilities has been part of the reasoning behind aid-to-transit legislation.[53] This recognizes both the extensive capital investments by government in roads, as well as the general failure of government planners adequately to comprehend and control the revolutionary changes set in motion with the highway aid programs.

Perhaps more important is the recognition of the limits of transportation systems totally dependent upon autos and roads. While automobile ownership is widespread, a significant number of Americans do not have access to an auto. Their mobility in the absence of transit systems is extremely limited. The people most likely to be denied continual access to a car are the young (who cannot get a driver's license), the elderly (who may never have driven or are too old to continue to drive), the infirm, and the poor. Moreover, in families owning only one car used for commuting purposes the mobility of the rest of the household is limited. The adverse impact on mobility of transportation systems based on autos helps create government policy supporting transit.[54]

Environmental considerations are equally important. There is no doubt that automobiles in our society have helped create suburban sprawl. This has led to familiar problems: unregulated consumption of land and natural resources, high energy costs, and pollution, to list a few. Environmentalists and planners concerned with a more balanced use of land and a more orderly form of suburban development have long been among the most vocal advocates of transit alternatives to automobiles. Given the present energy crises, these demands will probably continue and be given more attention in the future.

Finally, the adverse effects that dependence on the automobile has on the central business districts has also created concern about transit systems. Central business districts and central cities in general are deteriorating. Much of the cause for this deterioration is laid to the automobile and highways which have allowed and encouraged the unplanned outmovement of people and industry. Given these facts, more balanced transportation networks in metropolitan areas seem desirable. Public policy, especially through federal aid, has moved in the direction of providing such balanced systems. However, the outlook for success of mass transit is not promising. But perhaps even less promising is the actual ability of mass transit to promote more orderly suburban growth and metropolitan development, which is one goal set in federal policies supporting transportation policies.

The Limits of Transit in an Automobile Based Society

By their very nature, mass transit lines are most successful servicing compact urban centers. Most important is the existence of centralized business and employment locations that can be easily serviced by concentrated rail and bus lines. Compact residential development is also easy to service with mass transit. Connecting compact residential areas to a central business district is the task to which mass transit is best suited. Yet, after 50 years of highway construction and the suburbanization of population and industry, development patterns in most metropolitan areas do not conform to those most amendable to mass transit. As a result of suburban sprawl and scatteration of employment throughout suburban areas, it may be impossible to support the future growth of transit systems. Thus the financial health of metropolitan transit systems may be totally undermined by the nature of present day metropolitan growth.

Similarly, even if mass transit is subsidized to the extent it needs, the ability of mass transit to foster orderly growth in the future may still be limited. In the not distant past, the effects of transit on the shape of metropolitan growth was significant. New development was tied to the opening of areas by transit lines. Residential growth (such as "streetcar suburbs") and commercial development followed the construction of transit lines into previously undeveloped areas.

At present, however, transit systems can no longer radically affect patterns of growth, largely because they do not represent the extensive change in an area's accessibility they once did. Automobiles and highway construction have made most parts of metropolitan regions easily reachable. As a result, introducing buses or rail systems into an area already served by freeways, cars, and trucks only incrementally changes accessibility and resulting patterns of growth. Further, maximizing whatever impacts mass transit can have on development requires that comprehensive planning occurs and that mass transit development be supported by zoning and other land use regulations. Usually, however, government agencies in the United States do not have or choose not to use zoning or taxing powers in conjunction with transit development to foster compact growth.

The easiest way to understand this point is to compare the planning and development of mass transit in the United States with its traditions of minimal government intervention with transportation planning in other countries, such as Canada or Sweden, where integration of land use and transportation planning is the expected norm.

Frank C. Colcord, for example, argues that the impact of automobiles in most continental European cities has been less than in the United States "primarily because European governments have played a much stronger role in shaping land use."[55] In particular, he compares the United States and Sweden and finds that Sweden has vigorously promoted high density housing development planned and coordinated with transit systems. This coordination has encouraged the use of mass transit and discouraged the use of automobiles for commuting.

Similarly, an intensive U.S. Department of Transportation study of the land use impacts of mass transit notes that European cities routinely coordinate transit and housing development. According to this study, building suburban communities in Europe without providing good and reliable mass transit facilities would be unthinkable.[56]

Thus Europeans assume that mass transit and community development go hand-in-hand. Planners make sure that the two actually develop together, and government powers are routinely used to make sure that coordination is achieved. By contrast, in the United States, with its widespread reliance on automobiles, the link between transit and community development is weaker. In addition, given the historical traditions of limited government in the United States, policies promoting coordination are infrequent, or are unenforced. This failure of coordination is evident in recent mass transit projects undertaken in this country.[57]

The BART system (Bay Area Rapid Transit) in San Francisco and METRO in Washington, D.C., are two of the newest mass transit systems in the world. These systems are based on "heavy rail" technology and both are designed to serve as metropolitan-wide systems. They are expected to have a major impact on suburban development, controlling sprawl, and on the relationship between the central city and suburbs, improving the condition of the city.

However, empirical evidence of the impact of these transit systems on metropolitan development is ambiguous. Washington, D.C.'s METRO was originally planned as a regional system with eight separate lines and over 100 miles of track. However, at present, only a small proportion of those tracks are in service and given escalating construction costs, it is highly unlikely that more than 50 percent of the planned system will ever be built. At this early stage, the impact of the rail system on land use and community development is not measurable.

The San Francisco BART system is more developed and its impact more measurable. BART is a regional system serving 3 of the 9 Bay Area Counties (Alameda, Contra Costa, and San Francisco). The system is designed both to serve the central city itself and to bring suburban commuters into downtown. In fact, the average distance between stations is over 2 miles, indicating their relative dispersion. Yet, while the transit system has had some impact on revitalizing central city growth, the city of San Francisco was not in poor shape to begin with, and the potential impact of new mass transit on a seriously deteriorating city cannot be ascertained from BART. Furthermore, the impact of BART on suburban development is at best debatable. First, the BART system is not servicing the areas of most rapid suburban growth. BART does not reach Santa Clara County, where growth is most intense. Nor does BART service the southeast, towards

Livermore, or the North Bay Counties. All these suburban areas are experiencing higher rates of growth than the three counties BART does service.

In addition evidence of BART's impact on the areas it does penetrate is conflicting. This lack of impact results in large measure from the fragmentation of suburban land use powers, and the inability of government to coordinate development and transit systems. Thus while some suburbs have rezoned for higher density development along the BART station system, other suburbs have "downzoned" to prevent any intense development. Further, in places along the BART system where growth has taken place, it is likely that factors other than BART had already produced growth and that the independent effects of BART creating new planned developments are small.[58] In short, an extremely expensive investment in transit system in part designed to provide orderly suburban growth has not proven unequivocably successful.

The success of heavy rail transit systems in other areas is also mixed. For example, in 1969 an extension of a commuter line was built from Philadelphia into its New Jersey suburbs, called the Lindenwold line. Service was extended and equipment upgraded. This single line was conceived as a regional system connecting six suburban areas with stations in downtown Camden and Philadelphia. The single transit line carries a considerable number of people, about 17,000 per day. This is more people than carried by the 17 commuter bus routes serving the area and more than any of the other 13 commuter rail lines that also service the region. Yet the impact of this system on suburban growth again is not totally clear.

Apparently a major concentrated area of suburban development, the Echelon Urban Center, was in response to the existence of the Lindenwold renovation. The Urban Center combines shopping, housing, and commercial offices, and does provide a growth focus as an alternative to suburban sprawl. Concentrated development at other points along the line, especially the Borough of Haddonfield, also is cited as an example of coordinated growth and transit development. But despite these isolated examples of success, the necessary coordination of transit and articulated suburban growth plans has not been fully forthcoming. Similarly, the extension of the "Orange Line" into the suburbs north of Boston and the "Red Line" south to Quincy has had an effect on concentrating growth in these suburban areas. While there is some evidence of impact, the extent is not great and is probably not commensurate with the costs of the expansion or construction of heavy rail transit systems.

Because of the expense and problems of heavy rail technology, and because clear results are lacking, it is probable that more investments in suburban bus routes will be forthcoming rather than for rail mass transit.

Studies on the impact of commuter bus services have been funded by the Urban Mass Transportation Administration. These studies have included the provision for express bus services in Washington, D.C., along Interstate 95 linking the city with its northern Virginia suburbs. Similar express bus systems in San Bernadino, Seattle, and the Miami region have been instituted. These systems usually provide an express lane on highways reserved for designated buses. Despite studies, the impact of busways on suburban growth is not yet measured.

There have also been several attempts to use buses to provide "reverse commuting" facilities in metropolitan areas, allowing underemployed inner-city residents access to jobs in suburban areas. The largest such program was an attempt to link Boston's Roxbury ghetto with the concentration of industry along Route 128 surrounding Boston. The program lasted for 6 months and was judged a failure. Similar programs in Chicago and St. Louis also were unsuccessful.[59] In general, then, the impact of buses on suburban development and metropolitan inequalities have not been very great.

Other forms of mass transit — trolleys, cable cars, streetcars — will not have an appreciable impact on suburban development. Given the diffusion of government power in suburban areas, and the historical lack of coordinating development and transit, the impact of transit on suburban development will be small at best.

Transit impact is further weakened by the extensive system of highways and heavy reliance on automobiles that makes transit systems nonessential for movement and development in suburban areas. Given the high accessibility of most areas because of automobile ownership, we cannot expect that the provision of mass transit will have a major impact on metropolitan development.

In short, it may be too late for the United States to rationalize the provision of metropolitan transportation systems. For too long U.S. policy makers have acceded to the wishes of the population for low density, single family, sprawling development supported by automobile ownership and highways.[60] Given the low commitment to an active and coordinated response and given the physical shape of sprawling suburban development, it may forever be impossible to provide an alternative means of transportation in suburban areas other than ones based on autos and highways.

Summary: Service Delivery in Metropolitan Areas

In the preceding three chapters some of the major issues confronting government organization in metropolitan areas have been highlighted.

Inequalities between various communities in the level of services received is one major issue frequently addressed in the examination of metropolitan governance. This concern has been most evident with regard to educational finance, where a heavy reliance on local property taxes has meant that the rich school districts have had well-supported schools while poor districts are hard pressed just to provide a basic educational foundation. These inequalities are often traced back to fiscal zoning, where competition between communities creates "winners" and "losers" and fosters a general system of "separate but unequal" services.

Another area where unequal level of services has been investigated, albeit to a considerably lesser extent than education and zoning, is police. In policing there is evidence of wealthy communities being able to provide more extensive and "personalized" police services than less well-to-do communities. While unequal levels characterize other public goods and services delivered by local governments in metropolitan areas, the intensity and frequency of debate has tended to be less than in the issue areas discussed. However, unequal coverage for other services does frequently become an important issue in metropolitan areas.

If inequality in services is one theme in the governance of metropolitan areas, so are questions of efficiency in the provision of such services. Two particular dimensions of efficiency are usually brought into central focus. First, local government actions may be inefficient in a technical sense in that individual local governments may be able to escape the full consequences of their policy choices by imposing costs on their neighbors, that is, they may generate "negative externalities." For example, an upstream community may pollute a waterway with inadequately treated sewage. Or a community may zone to allow the building of new factories or commercial development but refuse to allow the building of housing units for the low income workers needed to staff those new business concerns. In either case, some other community must "pay" for the actions of its more successful neighbor. In the first case, the downstream community must bear higher costs for water treatment. In the second case, the "losing" community will most likely be forced to impose a higher tax rate because of a lower property tax base resulting from low income development. Such "externalities" create inefficient public policies in a technical sense because they hide the true costs of the goods generated by individual governments. It is usually argued that the fragmentation of suburban areas into small and relatively autonomous jurisdictions creates the conditions that maximize the possibilities of externalities in the provision of services.

The other manner in which the provision of services is viewed concerns "economies of scale." It is often argued that most local governments are inefficient providers of goods and services because their small size makes them unable to purchase the newest most up-to-date equipment and unable to hire the best trained personnel. It also is often argued that fragmentation creates overlap and duplication in the provision of services.

Governments in metropolitan areas have tried to respond to these shortcomings for providing services in many ways. The creation of larger units is one traditional response. This is most common with schools. States have made it advisable for many small local school districts to consolidate with their neighbors.

Regional provision of other services such as sewering or solid waste disposal is also common. One further step along this "consolidationist" approach is the restructuring of local governments themselves, creating one regional government to replace the fragmented system of local governments in an area. As illustrated in the next chapter, this approach is evident in such metropolitan regions as Nashville, Tennessee, and Jacksonville, Florida.

Increased government cooperation between existing governments is also possible. Such cooperation is seen in the provision of police services, where independent police forces have developed cooperative agreements for the apprehension of criminals as well as for the provision of certain expensive services, such as pretrial detention and radio communications, that are more efficiently handled on a cooperative basis between neighboring jurisdictions. The possibility of improving services in metropolitan areas through such cooperative arrangements is also discussed in the next chapter.

In short, problems of governance and the provision of services in metropolitan areas focus on at least three issues: inequalities between communities in the same region; the "external" effects that small local government policy choices have on their neighbors; and, the failure of local governments to achieve economies of scale in the provision of services. Responses to these problems fall along a broad spectrum. On one end of the range, some students of local government hope to improve the performance of local governments by seeking ways to increase the level of voluntary cooperation between existing independent local governments. While hoping to improve performance through cooperation, such reforms would leave the structure of local governments essentially intact, changing the existing system of multiple local governments in only a marginal fashion. Almost totally opposed to this position are those students of metropolitan government who seek to improve the delivery of services and the general level of governance by the eradication of most existing units of local government by their consolidation into one large-scale unit governing the entire metropolitan region. It is to these issues concerning government organization in metropolitan areas that we now turn.

Notes

1. The literature on "Lilliputs" and metropolitan policing is quite extensive. See, for example, Elinor Ostrom and Dennis C. Smith, "Are the Lilliputs in Metropolitan Policing Failures?" paper presented to the annual meeting of the American Society for Public Administration, 1975; Elinor Ostrom, Roger B. Parks, and Gordon P. Whitaker, "Do We Really Want To Consolidate Urban Police Forces?" *Public Administration Review*, 33 (September/October, 1973), pp. 423-432; Elinor Ostrom and Roger B. Parks, "Suburban Police Departments, Too Many and Too Small?" in Louis Masotti and Jeffrey Hadden, eds., *The Urbanization of the Suburbs*, volume 7, Urban Affairs Annual Review (Beverly Hills, California: Sage Publication, 1973), pp. 367-402.

2. The following discussion is drawn from James Q. Wilson, *Varieties of Police Behavior* (Cambridge, Massachusetts: Harvard University Press, 1968).

3. *Ibid.*, p. 209.

4. President's Commission on Law Enforcement, *The Challenge of Crime in a Free Society* (Washington, D.C.: Government Printing Office, 1967), p. 119.

5. *Ibid.*, p. 308.

6. (New York: Committee for Economic Development), p. 31.

7. Wilson, *Varieties*, p. 214.

8. Harry P. Pachon and Nicholas P. Lovrich, Jr., "The Consolidation of Urban Public Services: A Focus on the Police," *Public Administration Review*, 37 (January/February, 1977), pp. 38-47. Also see the data in Ostrom and Parks, "Suburban Police Departments."

9. Pachon and Lovrich, "Consolidation."

10. Elinor Ostrom, Roger B. Parks and Gordon P. Whitaker, *Policing Metropolitan America* (Washington, D.C.: Government Printing Office), p. iii. Also see the works cited in footnote 1.

11. Ostrom, *et al.*, *Policing*.

12. *Ibid.*, chapter III.

13. *Ibid.*, p. 32.

14. William B. Neenan, *Political Economy of Urban Areas* (Chicago: Markham Publishing Company, 1972); Pachon and Lovrich, "Consolidation," pp. 39-40. Norman Walzer, "The Economies of Scale and Municipal Police Services: The Illinois Experience," *Review of Economics and Statistics*, 55 (November, 1973), pp. 431-438.

15. Harry Hatry, "Wrestling with Police Crime Control Productivity Measures," in Joan Wolfe and John H. Heaply, eds., *Readings on Productivity Measures* (Washington, D.C.: Police Foundation, 1975). Wesley G. Skogan, "The Promise of Policing," *Journal of Urban Analysis*, 5 (Winter 1978), pp. 203-222.

16. George Kelling, *et al.*, *The Kansas City Preventive Control Experiment* (Washington, D.C.: The Police Foundation, 1974).

17. Skogan, "Promise of Policing."

18. Lois MacGillivray, "Measuring Fire Protection Service Delivery," paper presented at the Workshop on Policy Analysis in State and Local Government, State University of New York, Stony Brook, May 1977, p. 31.

19. Philip B. Coulter, Louis MacGillivray and William Edward Vickery, "Municipal Fire Protection Performance in Urban Areas," in Elinor Ostrom, ed.,

The Delivery of Urban Services, Urban Affairs Annual Review, volume 10 (Beverly Hills, California: Sage Publications, 1976), pp. 231-260.

20. Michael R. Greenberg, *et al.*, *Solid Waste Planning in Metropolitan Regions* (New Brunswick, New Jersey: Center for Urban Policy Studies, 1976), chapter 1.

21. This discussion draws heavily on Christopher Niemczewski, "The History of Solid Waste Management," in E.S. Savas and Barbara Stevens, *Evaluating the Organization of Service Delivery: Solid Waste Collection and Disposal* (Washington, D.C.: National Science Foundation, 1977).

22. Savas and Stevens, *Solid Waste*, Table 4-13, p. 89.

23. Eileen Berenji and Daniel Baumol, "The Role of Local Government in Regulating Solid Waste Disposal," in Savas and Stevens, *Solid Waste*.

24. Frank Grad, "The Role of Federal and State Governments in Solid Waste Management" in Savas and Stevens, *Solid Waste*.

25. *Ibid.*, p. 333.

26. Greenberg, *et al.*, *Solid Waste Planning*, pp. 133-134.

27. *Ibid.*, p. 177.

28. *Ibid.*, pp. 185-188.

29. Council on Environmental Quality, *The Growth Shapers* (Washington, D.C.: Government Printing Office, 1976).

30. George Carey, *et al.*, *Urbanization, Waste Pollution and Public Policy* (New Brunswick, New Jersey: Center for Urban Policy Research, 1972), pp. 1-7.

31. John A. Black, *Water Pollution Technology* (Reston, Va.: Reston Publishing Company, Inc., 1977), p. 137.

32. John J. Hartigan and Gener E. Willeke, "Land Disposal of Wastewater: An Annotated Bibliography," Council of Planning Librarians Exchange Bibliography, 837 (July 1975).

33. Black, *Water Pollution*, p. 137.

34. *Ibid.*, chapter 9.

35. It should be noted that regardless of the level of treatment, sewer plants produce a solid waste product called sludge. A large regional plant can produce large amounts of this solid waste that must be disposed of. For example, the Metropolitan Sanitary District of Chicago generates about 1,000 metric tons of sludge every day. Thus, wastewater treatment may produce significant effects for solid waste disposal systems.

36. Recognizing this relationship, many suburbs seeking to limit growth impose sewer moratoria on new hook-ups to sewer plants or ban the construction of new sewer lines. These moratoria can be an effective means of regulating growth.

37. CEQ, *Growth Shapers*, p. 19.

38. *Ibid.*, p. 48.

39. *Ibid.*, p. 53.

40. William G. Colman, *Cities, Suburbs, and States* (New York: The Free Press, 1975), pp. 74-76.

41. Hartigan and Willeke, "Land Disposal," p. 5. Also see Lee Koppelman, "Policy Issues in Waste Treatment Planning," *Journal of Urban Analysis*, 5 (Winter 1978), pp. 251-274.

42. Herman Martins, Jr. and David R. Miller, "Urban Transportation Policy: Fact or Fiction?" in David R. Miller, ed., *Urban Transportation Policy* (Lexington, Mass.: D.C. Heath, 1972), pp. 19-36.

43. Palley and Palley, *Urban America and Public Policies*, chapter 9. George Smerk, "The Urban Transportation Problem," in Miller, *Urban Transportation*, pp. 5-18. Frank J. Kendrick, "Urban Transportation Policy: Politics, Planning, and People," in Robert L. Lineberry and Louis H. Masotti, eds., *Urban Problems and Public Policy* (Lexington, Mass.: D.C. Heath, 1975), pp. 129-138.

44. K.H. Schaeffer and Elliot Sclar, *Access for All* (Baltimore, Maryland: Penguin Books, 1975), p. 39.

45. Melvin R. Levin and Norman A. Abend, *Bureaucrats in Collision* (Cambridge, Mass.: MIT Press, 1971), chapter 2.

46. *Ibid.*, p. 34.

47. *Ibid.*, chapter 10.

48. *Ibid.*, passim.; Smerk, "Urban Transportation."

49. Martins and Miller, "Urban Transportation Policy."

50. Frank J. Colcord, "Urban Transportation and Political Ideology," *Policy Studies Journal,* 6 (Autumn 1977), pp. 9-20.

51. Between 1946 and 1970, the annual ridership on mass transit and commuter trains dropped from 23 billion to about 8.5 billion. While all forms of mass transit suffered loss, buses experienced the heaviest decline in ridership (Schaeffer and Sclar, *Access*), p. 46.

52. George W. Hilton, *Federal Transit Subsidies* (Washington, D.C.: American Enterprise Institute, 1974), p. 89.

53. *Ibid.*, p. 6.

54. Anthony R. Tomazins, "Transportation Policies and Urban Development," in Miller, ed., *Urban Transportation*, pp. 129-140; Kendrick, "Urban Transportation Policy," Schaeffer and Sclar, *Access*.

55. Colcord, "Political Ideology," p. 10.

56. Robert L. Knight and Lisa L. Trigg, *Land Use Impacts of Rapid Transit* (Washington, D.C.: U.S. Department of Transportation, 1977).

57. *Ibid.*

58. *Ibid.*, p. 90.

59. Hilton, *Subsidies*, pp. 14-33.

60. Colcord, "Political Ideology", p. 16.

Chapter 6

Governing Suburban America

By now, the real and assumed ills and shortcomings of government and service delivery in metropolitan areas of the United States should be well known to the reader. The failures in government of suburban and metropolitan areas in general relate to the social stratification of the population, the development of fiscal imbalances between metropolitan communities, and the inefficiencies and lack of coordination and control over public services as presently supplied in the metropolis. Oversimplifying the arguments previously developed in the first chapters of this book, criticisms of local government in metropolitan America can be grouped into several categories.[1]

First, the most frequently cited complaint concerning suburban government is the division of metropolitan areas into central cities and suburbs. Suburbs, while socially, economically, and physically intertwined with the central city are politically separate from it. Given patterns of migration and the resulting class and racial imbalances that result, the separation of cities and suburbs produces major problems of governance. In particular, these problems revolve around the concentration of low income and racial minority groups in the central cities and the settlement of white upper and middle class groups in the suburbs. Central cities, especially older larger ones, have low income populations with high service demands and declining tax bases to finance these services. In contrast, suburbs on the whole, represent higher status populations — with lower service demands and hence a more beneficial fiscal mix from which to finance government services.

Much of the stratification between cities and suburbs is often seen as the direct result of exclusionary growth policies undertaken by suburban governments to build "invisible walls" around themselves, thereby excluding low income residents. While this line of argument can be exaggerated[2] and while speculation exists that city and suburban differences may be declining,[3] large and persistent class and racial balances do exist and seem to *grow* over time. This is particularly true in the oldest and largest metropolitan areas in the country, especially those located in the northeast and Great Lakes regions.[4]

The separation of racial and class groups between cities and suburbs implies a *social* stratification that is of concern, but it also implies a *fiscal* problem in terms of the provision and funding of services. Similarly, the fragmentation of suburbia itself into autonomous independent local governments creates the same results. Some suburban communities succeed in the "competition" for desirable residents and "specialize" in large homes and countrified estates for rich people. Other suburbs succeed in attracting upper middle income residents who can also pay taxes necessary to support local services. Still other suburbs succeed in attracting business and industry to bolster their local property tax base. In recent years, some evidence exists suggesting that the most well-off suburbs now attract *both* wealthy suburban residents *and* commercial development, producing the strongest possible local tax base.

There also exist suburbs that fail in a competitive growth process — suburbs that attract neither residents nor business that add to local property tax base. These "unannointed" suburbs face the constant battle of financing public services from an inadequate tax base. The funding of local government services, heavily paid for out of local property taxes, becomes mired in the inequalities in local tax base between neighboring communities. In its social dimension, the process of separation between racial and class groups has been termed "areal specialization" and the result of such specialization in social terms is well known: each individual suburb is more homogeneous than the metropolitan area as a whole.[5] In fiscal terms, areal specialization is mirrored in the "separate and unequal" nature of government services and finance.

Further, the provision of local government services in suburban areas often is criticized for being wasteful and inefficient. Unregulated growth resulting in "suburban sprawl" wastes large quantities of land and imposes high service costs on local governments through the need to construct more widespread service delivery systems such as water supply, sewage disposal, roads, and schools. In addition, because suburban areas are divided into a multitude of government jurisdictions, it is frequently argued that the provision of these services on a coordinated and integrated basis is impeded. The resulting inefficiencies, duplication, and overlap between local government delivery systems is thought to impose higher costs than necessary on local governments and to prevent the production of essential areawide services. As the Committee for Economic Development (CED) notes in its study of *Improving Productivity in State and Local Government:*

> Local government in the United States continues to be characterized by unnecessary duplicative and overlapping jurisdictions. There is a need for local jurisdiction of sufficient size and authority to plan, administer, and provide financial support for solutions to areawide problems.[6]

According to the CED, government reform is necessary to provide more coordination in the provision of services. Larger scale governments of "sufficient size and authority" are probably necessary to provide areawide services and to equalize the funding of such essential services. The reform of suburban government to improve the productivity of government services becomes a theme in the discussion of suburban government.

Moreover, given skyrocketing service costs and the inability of most local governments to generate sufficient revenues from local taxes to meet demands, interest in increased productivity has moved to center stage in recent years. Caught in a fiscal squeeze, local governments must either raise tax rates, reduce services, obtain revenue from higher levels of government, or try a combination of these. Raising taxes and cutting services are among the most difficult policy choices local governments face and are avoided for as long as possible. Improving the productivity of existing resources seems to be the most viable short-term solution to the problems of financing local government service delivery. Hence, increasing productivity through the upward shift of services (as seen in Chapters 4 and 5) and through the creation of new means of delivering such services more efficiently is of growing importance to the functioning of metropolitan areas.

Finally, on a somewhat different level, very practical criticisms of suburban government have been embodied in the actions of the state and federal governments to which local suburban governments must ultimately respond. During the 1960s, the federal government had a big-city bias in it policies and was itself concerned with actually implementing social programs and with the day-to-day problems of service delivery. Since the administration of Richard Nixon, the federal government under the general term "The New Federalism" has turned more and more to the use of local governments to implement national policies.[7] Subsequently, the importance of local government in achieving federal objectives has increased. In turn, the federal government continues to express its concern for the effects of present local fragmentation on the efficiency of suburban government. In fact, pressure from the federal government to modify the government of suburban regions is one of the prime forces urging reform of suburban government and service delivery systems.

Similarly, state governments have also been concerned with the effects and the costs of present suburban government. Responding to their own interests and their felt needs for better coordinated services in metropolitan areas, as well as reflecting pressure put on them from the federal level, state governments have increased the demands on suburbs to improve coordination of their policies. Furthermore, as the fiscal squeeze on all levels of government continues to mount, reforms designed to maximize service output and minimize service costs undoubtedly will be more popular. Inevitably, the reform of suburban government will be seen as an area where significant savings in service costs can be realized.

An Inventory of Forms of Local Government

Before going into more detail concerning changes in government in suburban areas, it is useful to list and briefly describe the forms of local government most widely used in metropolitan areas at present. These forms of local government can be classified into two broad categories, general purpose local governments and special districts.

General Purpose Governments

There are at present some 38,000 units of general purpose local governments in the United States which can be divided into the following categories:

Municipalities These are incorporated local governments — that is, they possess a municipal corporation charter giving them state powers as well as the right to exercise certain corporate responsibilities. This gives municipalities flexibility in the provision of urban services. Depending upon the region and state, municipalities are called cities, boroughs, or villages. In 1972, the U.S. Census of Governments enumerated over 18,000 municipalities.

Counties Currently, counties are potentially the most important level of government in suburban regions. Counties are units of local government historically used by state governments to administer state programs and functions. They handle certain important state functions such as the administration of justice (sheriffs, courts, jails), property assessments for tax purposes, and health care and hospitals. Counties have the size and geographic scope to provide services to suburban areas efficiently and to equalize unbalanced finances and services. Indeed, the use of "urban counties" to deliver essential services is increasing. Yet, despite the growth of the importance of counties in many states, counties are still weak governments in most places. Counties often do not have the independence or the power of municipalities and most have not been granted autonomy or "Home Rule" by their state governments.

New England Towns Because of historical settlement patterns, mostly the importance of church parishes in the development of the New England colonies, unincorporated towns in New England, areas roughly corresponding to historical church boundary lines, play important local government roles in that region of the country. The 1400 New England towns provide a wide range of services handled in other places by county or municipal governments. In addition to general municipal government functions, New England towns also are often responsible for the governance and funding of local education.

Townships These local units of government are found in a large number of states but are actually important in providing services only in five: Michigan, New Jersey, New York, Pennsylvania, and Wisconsin. In the other midwest states in which townships exist, they are concerned mostly with the condition of roads and are not involved in other municipal services. However, since townships in the midwest have received federal aid from the General Revenue Sharing program in excess of their needs for road maintenance there is some evidence that townships in suburban areas of Michigan and Wisconsin are now expanding their role in providing other urban services.

Special Districts

In contrast to general purpose governments providing a variety of services, special districts often are formed to supply a limited set of services. Frequently a special district will provide only one service. In contrast to general purpose governments which usually provide a multitude of services within one set of defined government boundary lines, the size and shape of special districts are more flexible. Thus, special districts can be formed to provide a service to a subset of a municipality where the need for a particular service, e.g., sewers, is particularly severe. A special district may also cut across existing general purpose government boundary lines to provide services to residents in a number of municipalities. Or, as is most frequent, special districts can be created to deliver an urban type service to an unincorporated area in need of the service but without a general municipal government readily available to supply it. The most common form of special district is the school district and special districts for water, fire, transportation, housing, drainage, soil conservation, or mosquito control are common.

While special districts have been criticized for fragmenting local government and weakening general purpose governments in favor of functional specialization,[9] they do represent a flexible organizational response to service delivery problems.[10] They are frequently used to provide a service that a municipal government either does not want to supply or is financially constrained from supplying because of state regulations governing taxing or debt limitations. While single purpose special districts predominate, there is some speculation that multi-jurisdictional special districts encompassing a variety of governmental services may provide one "back door" approach to areawide government in metropolitan regions.

It is within this multitude of local government forms representing a wide variety of areawide governing potentials and of different responsibilities for services that the question of what reforms and improvements in local government have been suggested and what reforms have actually been implemented can be studied.

The Response to Problems of Government in Metropolitan Areas: Consolidation

For the greater part of this century the predominant attitude toward reform has favored the elimination of most local units of government and the creation of larger, more comprehensive metropolitan government. Since the Sixties the Committee for Economic Development has been one of the leading proponents of this "consolidationist" position. Their document, *Modernizing Local Government,* is the classic statement of the presumed benefits that would accrue to metropolitan areas as a result of consolidation of local governments. Thus, according to the CED, "the most pressing problem of local government in metropolitan areas may be stated quite simply. The bewildering multiplicity of small, piecemeal, duplicative, overlapping local jurisdictions cannot cope with the staggering difficulties encountered in managing urban affairs."[11]

The failure of small-scale suburban government can presumably be traced to several characteristics inherent to that system of government. According to the CED, very few units of local government at present are large enough to command the resources necessary to support modern methods of policy analysis and problem solving. Their ability to support professional analysts and government officials is limited by their resources. This is particularly true for long-range planning where high quality personnel are essential. Furthermore, the fragmentation of local government produces competition between neighboring jurisdictions. But just as importantly, the overlapping and divided responsibility for services in the metropolis means that no single decision center for policies and services is identifiable. According to the "consolidationist" argument, this multi-layer system creates an inability to set regional priorities in the allocation of resources and makes the identification by citizens of government officials responsible for the existing level of services difficult. As a result, according to this position, citizens lose interest in government because they are confused by the vagueness of the government structure deciding policy.[12]

Given these problems inherent in the fragmentation of metropolitan areas, the consolidation of government functions and policy making into one comprehensive government for an entire metropolitan region is the preferred policy response of many reform organizations. While the "consolidationist" position has been the dominant theme of metropolitan reform throughout the last decades, its peak of importance was embodied in the 1966 publication of the CED report on *Modernizing Local Government*. Since that time, considerable interest in alternate paths to improving government in metropolitan areas has arisen. In particular a school of thought generally referred to as a "political economic" framework has been in vogue.

Polycentricity and Political Economic Approach to Government Reform

The political economic approach to government reform begins by stating that support for the multiplicity of local governments rather than their elimination is desirable. This position rests on two lines of argument, both derived from a preference for a "free market" solution to government problems over a coercive "monopoly" embodied in a single large-scale government.

First it is assumed that the existence of a multitude of small local governments, each with a different mix of local services, allows citizens of a metropolitan government to move to and live in a community that most closely reflects their preferences for different types of services. Thus, the existence of small and competing local governments creates "a quasi-market choice for local residents in permitting them to select the particular community in the metropolitan area that most closely approximates the public service levels they desire."[13] Rather than being coerced into "purchasing" a mix of services the same over one large metropolitan government, a "polycentric" system of small governments theoretically allows greater choice in public services by individual citizens.

This line of argument has recently been bolstered by concern for community control and the decentralization of government in large cities. Living under a large-scale urban government that has eliminated the kind of fragmentation that allegedly hinders the governance of suburbia, many central city residents complain bitterly that their government is not responsive to their interests and needs. In response, they advocate the decentralization of central city government into neighborhood government. Such decentralization clearly seeks to establish within the central city local governments not unlike those already existing in suburbia! Hence the assumed benefits of large-scale consolidated metropolitan government may not be felt by the citizens of the region. This point is so telling that in most recent arguments in favor of consolidation some provision for a two "tier" system of government is now advocated — a centralized large-scale consolidated government in charge of metropolitan area-wide needs and priorities coupled with a continuation of small-scale neighborhood governments subservient to the larger government, but still responsive to local needs.

Second, political economists dispute the view that large-scale governments can produce services more efficiently than small units of government. This denial is based on several beliefs. Political economists tend to be economists first and analysts concerned with government organizations delivering services second. As a result, the number of units of local government involved in service delivery in a metropolitan region may not seem large to an economist accustomed to problems of the coordination of an even greater number of competing firms operating in the same private marketplace. Hence the extent of fragmentation may be minimal in the eyes of the political economists. Further, if, as economists believe, competition in the marketplace can produce satisfactory coordination between a large number of competing private firms, competition between the number of local governments in a metropolitan area may also produce satisfactory coordination.

Finally, political economists do not believe that all services are amenable to delivery by large-scale units. Neither do they believe that all services should be retained in smaller ones. However, according to political economists, this is an *analytic* question that must be answered empirically for each policy area, rather than simply assuming *a priori* that large-scale governments are best. The issue of police work is a case in point. Clearly police departments run by large governments can produce certain expensive police services more efficiently than small local suburban departments. Yet other police services, most notably patrol, seem to be easily and efficiently delivered by small departments. Therefore, the creation of just one large single department delivering *all* police services is unnecessary, and may be wasteful. The argument can obviously be extended to other services.

In general, much of the continuing debate concerning the "proper" size of government units can be conceptualized as falling into two lines of argument, both drawn from economic reasoning. One concerns "economies of scale." The other concerns the concept of "externalities."

Externalities and Suburban Government

The existence of a multitude of autonomous suburban governments gives rise to the possibilities that some local governments can undertake policies that benefit themselves while passing on the costs of such action to other local governments. Take for example the case of housing policies and the fiscal impact of low income residents on suburban services. Each local government wants to maximize its tax base in relation to service costs. Therefore, each local government may seek a housing policy that attracts the most fiscally productive residents, e.g., high income families. Yet there are not enough of these "desirable" residents to go around. A "successful" suburb will attract these residents, and leave an "unsuccessful" suburb to house lower income residents. To the extent that some suburbs are successful, other communities will suffer. In other words, the successful suburb has created "spill over" effects or "negative externalities" for other local governments to absorb.

Consolidationists recognize this problem. Their argument for expansion of government boundary lines to create large-scale area-wide decision units is a not unusual response to the general problem of externalities — boundary lines are redrawn to encompass all affected units and externalities are "internalized" within one larger government unit. As a result of this internalization, no local government can escape the costs it imposes on others.[15]

In contrast, political economists note that the market can take care of spill over short of creating large scale consolidated government. Political economists favoring the continuation of multiple or "polycentric" government stress the use of intergovernmental agreements to ameliorate the effects of interjurisdictional problems.[16] This means that local governments bargain with one another to arrive at compensation for externalities imposed.

The relative effectiveness of each system of dealing with externalities is essentially unknown. But it is an issue that pits consolidationists against political economists and is central to the debate concerning reform of metropolitan government.

Economies of Scale

Economies of scale are also an underlying theme in the analysis of government organization in metropolitan areas. As noted, consolidationists assume that larger governments can produce services at greater efficiency and less expensively by achieving economies of scale associated with large-scale services. Political economists, on the other hand, argue that the achievement of economies of scale is not insured and, in particular, economies of scale associated with different services may vary widely. Most arguments attacking the assumption that economies of scale are achievable through consolidation turn to the work of a leading urban economist, Werner Hirsch. In a seminal article on expenditure implications and size of local governments, Hirsch argued that there exist three types of services in metropolitan areas.[17] First, there are certain services that are capital intensive and require large physical plants for their operation. These are such services as water supply, utilities in general, or transportation. These capital intensive services are capable of "vertical integration" and effective coordination could clearly achieve economies of scale — e.g., a regional utility is more economically efficient than a large number of small community systems.

However, other services are not as easily integrated. Certain urban services are what Hirsch refers to as "circularly integrative." Included are services such as general planning and government administration. Coordination and integration of these services in metropolitan areas could conceivably achieve some economies of scale, but not significant ones.

Finally, most services delivered by government in metropolitan areas are labor intensive (e.g., police, education, fire) and not amenable to close integration. To use Hirsch's terms, they are "horizontal" services and there is no evidence that integrating such labor intensive "horizontal" services would produce any economies of scale. In fact, Hirsch has gone so far as to argue that creating larger units of government delivering these labor intensive services may ultimately be responsible for *higher* government costs because the larger bargaining unit responsible for workers in the expanded service unit would have increased power over local governments.[18]

The issue of the economies of scale associated with any given service is still subject to intense debate. But at this point in time, it seems fair to say that only certain services are in fact amenable to coordination to achieve economies of scale in production, while others are not. This conclusion has been used by political economists to attack the consolidationist position — political economists arguing that the creation of large-scale governments will not solve many existing inefficiencies in service production, only transform them.

Finally, political economists also note that it is possible to separate the *production* of services from the *provision* of services. It is possible for a large-scale unit of government to achieve economies in the production of some services. Local governments could contract with this larger and more efficient producer of services and then "retail" the service to its local citizens. The large-scale government then provides the "wholesale function" while local governments retain flexibility to choose a particular level of service or a particular combination of services to meet the demands of its local residents. In this manner, economies of scale are realized but the independence and existence of local governments are preserved.

The attacks of political economists on the assumed benefits of consolidation have been telling. Recent proposals for reform have responded on one level by modifying the proposed structure of metropolitan government to continue the use of local units of governments to represent the desires of local citizens. The debate concerning externalities and economies of scale has not yet forced equally extensive modification of reform proposals. While the concepts have undoubted validity and the questions raised by political economists concerning the presumed benefits of large-scale government are basic, further empirical research documenting the relative ability of different types of governments to deal with these questions is essential.

Some criticisms concerning the validity of the political economic framework have also been raised. Political economists seek to emulate the "free market" to maximize individual freedom in the consumption of public goods and services. The model assumes that individuals are free to move into different communities representing different mixes of public goods. Yet the social stratification process enforced by local government zoning laws means that choice for low income individuals is limited. The "separate and unequal" nature of existing services in local governments creates a class bias in the choices available to metropolitan residents. For certain services, such as education, this may create a violation of essential constitutional requirements for "equal protection of the law."[19] Further, the political economic approach assumes that when necessary, local governments will in fact find satisfactory means of cooperating to produce services efficiently and effectively. Yet many essential services continue to fail in suburban areas and that effective voluntary coordination is not forthcoming. Reform of the structure of suburban government in areas as diverse as Minneapolis, Jacksonville, and Nashville occurred because local governments were not able to produce an essential service. In short, a higher level of coordination in the provision of public services may be necessary than is assumed in the political economic model. But nonetheless the impact of political economists on the dominant position of consolidationists should not be minimized. Further research concentrating on the questions of externalities and economies of scale certainly will be forthcoming and will be essential to the debate.

Several other issues influence the debate concerning the government of suburban areas and its reform. At least three such issues deserve comment. First, analysts have tried to distinguish between the need for coordination and the willingness of local governments to cooperate concerning "life style" policies compared to "system maintenance" services. Further, concern for the conflict between functional specialists and "generalist" local government officials has been important. And finally, interest in the effects of government reform on minority group representation has been expressed.

Life Style Versus System Maintenance

According to Oliver P. Williams, a political scientist, questions concerning the provision of government services in suburban areas and the general question of government itself can be understood by distinguishing between two types of conditions or needs found in suburbs.[20] First, each individual suburb is more homogeneous than the metropolitan area as a whole — that is, there is areal specialization between suburbs. This areal specialization results in part because people who have similar life styles usually choose to live near one another and apart from others with conflicting life styles. In suburban areas government boundary lines institutionalize these life style differences. The coincidence of political boundary lines over social life style choices creates what Williams calls "sociopolitical units." These sociopolitical units then use government powers and policies to protect and further the attainment of their preferred life style values. In contrast, there are other services in the metropolitan region that are essential to continue the functioning of the entire region. A general system of transportation and communications throughout the region must be provided and other essential services similarly must be available to allow the continued functioning of the economic and social system of the region. According to Williams, the ability and interest of local communities in coordinating services vary according to whether or not they feel a service is a "life style" function or a "systems maintenance" function, the latter being more amenable to cooperation.

The general validity of this distinction between life style and system maintenance activities can be implied by the discussion of the forms of service delivery described in Chapters 4 and 5 above. Education, one of the most basic life style policies, is most locally oriented. Police services, especially patrol, and fire protection are also heavily rooted in local communities. On the other hand, larger scale public services such as transportation, waste removal, and mass transit are clearly more amenable to higher level control and intervention. Indeed, local community input into transportation decision making for regional networks of roads is minimal. Thus the policies surveyed tend to support the life style versus system maintenance concept. Furthermore, as will follow, the actions undertaken by regional areawide governments also are explicable to a considerable degree by the distinction in these two types of policies. Unfortunately, however, while the extremes of public services with life style implications can be compared to those with more system maintenance implications, most government services have *both* types of impact, and the true utility of this dichotomy is debatable.

Functional Expertise versus General Purpose Government

The most common arrangement for delivering local government services is for residents of a. community to elect representatives such as a mayor or city council members who are charged with formulating policies and determining priorities in public policies. The actual implementation of such policies is parceled out to "line agencies" of government — that is departments or bureaus with functional expertise and specialization for a particular service. For example, a municipality may have a department of public works, a parks department, and a police department. These agencies are supposed to be responsive to the directives issued by the policy making body of the local government. However, many of these functional agencies develop independent power bases. This problem is particularly severe in larger metropolitan communities, where the sheer size of the workforce and its ability to defend actions by use of expert knowledge may make it especially hard to control.[21] The extent to which these types of "islands of functional autonomy" have developed in suburban government is not known.

What is known, however, is that in suburbia another type of functional government has been heavily used and that this has limited the ability of general purpose governments to control policy and services. What is referred to here is the use of special districts charged with providing a public service such as education, water, sewers, mosquito control, soil conservation, etc. Most special districts are concerned with only one service, although multi-service districts are also found. The decision makers in charge of the services provided by special districts are functional specialists. Their overwhelming concern is with the service(s) the district provides. The implications of their actions on the general nature of government in metropolitan areas and the balancing of services one against another are not within their purview — their responsibilities lie with a limited set of service questions.

Special districts have been severely criticized in the past. They are viewed as further fragmenting government in metropolitan areas by creating new levels of government. Moreover, most special districts are relatively invisible to local residents. This means that most individuals will be unaware of important government policy decisions being made. This lack of citizen control helps create "functional government" at the expense of general purpose governments.

The concern for controlling the effects of functional government has become important in the analysis of suburban government. But perhaps more important than the actions of local governments themselves is that higher level governments now recognize the need to bolster general purpose local governments and control special districts and functional expertise. The number of special districts in the United States has doubled in the past 25 years. But many of these special districts were formed to take advantage of federal, and to a lesser extent, state programs that required the formation of such functional governments. Furthermore, most federal and state aid to local governments was in terms of grants-in-aid. That is, the state and federal governments made money available to local governments which was tied to the attainment of specified and detailed functions and services.

The emphasis on grants-in-aid created functional experts who developed independent ties with federal agencies, thus bypassing local political executives. At the same time, while federal and state governments were investing heavily in functional expertise, virtually no aid was made available to support general purpose government planning and policy analysis. As a result local government frequently became divided into functional fiefdoms and special districts. Functional agencies prospered at the expense of general purpose local governments.[22]

Yet there exists a strong recurring belief in the United States that general purpose local governments should be supported and revitalized while functional autonomy is brought under control. Local government reforms often try to tie the operations of special districts more closely to the desires of a general purpose governing council. Similarly, the structure of local executive leadership is sometimes strengthened by giving a mayor or city manager more direct control over agency budgets and personnel. These techniques can bring functional experts under greater political control.

But just as important as any local action, the policies of the federal government toward local general purpose governments have changed considerably in the past decade. In 1968, the federal government passed the Intergovernmental Cooperation Act specifically favoring applications for federal grants coming from general purpose local governments over similar applications coming from special districts. This policy goal was strengthened in 1972 with the passage of General Revenue Sharing. Under this program, the federal program returns to local governments a share of its tax revenues. However, these revenue sharing funds are made available only to general purpose local governments. Special districts are not eligible to receive them. This has had some effect in strengthening general purpose local governments.[23] Furthermore, the federal government has made more money available for general purpose planning, hoping to improve those capabilities as compared to specialized functional planning which it has generously supported for decades. These trends together may increase the capabilities of local governments to control functional experts. Yet the tension between the needs of general local government and functional government continues to be a central concern in governing suburban areas.

Minority Representation and Metropolitan Government

One of the most frequently advocated methods of reforming local government in metropolitan areas is to consolidate the central city with surrounding suburban communities to create a single metropolitan government. However, one major issue confronting proponents of this type of reform is the impact of consolidation on black and minority group representation. Minority groups are disproportionately concentrated in the central city. Within that political jurisdiction blacks are often a majority or the single largest ethnic minority group. This numerical strength is reflected in the growing political representation of minorities on city councils and in the number of black mayors. Yet combining the central city with an overwhelmingly white dominated suburban ring inevitably dilutes the numerical strength that blacks have in the smaller central city jurisdiction. Consolidation reduces the percentage of the voting population that is black.

Counterbalancing black and minority group representation with the needs for better government in metropolitan areas is another issue that must be faced in reforming local government.

Reforming Local Government: The Range of Responses

In response to the needs for better and more productive local government in metropolitan areas, a variety of reforms have been proposed and implemented. Most reforms are aimed at improving the existing system of polycentric suburban government, emphasizing negotiation, bargaining, and improved communications between local government officials while leaving the basic structure of local government intact. The goal is to allow the multitude of local governments in a region to achieve economies of scale, receive compensation for externalities, and avoid duplication and waste in local services in a cooperative manner. Other reforms seek to achieve these same goals by the establishment of more formal areawide government. Extensive structural reform involving the elimination or reduction in the number of independent local governments or the more formal subordination of local governments to an areawide governing body is advocated.

The Cooperative Approach

Retaining the existing system of local government, many reforms aim at improving the level of existing services through facilitating the voluntary cooperation of local governments. Some changes advocated under a cooperative approach include an increased use of service contracts, joint service agreements, or the transfer of services between different levels of government.

Contracts by Governments

One source of inefficiency in suburban government is the

attempt by many small governments to produce by themselves all the urban services they would like their citizens to enjoy. Given the small scale of many local governments, inefficiencies in service production result. Service contracts may be one way of solving this problem. Instead of each individual government producing every service, a small local government can enter a contractual arrangement with a larger more efficient producer of a desired service. For example, a county can build and operate a countywide water supply system. The county agency can sell the water to a local government which can in turn retail the water to its local residents. Or, a city can contract with a county for the placement of city prisoners in larger, more efficient county-run detention centers.

The most widespread use of contracting is found in Los Angeles County and is usually referred to as the "Lakewood Plan," after the first suburban city that relied almost exclusively on contracting for services.

Lakewood, a city of about 60,000 residents in Los Angeles County, was incorporated in 1954. Despite its rather substantial population size, the number of individuals directly employed by the city was extremely small, less than one dozen. The reason for the small staff was the decision by the city to contract with other governments and private firms for urban services. As a result, Lakewood's employees are concerned mostly with drafting contracts and monitoring the quality of services and not with service production itself. Lakewood contracts heavily with Los Angeles County, with surrounding municipalities, and with special districts. Therefore, Lakewood can shop for the most efficient and least expensive service producer and contract with that government or private firm.

The success of the city in minimizing its expenses while at the same time securing good services for its residents was considerable. During the 1960s the concept of service contracting grew throughout Los Angeles County. By the mid-1960s, there were almost 1500 service contracts covering over 75 purchasing cities and producers (see Table 6-1). These producers included 16 Los Angeles County Departments, and five special districts (fire, library, lighting, parks, plus recreation and sewer maintenance).

Table 6-1 The Lakewood Plan: Contracting with County Government for Urban Services, Functions and Recipients, 1972

| | Cities Contracting for Service | |
Function	Number	Percentage of all cities in the county
Maintenance of city prisoners in county jail	76	99
City health ordinance enforcement	74	96
Subdivision final map checking	70	91
Emergency ambulance program	67	87
General services agreement	65	84
Animal control services	38	49
Hospitalization of city prisoners	37	49
Industrial waste	31	40
Building inspection	30	39
Law enforcement services	29	38
Street construction and maintenance	28	36
Parcel map checking	14	18
Tree planting and maintenance	5	7

Source: Advisory Commission on Intergovernmental Relations, *Report A-44. Substate Regionalism and the Federal System: The Challenge of Local Governmental Reorganization* (Washington, D.C.: U.S. Government Printing Office, 1974), vol. III, page 71.

Under the Lakewood Plan, at least five service options are available. A local government can: (1) organize its own service; (2) contract the service from another government jurisdiction such as Los Angeles County; (3) contract to buy the service from a private company; (4) enter into a service arrangement on an equal basis with another unit of government (a joint services contract); or (5) form or participate in a special district to provide the service.

Proponents of the Lakewood Plan and the use of contracting see several benefits from this approach to providing local government service. First, economies of scale can be achieved by using larger service producers. Yet small local governments retain their independence and their flexibility by having a range of service options and service producers from which to choose. Second, contractual arrangements frequently create conditions allowing for competition between private firms or other units of government desiring to produce a service. This competition can help keep the cost of service down. For example, competition between private firms wanting to contract with suburban cities for municipal solid waste removal often keeps service costs lower than if the municipality collected the waste itself.[24] Finally, contracts and negotiations between local governments may allow the opportunity for compensation for externalities to be realized. The price for a service or the terms of a contract may be able to compensate a local government suffering negative externalities from the actions of a neighboring community. While these substantial benefits can be achieved through contracts, local autonomy is preserved, and local governments can retain their responsiveness to local citizen preferences.

While contracting is now viewed as a powerful means of reforming service delivery systems in suburban areas, service areas in which contracts can be used are probably limited. Contracting has been most successful in service areas with clearly definable outputs through which the effectiveness and efficiency of the service producer can be judged. This means that contracting is most useful for services such as refuse collection, street cleaning, snow removal, and road maintenance.[25] In general, the use of contracting requires that "hard" output measures be available, that competition exists between potential service providers, and that the contracting municipality has the credibility to threaten intervention if performance by the contracted agency falls below specified performance levels. Again, this limits the range of services to which contracting can be applied. But for those services in which it is possible, agreement exists at present that contracting is an attractive alternative for local governments in the provision of services.

Joint Service Agreements

Contracting is just one form of a general approach to providing services that leaves the structure of local governments untouched. Under the contractual approach, one unit of government or a private firm produces a service for consumption by residents in another locale. It is also possible for several local governments to either formally or informally enter into a joint service agreement for the production of a desired service. The benefits from this form of service agreement are similar to that involved in contracting —

more economical provision of services while retaining local government independence. Both contracting and joint service agreements are politically attractive. They can be entered into without voter approval and usually can be terminated easily. Hence, through contractual or joint service agreements the provision of services can be made more efficient without necessitating a major redesign or restructuring of local government.[26]

Intergovernmental Transfers of Functions

A third form of service agreement is the transfer of function from one government unit to another. In this form of agreement, a local government usually asks a higher level government to take over policy and financial responsibility for a service the local government had previously supplied itself. While the transfer of functions from local government to county governments is the most frequently found transfer of service function, other arrangements are possible. Thus while a recent survey of transfers of municipal functions found that fully 56 percent were from local government to the surrounding county, 19 percent were from municipal government to a special district, 14 percent were to the state, 7 percent were to other municipalities, and 4 percent were to regional level Councils of Government.[27] As with other forms of service agreements, transfers of functions seek to achieve economies of scale in service provision and enable a local government to obtain services for its residents that it cannot produce economically or efficiently.

However, even if these service agreements leave the existing structure of local government intact, local government officials still fear the loss of local autonomy and independence they represent. As a result, most service agreements tend to be limited to a single function. There exists no evidence that satisfactory experience with service agreements is associated with more positive attitudes toward the need for areawide government or service delivery mechanisms. Given these limitations, the Advisory Commission on Intergovernmental Relations provides the best summary of the merits of this approach to intergovernmental cooperation in metropolitan regions:

The use of agreements for the provision of services appears to be a limited and rather temporary form of functional consolidation based upon a partnership approach in which administration is centralized and policy making is decentralized . . .

This approach has been most popular because it is pragmatic, piecemeal, permissive, and has a minimal disruptive impact on the structure of local government.[28]

Service agreements represent an attempt at improving local government services by relying on voluntary and cooperative arrangements. However, these service agreements are both limited and piecemeal. Attempting to deal more systematically with the problems of area-wide government, while still retaining the voluntary nature of service agreements, the creation of regional forums of local government officials and metropolitan residents has been frequent. These regional forums seek to improve the level of area-wide governance by providing a place in which area-wide problems of service delivery can be addressed and through which intergovernmental cooperation can be achieved more systematically than at present. Concurrently, by relying on voluntary cooperation and intergovernmental communications, the use of regional councils seeks to minimize or avoid the need for more comprehensive structural reform of local government.

Cooperative Regionalism: Councils of Government and Regional Planning Agencies

Most metropolitan areas now have a regular forum for intergovernmental cooperation and discussion operating at the regional level. These are either Councils of Government (COGs) which consist of elected officials from local governments, or they take the form of Regional Planning Agencies (RPAs) which usually consist of a broader range of local government officials, including elected and appointed ones, plus non-governmental local residents.

Generally, these forums have been created in response to interest expressed by the federal government for areawide governing bodies and in response to the federal government's willingness to pay most of the costs of such regional bodies.

The creation of COGs and RPAs has always been highly responsive to federal initiatives. Before the 1950s, only about 35-

40 regional councils had been established throughout the United States. Most of these were formed by "good government" reform groups and funded out of private contributions. However, in 1954, the Federal Housing Act established a program of support for urban planning ("Section 701"). The original federal support for planning was concentrated on central cities, although some support for regional planning was also included. Within three years of the availability of Section 701 funding, many new planning agencies came into existence specifically to compete for these federal monies. As a result, requests for Section 701 planning grants far exceeded the limited funds available.

In 1959, Section 701 planning grants were made available to support intergovernmental planning efforts in metropolitan areas and support for "urban planning" was expanded to include "comprehensive planning." In 1961, Section 701 was again changed. Federal money available increased from $20 million to $75 million and the federal share of support was increased from 50 percent to 75 percent. Other regional planning efforts were also authorized at about the same time, including area transportation studies that sought to measure the impact on regional development of highways and transportation investments. Each of these changes in federal policy spurred interest in the creation of regional planning agencies or councils of government.

Yet the infusion of federal funds for comprehensive regional planning was just beginning in the early 1960s. The Housing and Urban Development Act of 1965 specifically expanded federal planning support to regional councils of local government officials (COGs). In response, the number of COGs increased from less than 50 in 1965 to over 100 in 1968 and over 200 by 1970. Furthermore, in the mid-1960s the federal government decided to increase the strategic importance of COGs and RPAs in the flow of federal funds to local governments. In Section 204 of the Demonstration Cities and Metropolitan Development Act of 1966, regional councils were given the right to review and comment upon the regional implications of local government applications for over 30 federal urban development programs. While these comments by regional councils were not binding on the decisions of federal agencies, that is, federal grants to local governments could be made despite negative comments, the expectation was that regional review would increase the negotiating position of regional governments relative to local ones. In addition to controlling the actions of local governments to achieve regional purposes, regional review was also an attempt to control functional fragmentation. The regional council was hoped to be an arena in which the multitude of federal programs in a region could be sorted and priorities on federal grants and programs established.

These hopes were given further support in Title IV of the Intergovernmental Cooperation Act of 1968 and were supported again in what has often been called the "magna charta" of regional government — Circular A-95, issued by the (then) Bureau of the Budget, now the Office of Management and Budget (OMB). Under the provisions of A-95, regional clearinghouses have been set up to review and comment on local government applications for federal funds. Building on earlier review procedures, Circular A-95 procedures at first covered 50 federal programs, mostly in direct physical development and planning. By 1971, coverage was expanded to more than 100 federal programs, including social and human resource programs such as housing, neighborhood development, law enforcement, education facilities and others. In November 1973 an additional 35 human resource programs were also brought under regional review, and the list of covered programs continues to expand.[29]

Proponents of A-95 Review see the power vested in regional clearinghouses as an indication of the continuing evolution of regional government. One consistent emphasis in A-95 Review is the early and continuous involvement of higher level governments in the actions of local units. Moreover, there is some evidence that over time, not only is the scope of A-95 Review expanding to cover more programs, but an emphasis on hierarchical authority and central direction at the expense of local autonomy in service choices has been developing.[30]

Yet problems exist with relying on A-95 Review as a means of evolving regional government. First, there are reservations about the ability of regional councils actually to prepare the plans necessary to provide the standards by which to judge the requests of local governments.[31] As a result, A-95 Review is often a regional "rubber stamp" of local government proposals. The knowledge of local officials regarding the requirements of the Project Notification and Review System (PNRS) that is at the heart of the A-95 process is also probably inaccurate and incomplete.[32] Further, the regional agencies invested with review powers usually have little or no formal power over the behavior of local governments. These councils are most often strictly advisory bodies with little or no actual responsibilities for the delivery of urban services in the region. A-95 Review is also itself advisory and not binding on local governments or federal granting agencies. Hence, regional councils can review and comment upon local government requests for funds but cannot force any change in local government policy. Federal agencies can and do make grants to local governments even in the face of objections by regional government councils. In fact, most A-95 clearinghouse staff members complain that there is no feedback whatsoever from federal agencies concerning their comments. In short, the A-95 Review agency does not know what the federal granting agency thinks or feels about its review, and the agency does not know if its efforts at regional coordination are at all effective. Some recent changes in the A-95 Review process more closely tying regional reviews to the notification of federal grant awards are now aimed at changing that condition.

Finally, despite the extension of A-95 Review into social policy, there is still a systems maintenance and "bricks and mortar" orientation to the Review Process. The federal agencies most responsive to A-95 Review procedures are agencies such as Interior, Transportation, and Housing and Urban Development, those most concerned with construction and public works projects. The federal agencies most responsible for human resources-related programs such as the Department of Labor, the Law Enforcement Assistance Administration (LEAA), and the Office of Economic Opportunity are much less responsive to A-95 Review procedures. At the same time, most applications processed by A-95 agencies tend to be concerned more with physical development (e.g., highways, mass transit, sewers) rather than with social programs.

This general dichotomy between success in social and physical planning functions is apparent in a 1972 survey of the directors of regional councils. According to the survey, most directors felt that their agencies have had the most success in the development of functional plans for physical development and least success in comprehensive social planning.[33] But, they also felt that their ability to implement any type of plan (as compared to just formulate them) was also severely limited.

A Summary

Regional councils, intergovernmental service agreements, and transfers of functions are limited means of improving the level of services in metropolitan areas. Since they are all essentially voluntary and do not pose threats to the existing structure of local government, they are usually well-received by local government officials. Successful use of these mechanisms can introduce regional concerns into local decision making, can allow local governments to achieve economies of scale by having services produced by larger units, and can, through negotiation, introduce means of controlling some of the externalities of the actions of local governments. Given these benefits and the low level of threat to existing forms of government, it is not surprising that "procedural responses — assigning functions without changing governmental structures — to service allocation are more popular than structural ones."[34]

By using these procedural responses and leaving the structure of local government intact, government officials seek to improve the level of public service while avoiding the issue of suburban autonomy and without opposing local community sentiments for independence.

Structural Reform of Metropolitan Government

Despite the obstacles to structural reform of local government, and despite the existence of procedural arrangements that can solve service delivery problems on an *ad hoc* basis, major reforms changing the basic structure of local government in metropolitan areas do occur. In part, Americans love to tinker with existing forms of local government and this explains part of the persistence of reform movements.[35] Further, in some instances services in suburban areas deteriorate to a point where a serious crisis emerges and major structural reform of local government is enacted in response. And finally, despite recent opposing intellectual arguments, the persistent call for structural reform by good government groups has created the impetus for wide-ranging structural reform.

Just as a variety of mechanisms exist for improvements in service delivery that rely on cooperative agreements, a variety in structural reforms that more radically affect the organization of local governments are also possible.

Urban Counties

Perhaps the "mildest" form of structural reorganization involves the strengthening of a level of government already in existence in most suburban areas — the county. By improving their governing capabilities and their ability to deliver urban services, proponents of strong counties hope to increase the ability of counties to act as areawide governing bodies.

The importance of counties as potential areawide government is particularly pronounced in those areas where a single county's boundary lines define the metropolitan region. This includes over 125 SMSAs at the present time. In these single county regions, a strong county government delivering urban services would, in fact, provide a comprehensive areawide governing mechanism.[36] But even in multicounty regions, the existence of strong urban counties would reduce government fragmentation and provide a means of reducing service delivery problems. Counties in suburban areas often have the size, geographic scope, and fiscal base to allow them to achieve economies of scale in the production of services while at the same time reducing externalities and inequities in the financing and in the level of suburban services.

However, while reform proposals emphasizing the county are frequent (some states have increased the importance of county government), their present role in most regions is limited. In most states, counties still act as predominantly administrative agents of state laws and do not have home rule power to increase their own control over urban services. In a recent survey of urban counties, the role of county government and its limitations were highlighted. Table 6-2 shows the percentage of approximately 150 urban counties involved in delivering certain important urban services. Most of the counties surveyed are involved in administering the functions traditionally assigned to them by the state: jails, courts, tax assessment, public health. But far fewer are involved in delivering other urban services. Only 55 percent report involvement in zoning, and even less report involvement with subdivision control. While close to 80 percent were concerned with some aspect of police work, only 31 percent were involved in fire services. Less than one-third of the counties sampled played a role in such essential infrastructural investment policies as sewers, airports, or water supply. Fewer still were involved with mass transit, public housing, and urban renewal. In short, even in the most developed urban counties surveyed, the range of services actually provided by county government is limited.[37]

Attempts to improve the functioning of county government in a suburban area usually begin with a proposal to restructure the form of county government. In most regions, counties are administrative arms of the state with no independent power to make policy other than as specified by state law. A county home rule charter increasing the policy independence of the county is often advocated as a first reform. Home rule increases the power of the county independently to intervene in a wider range of urban services than it possesses as only an administrative arm of the state. Furthermore, most counties operating under a home rule charter enact wide-ranging changes in the form of county government. At present, most counties are governed by a commission form of government in which certain county-wide elected officers (e.g., county tax assessor, sheriff, or justice of the peace) act together as both the legislative and executive branches of county government. This plural executive form of government is weak and usually unable to respond effectively to new demands from rapid suburbanization placed on county government. Charter counties usually replace the commission form of government with a strengthened single executive. This more centralized form of government can use a county administrator selected by the county commissioners but with independent

Table 6-2 Rank Order of Selected Function Performed by 150 Metropolitan County Governments

Function	Number	Percent of total
1. Jails and detention homes	145	97
2. Coroner's office	130	87
3. Courts	130	87
4. Tax assessment collection	125	83
5. Public health	120	80
6. Prosecution	120	80
7. Probation and parole service	119	79
8. Police protection	117	78
9. Roads and highways	117	78
10. General assistance public welfare	114	76
11. Planning	114	76
12. Agricultural extension services	112	75
13. Medical assistance	105	70
14. Mental health	104	60
15. Libraries	86	57
16. Veteran's affairs	86	57
17. Parks and recreation	83	55
18. Zoning	82	55
19. Crippled children	78	52
20. Public defender	77	51
21. Subdivision control	77	51
22. Animal control	75	51
23. Data processing	65	43
24. Code enforcement	63	42
25. Hospitals	61	41
26. Central purchasing	60	40
27. Soil conservation	59	39
28. Secondary schools	58	39
29. Special education programs	57	38
30. Mosquito abatement	56	37
31. Elementary schools	56	37
32. Solid waste disposal	55	37
33. Air pollution	55	37
34. Personnel services	52	35
35. Flood and drainage control	51	34
36. Sewers and sewage disposal	50	33
37. Fire protection	47	31
38. Water pollution	45	30
39. Junior colleges	40	27
40. Airports	36	24
41. Livestock inspection	34	23
42. Ambulance service	34	23
43. Industrial development	32	21
44. Refuse and garbage collection	31	21
45. Water supply	31	21
46. Public Housing	28	19
47. Museums	25	17
48. Parking	17	11
49. Urban Renewal	13	9
50. Mass Transit	7	5

Source: Advisory Commission on Intergovernmental Relations, *Profile of County Government* (Washington, D.C.: Government Printing Office, 1972), p. 23.

budgetary and personnel policy powers, or, in its most developed form, an independent *elected* county executive can occupy the crucial focal point in reformed county government. In either case, the single county executive, with increased powers over county policy, often creates a political force for further strengthening county services and functions.

Counties can also incrementally increase their importance in the delivery of services in a region. It is relatively easy for county governments in most parts of the country directly to deliver services to unincorporated areas — the county may be the only general purpose government in existence and is thus not threatening existing local governments. Counties can also begin to offer more services to incorporated areas. This can be done through contracts, joint service agreements, or transfers of functions. In this way, the strategic importance of the county as a provider of services and as a focal point for areawide government can increase. Further, the county can deliver *new* services to the entire county — again increasing its importance but avoiding competition with existing municipal governments. And finally, the county can begin to offer more existing services on a county-wide basis. This might put the county directly into competition with its municipalities and is, therefore, potentially the most radical change in service arrangements.

Through the county home rule movement and the use of a strong executive form of government and through the expansion of the county role in the delivery of urban services, it is frequently argued that counties will provide one central link in suburban government improving the area-wide governing capabilities in a region. Moreover, this improvement in local government can be achieved without requiring a total restructuring of local government because existing counties can gradually increase their importance and control over local governments.

City/County Consolidations

More radical structural reforms of local government are embodied in attempts to consolidate the government of the central city of a metropolitan region with that of its surrounding county. The purpose of this type of reform is to achieve area-wide government by merging the central city government with the suburbs of the outlying county into a single entity.

City/county consolidations are not a new phenomenon in American urban history. The first major consolidation in the U.S. was in 1813 when New Orleans merged with its surrounding county. In 1821, a similar city/county consolidation took place in Boston, and in 1854, Philadelphia merged with Philadelphia County. The largest city/county consolidation took place in 1898 when the Greater City of New York was created through the consolidation of city government with the 5 metropolitan counties then defining the region. Several years later, in 1907, the City of Honolulu was merged with its surrounding county by action of the territorial legislature in Hawaii. However, after 1907 no significant city/county consolidations were recorded until 1947 when the City of Baton Rouge undertook partial consolidation of government functions with its surrounding county, East Baton Rouge Parish.

Consolidation in Baton Rouge

The Baton Rouge consolidation was partial in the sense that the City and the county did not totally merge into one single government.[38] Both governments maintained their identities, as did two smaller municipalities that had already existed in the Parish (county). Consolidation was accomplished by creating extensive overlap between the membership of the city council of Baton Rouge and the Parish council, and by having a mayor-president elected by the entire parish preside over both city and county councils. If the forms of regional government maintained a separation between city and parish, service delivery mechanisms also were consolidated only partially. Rather than services being uniformly provided throughout the parish, the area was divided into three types of districts: an urban services district, a rural district, and an industrial district. The boundaries of the City of Baton Rouge were extended to include the developed suburbs in the Parish; this expanded city became the urban services zone. The intensity and range of services provided to residents of the urban district were the greatest. Residents received normal county-wide services such as jails, street and highway maintenance, and tax assessment, but also received other essential urban services such as sewers, increased fire and police protection, and solid waste collection. In contrast, the needs for such services was not felt to exist in the rural and industrial service districts and more intensive urban services were not supplied. Hence, the existence of service zones gave the region more flexibility in providing services that matched existing needs. Moreover, by combining the suburbs and the central city into a single service zone, suburban areas which may otherwise have found it impossible to pay for needed services were able to receive them from the county. About 15 years passed after the successful consolidation in Baton Rouge before another major metropolitan region undertook city/council consolidation. This involved the extensive reorganization of government in the Nashville/Davidson County metropolitan region of Tennessee.

Nashville/Davidson County Consolidation

In the 1950s, Nashville was a growing metropolis beginning to face some of the problems endemic to urban growth in the United States.[39] Imbalances between local governments existed. Raising the funds necessary to support essential local services was becoming more difficult. Government fragmentation was seen as impeding the development of adequate responses to growing metropolitan needs. In response, interest in extensive government reorganization in the region began to grow in the Fifties. By 1958, interest in structural reform was so great that the issue of city/county reorganization was placed before the voters of the region in a referendum. But as in many other cases of extensive government reorganization, voter approval was not forthcoming.[40] Fearing loss of autonomy and local independence, suburban residents overwhelming opposed consolidation. Central city voters, on the other hand, were in favor of consolidation. But since a majority in favor of consolidation was required in *both* the city and the county sections of the region, the proposal was defeated.

However, the negative vote was not the end of the issue of government reorganization. Taking advantage of an extremely liberal annexation law enacted by the Tennessee State Legislature in 1955, the City of Nashville began to unilaterally annex large segments of the contiguous suburban area. Within a few years of the referendum, Nashville had expanded its geographic size by 50 square miles and its population by 87,000 residents. This unilateral action by the city began to make suburbanites somewhat nervous — they feared that they too would soon be swallowed up by the city. Many suburbanites and their government officials began to press for a renewal of the movement to restructure local government in the region. Their reasoning was that a wholesale annexation movement would destroy any hope they had for autonomy and isolation from the central city, while in a general government consolidation and reform movement, the suburbs might succeed better to preserve their power and position. When the Nashville City Council refused to participate in this new reform movement, suburbanites used their power in the state legislature to force the reconvening of a metropolitan reform commission.

The work of this commission proposing consolidation of city and county was placed before the voters in 1962 and was approved. This time support for reform was strongest in the *suburbs.*

Under the terms of the Nashville/Davidson County consolidation two major service districts were established — an urban service district, encompassing essentially the old city of Nashville, and a general service district, including the rest of the county. The separate identity of six suburban municipalities was retained, but their autonomy and control over services was limited. The consolidated government of Nashville was given all the powers of a municipality as determined by the laws of Tennessee plus those given to Tennessee counties.

Residents of the urban service district receive the most services including more intensive police and fire protection, sewers, street lighting, street cleaning, and refuse collection. Residents in the less densely populated general service district do not receive these services. But all residents of the Nashville region have services provided by the consolidated government such as courts, jails, hospitals, parks, libraries, code enforcement, and planning.

According to observers of the Nashville experience, several

benefits have been achieved by the consolidated government. First, by tapping a wider tax base and by achieving economies of scale, property taxes have been stabilized. Furthermore, by utilizing the wider county-wide tax base, service disparities and fiscal inequalities have been reduced somewhat and services have been improved. The exact extent of reduction in inequities is not measurable but the residents of old Nashville may have benefited by reduced property taxes and improved services. Services to the old suburban areas have also improved, especially those of police, health, hospitals, and welfare. Perhaps the most significant improvement in services was upgrading the region's school system. In general, these improvements were well received, and a majority of residents in the old suburban region seem to believe that the new metropolitan government is more efficient than the city/county system it replaced.[41]

After the success in Nashville, interest in consolidation in other regions grew. Two city/county consolidations involving relatively small metropolitan regions in Virginia were enacted soon after Nashville's reform. But the next major consolidation took place in 1967 and involved the merger of government in the City of Jacksonville with the government of surrounding Duval County.

Consolidation in Jacksonville/Duval County

By the mid-1960s, Jacksonville was in serious trouble as an urban center.[42] The city itself was stagnating, losing both population and tax base to its suburbs. Raw sewage was being dumped into the St. Johns River and the city's water supply was inadequate. At the same time, suburban residents were demanding more and better services from the county. The scope of governmental problems was so severe that a series of investigations into the mismanagement of local government was initiated. In 1966, a grand jury issued 104 separate indictments, naming city councilmen, city commissioners, and other city officials for corruption. The intensity of the scandal, coupled with the breakdown in services in both the city and the suburbs, provided a strong impetus for wide-ranging reform of local government. In August of 1967, residents of both the county and the city voted in favor of city/county consolidation.

In terms of political leadership, the consolidated government replaced a weak county commission government with a strong mayor/council government for the entire area. The mayor was given increased executive power over budgets and appointments. The executive staff was, in general, improved. In terms of services, Jacksonville followed previous consolidation experiences and established urban services districts and a general services district, allowing greater flexibility in distributing services. Since the tax rates in the urban services districts are higher, the districting system also links services received more closely to taxes paid. At present, there are five urban services districts in Jacksonville, one corresponding to the old city of Jacksonville, and four others corresponding to previously existing suburban municipalities. In terms of the effects of consolidation on the costs and quality of services, analysis seems to indicate that there was an increase in the overall costs of services provided by the consolidated government, but that the level and quality of services increased even more substantially.[43] This service improvement is especially true for the "systems maintenance" services such as sewers and water supply. However, the ability of Jacksonville to improve social welfare and "life style" services is less well agreed upon. Moreover, there is little evidence of redistribution of wealth or resources from the wealthy residents of the region to poorer ones.[44]

UNIGOV: Reform in Indianapolis

One final major consolidation deserves notice — the reform of government in the Indianapolis region creating what is called UNIGOV.[45] The merging of Indianapolis and Marion County into UNIGOV is interesting for several reasons. First, in contrast to Jacksonville or Nashville, UNIGOV was created without crises in public services acting as a catalyst. Furthermore, while many other local governments reforms required voter approval through a referendum, the UNIGOV consolidation was accomplished by the action of the Indiana State Legislature. This action was facilitated by a Republican sweep of Indiana in the local and state elections in 1967 and 1968 which created a Republican dominated state legislature, a Republican governor, Republican county leadership and a dynamic Republican Indianapolis leadership headed by Mayor Richard Lugar. This single party domination was rare in the political history of Indiana, traditionally one of the most competitive partisan states in the nation. The unity of party and government control and the absence of a referendum allowed the enactment of UNIGOV legislation within an extremely short time span — the period of public discussion began in November 1968 and ended with the Governor of Indiana signing UNIGOV legislation in March 1969. Finally, UNIGOV deserves special consideration because it is the largest metropolitan region enacting extensive government structural reform since the turn of the century and is the only major recent structural reform adopted north of the Mason-Dixon line.

The Extent and Limits of UNIGOV

The UNIGOV legislation provided for extensive political and administrative reform of government in Marion County. A single City/County Council was created headed by a strong mayor with extensive administrative power over local government agencies. The new council combined the activities of the old city council, the old Board of County Commissioners, and the activities of several previously independent boards and commissions responsible for such services as parks, sanitation, public works, and transportation. Yet, despite these political and administrative reforms, the actual reform of service delivery has been more limited.

In part, this limited impact on services results from the success of previous service reorganizations that had occurred in the county. After World War II, Indianapolis and the surrounding landscape in Marion County were subject to the same woes as most large metropolitan areas — outmigration of population and industry, declining central city services, and inadequate suburban services. In response, local governments in the area developed a variety of service responses to the emerging problems as well as to provide services to the outlying areas. Several functions administered by the city were extended to encompass the immediate surrounding suburbs. Other services were shifted to the county. In particular, through state legislative action, county-wide corporations were established to provide a variety of social services, such as health and hospitals, and to supervise capital construction projects. Sanitation services, provided mostly by the city, were transferred to a new sanitation service district that extended beyond the city limits. Other such service districts and *ad hoc* arrangements to deliver and administer essential services were developed, preventing any severe disruptions such as were occurring in Jacksonville or Nashville. By the time formal reorganization came in 1969, only the police and fire services were still handled by only the city government. Every other major service had been transferred or transformed into a larger region-wide service base.

However, while these arrangements enabled services to be provided to the areas of the region most in need, the *ad hoc* nature of the service arrangements began to upset local government officials. While many services were transferred to the county, the county was not administratively nor fiscally able to manage these services to the best extent possible. Furthermore, the existence of independent service agencies began to fragment political authority and responsibility. It was mostly in response to these administrative and political shortcomings that UNIGOV was enacted.

Formalizing existing service arrangements which were viewed as relatively successful, a complex system of taxing and service districts exists under UNIGOV. A central township covers the inner-city area. The Indianapolis School district supervises schools in the old city while 11 independent school districts continue to operate in the surrounding county area. A fire district, a police district, and a sanitation district exist to deliver services to the more densely populated areas of the county. Four independent suburban governments still retain their identity and control over services. The City of Indianapolis still exists as a separate political entity from the County government.

Within this rather complex "consolidated" UNIGOV system, the county is the basic unit of government. It is the functional and geographic base for the delivery of most urban services — health, hospitals, parks, planning and zoning, plus traditional county services such as jails, sheriffs, and tax assessment. The dominance of the county has reduced the extent of fragmentation and led to the coordination of many services. But in general, UNIGOV should be viewed as a substantial but not comprehensive reorganization of local government structure.

Perhaps the most severe limitation on the impact of UNIGOV is the continuation of the existing service arrangements that predated "consolidation" in 1969. The continuation of differential service districts prevents the equalization of tax burdens and service levels. The overriding philosophy of UNIGOV seems to be to tie the costs of services as closely as possible to those benefitting from the service. Thus, while the level of public services in the region has probably increased, these improvements have been matched by tax increases in the areas receiving those services, and no redistribution of tax burden or services in the region is evident. As a result, UNIGOV should be viewed more as an administrative and political organization rather than a rearrangement of service systems.[46]

Consolidation and Extensive Government Reorganization: Some General Observations

The structural reorganizations of local government achieved in Jacksonville, Nashville, and Indianapolis — while having long been advocated by good government groups and others interested in metropolitan reform — are relatively infrequent in the United States. Yet interest in such reform continues. For reasons related to political visibility, state capitals seem most open to city/county consolidation. At present at least nine state capitals operate under consolidated city/county government: Baton Rouge, Boston, Carson City, Denver, Honolulu, Indianapolis, Juneau, Nashville, and Richmond.[47] In addition, most of the city/county reorganizations that have been achieved in this century have been concentrated in the southern states: e.g., Baton Rouge; Nashville; Jacksonville; Lexington-Fayette County, Kentucky; Columbus-Muscogee, Georgia; plus several in the state of Virginia. This predominance of city/county consolidation in the South is the result of a greater use of county governments in the South than elsewhere in the country — that is, in the South counties already exist as significant providers of local government service.

Furthermore, because southern cities are "newer" than ones in the northeast and midwest, they are surrounded by fewer independent suburbs and are capable of annexing surrounding territory. This prevents the rise of significant opposition in suburban areas to city/county consolidation. But even in the South, opposition to city/county consolidation still exists and has prevented more widespread adoption of this form of local government reorganization.

Federation and Metropolitan Reform

While city/county consolidation merges local and county government boundary lines, and the most extensive consolidations would eradicate local governments entirely, still other structural reforms are not as sweeping. One major alternative to consolidation is the creation of "multi-tier" systems where local governments continue to exist as "first-tier" governments providing local services and avenues for local political participation, while their behavior is coordinated and regional services provided by a "second-tier," higher level government. However, if city/county consolidations are relatively rare in the United States, federation is even more rare. The only truly federated government existing in North America at present is Metropolitan Toronto, and the only existing regional government that comes close to approximating federation in the United States is the system of government in the Miami-Dade County area.

True Federation:
The Metropolitan Toronto Experience

Toronto has been one of the most rapidly growing metropolitan regions in North America.[48] In many respects, its patterns of growth were similar to metropolitan areas in the Great Lakes and northeast regions of the United States to which it is a contemporary. As in U.S. cities, through the 1920s growth was found in the City of Toronto itself, but even more rapid growth was taking place on the urban fringes. Again, not unlike large American cities, the City of Toronto usually annexed the areas of rapid expansion. However, in 1928, Toronto decided that it no longer wished to annex new territories. In response, urban fringe areas which had previously assumed that their services would eventually be provided by the city had to find an alternative means of service provision. They chose the most likely alternative and began to incorporate into suburban municipalities. By the late 1940s and early 1950s, the results of the patterns of urban growth and the existence of a central city surrounded by incorporated suburbs were apparent. The fragmentation of metropolitan government led to an inability to plan and coordinate essential area-wide services required by an expanding metropolitan population. Service problems with sewers, water, and transportation, in particular, began to emerge.

In contrast to the "hands-off" behavior of the legislatures in most American states faced with similar problems, the Provincial Government of Ontario took vigorous action. In 1953, the Provincial Government passed legislation creating the Municipality of Metropolitan Toronto as a federated metropolitan system of government. Under this legislation, the 13 municipalities in the Toronto region were federated with a newly created metropolitan government. Each of the 12 suburbs and the City of Toronto retained their own identities and control over local services. Meanwhile, passed on to the metropolitan government was responsibility for those services and policies which were felt to transcend local boundaries. The legislation created a Metropolitan Council of 24 members — 12 from the suburbs, 12 from Toronto. The Metropolitan Council was charged with supervising and administering services with clear regional impact such as expressways, roads, transit, transportation, sewers, and water supply. Local governments retained control over other services. However, when necessary, local governments and the Metropolitan government could share in the provision of any service. This arrangement worked reasonably well. The Metropolitan Government was able to supply the necessary services to support a growing region. Schools were built, roads were maintained, expressways expanded, and a regional transit system begun. The expanded tax base made these construction projects more possible. In particular, the improved financial standing of the Metropolitan Government was so great that it was able substantially to improve its bond rating. This alone may have saved over $50 million in interest costs compared to what the local governments operating independently would have had to pay.[49]

Despite these successes, a bitter policy dispute in the early 1960s over the provision of transit subsidies to subways, benefits thought to accrue mostly to residents of the City of Toronto, almost destroyed the Metropolitan Government.[50] The Ontario Provincial Government stepped in once again, appointing a one-man commission to investigate the need for reform. In 1965, in response to this report, the Metropolitan Toronto Amendment Act of 1966 was passed restructuring local government. Most notably, the suburban governments were combined into five boroughs and the City of Toronto was merged with three suburban governments into an expanded city. The representation on the Metropolitan Council was changed to reflect the predominance of population in the suburbs. But more importantly, the range of services over which Metropolitan Council had control was substantially increased, especially in basic "life style" areas such as education, welfare, and police. The present assignment of functions to local governments and to the metropolitan government is shown in Table 6-3.

These changes in the division of responsibility between local governments and Metro in Toronto reflect the continuing evolution of regional government. But, the continued existence of a regional government now seems beyond question. To a great extent, the endurance of Toronto's metropolitan government rests on its success in its ability to deliver quality services to residents of the region. It is widely believed that the metropolitan government in Toronto has done an excellent job in providing essential services while realizing significant economies of scale where possible. This, of course, means that its most notable success has been in large-scale physical development projects, such as the Toronto mass transit system. And there is evidence that its impact on "life-style" services, especially education, has also been measurable. In particular it is believed that metropolitan government has succeeded in reducing the extent of inequalities between local governments over a range of services.[51] However, despite the realization of economies in the production of many

Table 6-3 Functional Responsibility in a Federated System: The Case of Toronto Distribution of Responsibility

(M — Municipality of Metropolitan Toronto; A — Area Municipalities)

Finance and Taxation	
Assessment of property	M
Courts of revision	MA
Taxation of property	A
Debenture borrowing	M
Local improvement charges	A

Planning	
Official plans	MA
Subdivision approval	MA
Zoning	A

Recreation/ Community Services	
Regional parks	M
Local parks	A
Recreation programs	A
Community centers/ arenas	A
Municipal golf courses	M
Municipal zoo	M
Regional libraries	M
Local libraries	MA
Grants to cultural societies	MA

Road Construction/ Maintenance	
Expressways	M
Arterial roads	M
Local roads	A
Bridges and grade separations	MA
Snow removal	MA
Street cleaning	MA
Sidewalks	A

Traffic Control	
Traffic regulations	MA
Crosswalks	MA
Traffic lights	M
Street lighting	A
Pavement markings	MA

Public Transit	
Toronto Transit Comm.	M

Water Supply	
Purification, pumping and trunk distribution system	M
Local distribution	A
Collection of water bills	A

Sewage Disposal	
Sanitary trunk system and disposal plants	M
Connecting systems	A
Storm drainage	MA

Garbage Collection and Disposal	
Collection	A
Disposal sites	M

Air Pollution	
Air pollution control	M

Public Education	
Operation of school system	A
School sites, attendance areas, building programs	M
Operating and capital costs	M

Housing	
Low rental family housing	M
Elderly person housing	M
Moderate rental family housing	A

Welfare	
Welfare assistance	M
Hospitalization of indigents	M
Assistance to Children's Aid Societies	M
Homes for the aged	M

Health	
Public health services	A
Chronic and convalescent hospital	M
Hospital grants	A
Ambulance services	M

Police and Fire Protection	
Police	M
Fire	A

Administration of Justice	
Magistrates' courts	M
Court house and jail	M
Juvenile and family court	M
Coroner's office	M
Registry and land titles offices	M

Licensing and Inspection	
Business licensing	M
Dog licensing and pound	A
Marriage licenses	A
Buildings by-laws	A

Civil Defense	
Emergency measures	M

Other Municipal Services	
Collection of fines	MA
Collection of vital statistics	A
Distribution of hydro power	A
Harbor	A
Island airport	A
Municipal parking lots	A
Preparation of voters' lists and administration of civil elections	A
Redevelopment	MA

Source: Committee for Economic Development, Reshaping Government in Metropolitan Areas (New York: CED, 1970), page 83.

services, overall government costs in the region have increased substantially. This is the result of a greatly improved range and quality of services made available.

Despite the success of Toronto and despite the interest in federation as a means of reforming local government in metropolitan areas of the United States, Toronto is the only truly federated system on the North American continent.[52]

"Umbrella Agencies": The Gradual Creation of Regional Governance

Every attempt at comprehensive government reform in metropolitan regions detailed above involved the extensive restructuring or elimination of local governments. Given the tendency of politicians and local citizens to view such extensive changes with hostility, it is perhaps not surprising that so few major structural reorganizations of local governments in metropolitan regions have been achieved. Yet the voluntary approach to regionalism relying on Councils of Government, Regional Planning Agencies, and *ad hoc* intergovernmental service agreements sidesteps the emotional issue of local government autonomy. While popular among local government officials, voluntary schemes have been criticized as only a piecemeal and basically unsatisfactory solution to the problem of government service delivery. Given this deadlock, the *incremental* expansion of the power of regional forums is most likely the way in which regional government will develop for the immediate future. In particular, regional councils can be expected to act more and more as "umbrella agencies" more formally supervising and coordinating the actions of special districts and general purpose local governments in its region. Regional councils, now voluntary and advisory, will most likely develop stronger mechanisms by which to control regional policy and service delivery. They will become a regional "umbrella" under which local governments must operate. The most likely avenues through which regional governments will be strengthened center on making A-95 Review more binding on the actions of federal agencies, changing state laws to increase the power of regional councils over the actions of general purpose local governments, and giving regional councils more direct policy responsibility over the actions of special districts delivering services on a regional basis. Perhaps the clearest example of this approach to regional government is the Twin Cities Metropolitan Council now operating in the seven county region of Minneapolis-St. Paul, Minnesota.

The Twin Cities Metropolitan Council: An "Umbrella" for Regional Policy[53]

In the post-World War II suburban expansion, the Twin Cities area of Minnesota was probably slightly better off than the older more rapidly deteriorating cities to the east. Nonetheless, problems of suburbanization and service delivery were occurring and the fragmentation of the region into more than 300 local governments was beginning to create the usual problems of metropolitan governance. However, in the Twin Cities region there was an earlier and more intense interest in metropolitan coordination than found in many other areas. In part, this interest was the result of strong state concern for problems of the region — not only is St. Paul the state capital, but over one-half the state's population lives in the region, and most of the cultural life of the state is centered there. Furthermore, Minnesota has a long tradition of government reform[54] and it was a "natural" site for interest in regional government.

In 1957 a Metropolitan Planning Commission (MPC) was established to investigate service delivery problems and the need for policy coordination in the region. The need for regional policy intensified in 1959 when it was discovered that almost one-half of the water wells in suburban communities were contaminated by seepage from cesspools and that central water supply and sewering would therefore be necessary. While no similar crises in other services emerged, the need for regional policy in the placement of utilities, the construction of highways, and the provision of mass transit and other services was also becoming apparent.

While similar problems were found in other regions, unique to the Twin Cities was the intense involvement of the state government in metropolitan problems. By the mid-Sixties, it was not so much a question of creating a regional government with a strictly regional orientation, but rather "the critical need appeared to be the creation of a regional policy body capable of reaching a consensus on what kind of legislation the region wanted from the state."[55] In other words, the state was willing to use its wide-ranging powers to achieve reform of regional policy and was seeking a means by which to do so.

Indeed, while other metropolitan regions tried and often failed to find ways of implementing regional policy, it was the actions of the Minnesota State Legislature that created with relative ease the Twin Cities Metropolitan Council as a regional policy making body. Further, it was through policies of the state legislature that the Twin Cities Metro Council was able to pull under its umbrella crucial regional special district governments and the relationship between local governments and regional government began to evolve.

The Twin Cities Metro Council was created by an act of the State Legislature and, according to the legislation, its members are appointed by the Governor. This makes the Metro Council more an agency of the state than of local government. Further, it was state law that gave the Metro Council its greater coverage as an "umbrella" agency. Similar to most other regional councils, Twin Cities Metro Council does not have operational responsibility for any regional service. Instead, the Council focuses on regional *policy making,* leaving the actual *implementation* of its recommendations to a variety of special purpose agencies or to the local governments in the region. However, in contrast to other regional councils, Metro's policy decisions are not strictly advisory — its ability to have its decisions implemented are greatly strengthened under the state law that created the Council.

Special regional districts, such as the Metropolitan Transit Commission or the Metropolitan Sewer Board, own and operate their facilities and are legally separate from the Metro Council. But, the Council usually controls both appointments to the district's governing boards and the budgets of these operating agencies. This effectively makes special districts subordinate to Metro Council. The power of Metro Council is somewhat less over policies enacted by general purpose local governments. The Council is the A-95 Review Agency for the region, giving it some control over the actions of local government. However, state law strengthens that role. The Council is charged by the state with the preparation of a Regional Development Guide. To the extent that local governments undertake policies found to be in conflict with that Guide, the Council can suspend local policies for 60 days while seeking to mediate and change them. Obviously, these powers are less than the control the Council has over policy implemented by regional agencies directly responsible to the Metro Council. But the Council still has more power over local general purpose governments than Councils of Government or Regional Planning Agencies in other areas.

Using state law, the legislature also changed the relationship between local governments themselves, reducing the incentives for inter-community competition and reducing the possibilities of negative externalities. These changes can reduce the overriding parochialism of local government policy and make local governments more amenable to cooperation on a regional scale. In particular, the State Legislature in 1971 enacted the Fiscal Disparities Act to reduce the fiscal gains accruing to suburbs attracting industrial and commercial development.[56] Similarly, the entire system of local financing of schools was centralized more in the hands of state government, further reducing incentives for fiscal zoning.

In general, the philosophy of the state government in approaching metropolitan reform in the Twin Cities region has differed from that motivating regional government reform elsewhere. The overriding concern in the creation of Metro Council was *not* to achieve economies of scale and efficiency for services. While those were hoped for results, according to Ted Kolderie, the Executive Director of the Minneapolis Citizens League, regional reform was "advanced with the recognition that the regional agencies would undertake activities not being performed, and that costs previously absorbed by the environment or appearing as sub-optimal development would, in the future, be expressed in public budgets. And these budgets have in fact increased substantially."[57] Unlike service districts in other metropolitan reforms, in the Twin Cities area there has been an emphasis on the reduction of fiscal disparities through the provision of uniform services throughout the region and a concern for adjusting taxes according to the ability to pay.

Generalizing the Umbrella Multi-Jurisdictional Organizations

The experience of the Twin Cities Metro Council is often held as an example of successful government at the regional level. Metro Council has successfully coordinated many metropolitan services and has reduced many inequalities in tax burdens and services. Moreover, it has not required radical reorganization of local government structure in the region. Just as important, the building blocks upon which the Twin Cities Metro Council exists are found in many other metropolitan regions. Essentially, the Twin Cities Metro Council is a regional forum such as Regional Planning Agencies found elsewhere. But it has additional powers to implement its policy recommendations. In many respects, Metro Council can be understood as a continued evolution of the voluntary approach to achieving areawide government toward more formal and regularized means of attaining regional policy. However, since it stops short of abolishing or even radically reforming local governments, it sidesteps one of the crucial stumbling blocks of metropolitan government.

Based on the success of the Twin Cities Metro Council and a similar success of a strengthened regional council in Atlanta, the Atlanta Regional Commission,[58] the development of similar umbrella agencies in other metropolitan regions has been proposed as a short-term solution for the need for better government in metropolitan regions.[59]

The evolution of existing regional forums into more effective umbrella organizations would require several changes in existing powers and procedures. Federal policy toward regional governments, A-95 Review power, would have to be strengthened. In particular, the strictly advisory nature of A-95 Reviews could be changed so that regional views are made more binding on the granting of federal funds. Similarly, A-95 could be expanded to cover a wider range of policies in which the federal government has concern. Equally important, the concept of regional review in the allocation of "higher" level government grants could be extended to state government. In other words, *state* investments, policies, and programs affecting a region could be reviewed by a regional umbrella agency.

But perhaps more important is giving the regional agency greater control over the actual implementation of regional policy. At present, most regional councils undertake extensive regional planning but have no means of implementing those plans. Bringing special districts and other operating agencies more directly under the regional umbrella, through such mechanisms found in the Twin Cities Region, would strengthen existing councils. Alternately, regional councils could be given direct operating responsibility for regional functions as in Toronto. Such an approach to strengthening regional government might reduce the level of functional fragmentation in a region. Further, since councils are dominated by generalists rather than specialists, another goal of government reform can perhaps be realized.

Finally, the implementation of areawide government through strengthened regional councils is not dependent on the actions of local residents in a referendum nor does it require the extensive restructuring of local governments. Instead, improved regional government can be put "on-line" by building upon existing state, local, and federal programs and by strengthening existing mechanisms of regional coordination.

Despite the arguments in favor of "polycentricity" and a "political economic" approach to local government, growing regionalism in metropolitan areas seems to be an established fact. Yet given the strong resistance to formal structuring of local government, a "back-door" approach incrementally strengthening existing regional councils and planning agencies seems to be a most likely approach to the question of regional government and the areawide delivery of services.

Summary: Reforming Metropolitan Government

A wide range of possible reforms exists or has been proposed to improve the quality of services and government in suburban and metropolitan areas. These reforms range from the consolidation of all local governments into a single metropolitan government at one extreme to the use of confederation of local government officials into a regional forum for the discussion of regional perspectives. The goal of these reforms, regardless of how extensive, is to provide a means of integrating services between fragmented governments in metropolitan regions, to achieve economics in the production of those services, and in general to improve the level of governance. But empirically what is the evidence concerning the ultimate impact of reform on metropolitan government?

Economies of Scale

There are only scattered examples of the achievement of economies of scale in the production of services through reform of suburban government delivery systems. In part this may be the result of the nature of urban services — they are usually labor intensive and service integration cannot easily reduce labor costs. As a result, for most public services the existence of economies of scale are probably much more limited than previously thought.

Economies of scale are more likely to be found associated with services requiring large scale physical facilities. However, even in these service areas regional governments may be unable to realize any *new* economies in the provision of these services. For many services such as water supply, utilities, and sewers, special districts already exist in most regions that provide the service at an economical level. Thus, even when the conditions are amenable for a larger government to realize economies of scale, these economies may have already been achieved by existing government arrangements.

Further, as already noted, the truly expensive services with which local governments are concerned, most notably education, are labor intensive and no significant economies of scale may be achievable at all through the reform of local governments.

Total Service Costs

While economies of scale in some services may keep costs down, the labor intensive nature of most local government services means that the total costs of local government will continue to rise regardless of any reforms that may be instituted. In addition, there is some evidence that the total costs of services in reformed metropolitan regions may actually increase to higher levels than would be found in the absence of reform. These higher costs result because the *level* of services provided by a new regional government usually increases substantially over what was previously provided. Recall that many reforms of local government service systems are instituted because existing service levels are inadequate. To the extent that a reformed government comes into existence to meet a crisis in services, it must be expected to generate higher costs. There is also some evidence that in the few metropolitan areas, such as Toronto or the Twin Cities region, where equalization of services is an important goal of the metropolitan government, equalization is achieved by "levelling up" rather than levelling down service levels. This means that additional expenditures are made to bring low resource communities to higher service levels. In short, there is evidence that government reform leads to an overall increase in the level of government expenditures in a region — mostly because of improvements in services. Thus, improved services, not economies of scale, are the most likely achievement of government reform.[61]

System Maintenance versus Life Style Services

Reform governments in metropolitan areas, regardless of form, seem to have their greatest success in dealing with large-scale physical facilities planning and service integration. These physical system maintenance services require more coordination than more locally-specific "life-style" services. Therefore, the level of conflict involved in system maintenance services is less. As a long-term strategy for building support in the metropolitan region for area-wide government, a concentration on large-scale public works and physical construction projects may prove to be a viable approach. Historically, the party machines in urban centers during the late 1800s and early 1900s concentrated their efforts on large-scale physical construction projects as a form of "political advertising." These construction projects gave the nascent urban government resources by which to manipulate the general behavior of local residents and of government officials who might otherwise resist the centralization of power that the urban machines were trying to accomplish. In addition, the construction of large scale physical works conveyed the impression to the local citizenry of the capabilities and benefits of centralized urban government. In contrast, urban party machines often avoided social services because they lacked the visibility and concreteness of physical development while the political rewards were less certain.[62] The analogy is clear — present day metropolitan governments are trying to affect the centralization of government in a larger geographical region than urban machines of 75 years ago, but the problems and strategies are not uncommon.

Local versus Regional Government Control Over Services

One central issue that remains unresolved is the setting of clear objective standards by which to decide which level of government should have primary responsibility for which services. Except for the consolidation approach, most reforms of local government call for a sharing of service responsibilities between local governments and a regional government. While certain services are obviously amenable to regional policy, e.g., transportation, the list of such clearly regional services is short. And while local governments can claim that they should retain control over most other "non-regional" services, regional implications can be found in most local government policy decisions. As a result, the assignment of services to different levels of government varies considerably from region to region, and the assignment of functions is always a "political" question involving controversy, conflict, and continual evolution of responsibilities.

Redistribution of Services

There is very little evidence that most regional governments achieve any redistribution of services from wealthy residents to those more in need. In consolidated governments there is a tendency to use service and tax districts that tie closely together the costs of services, the taxes to pay for them, and the level of service provided. This means that the separation between low-resource, high-need populations in central cities and poorer suburbs from high-resource, low-demand population in wealthy suburbs is often continued. In the regional councils of confederated regionalism, the constituent unit voting scheme (one government, one vote) and the voluntary nature of local government participation limits the ability of regional government to address service and resource imbalances. Conflicts between central city government and suburban governments in regional councils are not uncommon. They mostly center on the issue of redistribution in the face of the apparent willingness of the majority of suburban government officials to ignore central city problems.[63]

Other Service Effects

There is some evidence that reformed government increases the impact of professionals in service delivery. Experts seem to gain greater control over any centralized and coordinated services provided by areawide government. One advantage is that these experts tend to be more responsible to a general purpose government organization rather than to be employed strictly by a single-function special district. This can, in the long run, lead to a strengthening of general purpose governmental capabilities in the region, an outcome desired by many government reform groups such as the ACIR, the Committee for Economic Development (CED), and the U.S. national government.

But the overall position of local government employees seems to be unchanged by the adoption of government reorganization. Indeed, in campaigns for major structural reform of local government, one issue that seems most in need of immediate resolution is the job tenure for present local government officials. Where existing government jobs seem threatened by reorganization, local government employee unions and associations are among the most vigorous and effective opponents of reorganization. As a result, most comprehensive government reform proposals usually guarantee the tenure of present employees. But this also means that the same people continue to deliver the same services before and after reform. In turn, the size of the local government labor force is not reduced, the labor costs of delivering services cannot be cut. In fact, improving the quality of services usually requires the hiring of *new* and more qualified employees — increasing labor costs. Furthermore, it is not surprising that many surveys of citizens attitudes before and after even the most sweeping government reforms show remarkably unchanged citizen satisfaction with the treatment they receive from government officials.

Reform and the Distribution of Political Power

Many reforms do not seem to alter the distribution of political power in the metropolitan region. This is especially true in confederated systems where the voluntary nature of membership and the one government, one unit method of voting seems to leave power undisturbed. In these regional councils, furthermore, local government officials usually see themselves as delegates of their local governments first, and "trustees" of the region second. Therefore, they are not willing to accede to programs or policies that might serve the regional interest at cost to *their* communities. Actions threatening the existing distribution of services and power are rejected and the distribution of any new services is viewed in terms of a fair and equitable "distribution" between all local communities rather than as needed "redistribution."

One particularly sticky question about the distribution of political power in local reform government is the impact of regional governance on minority group representation. Expanding the base of political representation from a central city that has a heavy black concentration to a city/county consolidation or into area-wide councils of government obviously lowers the proportion of blacks in the total population. Blacks that are, say, 40 percent of a central city population may be less than half that proportion in an expanded city/county consolidated government. For this reason, it is often feared by black leaders that metropolitan reform will "freeze" blacks out of government power and positions. However, the evidence on this is contradictory. The electoral arrangements adopted by reformed government in Nashville, Jacksonville, and Indianapolis, stressed district elections rather than at-large representation. Black presence on the new governing councils continued at significant levels. Indeed, in a study of the effects of consolidation on

Jacksonville, it was found that lower class whites, not blacks were the group most likely to be isolated under the system of reformed government.[64] Indeed, when the first sewers were constructed after consolidation, as an example of good faith, they were placed in black neighborhoods, not lower class white ones. While many have feared that metropolitan government would automatically dilute minority representation, the truth is more complicated and the effects of reform on minority power in the region more variable.

The Federal Governmental Role

The federal government continues to put pressure on local governments to reorganize their services onto an area-wide basis. A variety of federal programs are themselves organized on an area-wide basis (about 2 dozen federal programs have an area-wide component) and the use of A-95 Review provides a potent possibility for organizing and coordinating other federal government programs on a metropolitan basis. Furthermore, regional governments are heavily supported by federal grants, including: Section 701 planning grants from the U.S. Department of Housing and Urban Development; area-wide transportation planning grants from the Department of Transportation; and area-wide criminal justice planning grants from the Law Enforcement Assistance Agency. In fact, the very growth of regional councils of government and regional planning commissions is a phenomenon explained mostly by the increased availability of federal planning funds during the 1960s.

However, the federal presence favoring area-wide government is not totally consistent. Most importantly, while the federal government gives "lip service" to regional coordination through A-95 Review, its actual behavior with regard to the review process is not totally supportive. Thus, A-95 Review is strictly advisory and federal agencies do give grants for projects that are not favorably reviewed by the regional clearinghouse. Furthermore, not all federal projects are subject to A-95 Review. While the list of covered programs is growing, there are still many federal programs that are exempt. And, even the federal government's attempts at using area-wide districts is not consistent: the same district boundaries are not used for every federal government agency; additionally program provisions and guidelines for federal area-wide programs vary considerably. This creates fragmentation rather than unification. Finally, while there is a shift currently in federal government support from grants-in-aid to general revenue sharing, federal policies still maintain a functional orientation and rely on special districts to deliver urban services in metropolitan regions. While General Revenue Sharing and the Intergovernmental Cooperation Act of 1968 give specific preference to general purpose local governments over special districts, the shift is by no means complete.

The Role of the State

While the federal government occupies a strategic position in creating regional government, state governments obviously have the most power to intervene to change the structure of local governments. Boundaries of local governments are affected by state laws governing incorporation and annexation. State laws affect the ease with which consolidation of cities with counties can take place. Intergovernmental service agreements are also regulated by state legislation. States can also create effective metropolitan governing bodies such as the Twin Cities Metropolitan Council or the Atlanta Regional Commission to achieve coordination and reform of service delivery in suburban and metropolitan areas. Where the state government has had strong interest in the governance of a metropolitan region, such as in state capitals, it has been able to affect significant reforms in metropolitan governance. Truly, if cities and suburbs are "creatures of the state" then it is the states that have the greatest ability and perhaps the primary responsibility for improving the level of governance in the metropolitan areas.

The Role of Local Government

Despite the mixed record of reformed metropolitan government, the pressure to provide more and more services on an area-wide basis should be expected to grow. Over time, the role of local government in delivering services in suburban areas must be expected to decline. Yet that decline will take place incrementally as procedural changes slowly transfer services to higher level governments, in particular, reformed and invigorated urban counties. Wide ranging structural reform of suburban government will probably not be common, but greater area-wide governance will nonetheless be gradually achieved.

Notes

1. Mark Schneider, "Land Use, Suburban Fragmentation and Regional Control," Georgia Political Science Association *Journal,* 5 (Spring 1977), pp. 27-50.

2. Leo Schnore, *The Urban Scene* (New York: The Free Press, 1965).

3. Thomas P. Murphy and John Rehfuss, *Urban Politics in the Suburban Era* (Homewood, Illinois: The Dorsey Press, 1976).

4. John Logan and Mark Schneider, "Income Inequalities in Metropolitan Regions, 1960-1970," paper presented at the Ninth World Congress of Sociology, Uppsala, Sweden, August, 1978.

5. Michael Danielson, "Differentiation, Segregation and Political Fragmentation of the American Metropolis," in A.E. Kier Nash, ed., *Governance and Population* (Washington, D.C.: Committee on Population Growth and the American Future, 1972).

6. (New York: CED, 1976), p. 69.

7. Mark Schneider and David Swinton, "Policy Analysis in State and Local Government," *Public Administration Review,* 39 (January/February 1979), pp. 12-16.

8. Richard P. Nathan, Allen D. Manvel, Susannah E. Calkins, *Monitoring Revenue Sharing* (Washington, D.C.: The Brookings Institution, 1975), p. 287.

9. Advisory Commission on Intergovernmental Relations, *Problems of Special Districts in American Government* (Washington, D.C.: Government Printing Office, 1964).

10. Robert B. Hawkins, Jr., "Special Districts and Urban Services," in Elinor Ostrom, ed., *The Delivery of Urban Services* (Beverly Hills, California: Sage Publications, 1976), pp. 171-188.

11. Committee for Economic Development, *Modernizing Local Government* (New York: CED, 1966), p. 44.

12. *Ibid.,* pp. 11-13.

13. Vincent Ostrom, Charles M. Tiebout, and Robert Warren, "The Organization of Government in Metropolitan Areas," *American Political Science Review,* 55 (December 1961), pp. 835-842; Elinor Ostrom, "Metropolitan Reform: Propositions Derived from Two Traditions," *Social Science Quarterly,* 53 (December 1972), pp. 474-493; Robert Bish, *The Political Economy of Metropolitan Areas* (Chicago: Markham, 1971).

14. Committee for Economic Development, *Reshaping Government in Metropolitan Areas* (New York: CED, 1970).

15. Mancur Olson, "The Principle of 'Fiscal Equivalence': The Division of Responsibilities Among Different Levels of Government," *American Economic Review,* 59 (May 1969), pp. 479-487.

16. Bish, *Political Economy.*

17. Werner Z. Hirsch, "Expenditure Implications of Metropolitan Growth and Consolidation," *Review of Economics and Statistics,* 41 (March 1959), pp. 232-241.

18. Werner Z. Hirsch, *About the Supply of Urban Public Services* (Los Angeles: Institute for Government and Public Affairs, UCLA, 1967).

19. Thomas R. DeGregori, "Caveat Emptor: A Critique of the Emerging Paradigm of Public Choice," *Administration and Society,* 6 (May 1974), pp. 205-228. This question of equal protection of the laws and inequalities in services has been raised in a variety of policy areas, most notably education, but also with regard to zoning, street lighting, and other urban services.

20. Oliver P. Williams, "Life Style Values and Political Decentralization," *Social Science Quarterly,* 48 (December 1967), pp. 299-310.

21. Wallace Sayre and Herbert Kaufman, *Governing New York* (New York: Russell Sage Foundation, 1960).

22. Kenneth C. Olson, "The States, Governors, and Policy Management," *Public Administration Review,* 35 (December 1975), pp. 764-776.

23. Richard P. Nathan, Charles F. Adams, *et. al., Monitoring Revenue Sharing: The Second Round* (Washington, D.C.: The Brookings Institution, 1977), p. 133, passim.

24. E.S. Savas, "Municipal Monopolies versus Competition in Delivering Urban Services," in Willis D. Hawley and David Rogers, eds., *Improving the Quality of Urban Management* (Beverly Hills, California: Sage Publication, 1974), p. 477.

25. CED, *Productivity in State and Local Government,* pp. 62-64.

26. ACIR, *The Challenge of Local Governmental Reorganization* (Washington, D.C.: Government Printing Office, 1974), p. 30.

27. International City Management Association, "Municipal Transfer of Functional Responsibilities," Urban Data Service Report, Vol. 7 (September 1975).

28. ACIR, *The Challenge,* p. 52.

29. George J. Gordon, "The Office of Management and Budget and A-95 Review," *Publius,* 4 (Winter 1974), pp. 49-50.

30. *Ibid.,* p. 56.

31. Melvin Moguluf, "Metropolitan Councils of Government and the Federal Government," *Urban Affairs Quarterly,* 7 (June 1972), pp. 494-495.

32. B. Douglas Harmon, "Areawide Review of Federal Grant Application," ICMA Urban Data Service Report, 4 (February 1972), pp. 19-22.

33. ACIR, *Regional Decision Making* (Washington, D.C.: Government Printing Office, 1973), p. 100.

34. ACIR, *Governmental Functions and Processes* (Washington, D.C.: Government Printing Office, 1974), p. 31.

35. Lawrence J.R. Herson, "Pilgrim's Progress: Reflections on the Road to Urban Reform" in American Political Science Association, *Political Science and State and Local Government* (Washington, D.C.: American Political Science Association, 1973), p. 22.

36. Presidential Commission on Urban Problems, *Building the American City* (Washington, D.C.: Government Printing Office, 1968), p. 237; Committee for

Economic Development, *Reshaping Government;* Murphy and Rehfuss, *Urban Politics,* chapter 7.

37. ACIR, *Profile of County Government* (Washington, D.C.: Government Printing Office, 1972).

38. For a discussion of Baton Rouge see: Thomas A. Reed, "Progress in Metropolitan Integration," *Public Administration Review,* 9 (Winter 1949); John C. Bollens and Henry J. Schmandt, *The Metropolis,* 2nd edition (New York: Harper and Row, 1970); William C. Havard, Jr. and Floyd C. Carty, *Rural-Urban Consolidation: The Merger of Governments in the Baton Rouge Area* (Baton Rouge: Louisiana State University, 1964).

39. For a discussion of Nashville/Davidson County Consolidated Government see, e.g., Robert E. McArthur, "The Metropolitan Government of Nashville and Davidson County," in ACIR, *Regional Governance* (Washington, D.C.: Government Printing Office, 1973), pp. 26-35; Brett Hawkins, *Nashville Metro* (Nashville: Vanderbilt University Press, 1966); Daniel R. Grant, "A Comparison of Predictions and Experience with Nashville Metro," *Urban Affairs Quarterly,* 1 (September 1965), pp. 34-54.

40. Referenda calling for consolidation of local governments have not fared well with the voting public. See, e.g., Robert L. Lineberry and Ira Sharkansky, *Urban Politics and Public Policy* (New York: Harper and Row, 1972), p. 142.

41. Robert E. McArthur, *The Impact of Metropolitan Government on the Rural-Urban Fringe: The Nashville-Davidson County Experience* (Washington, D.C.: U.S. Department of Agriculture, 1971).

42. For a discussion of reform in Jacksonville see, e.g., John M. DeGrove, "The City of Jacksonville: Consolidation in Action," in ACIR, *Regional Governance,* pp. 17-25; Richard C. Martin, *Consolidation: Jacksonville Duval County* (Jacksonville: Crawford Co., 1968).

43. DeGrove, "Jacksonville," p. 21.

44. Joan Carver, "Responsiveness and Consolidation: A Case Study," *Urban Affairs Quarterly,* 9 (December 1973), pp. 211-250.

45. For a discussion of UNIGOV see, York Willbern, "UNIGOV: Local Government Reorganization in Indianapolis," in ACIR, *Regional Governance,* pp. 45-73.

46. *Ibid.,* p. 67.

47. Richard L. Forstall, "Annexation and Corporate Changes Since the 1970 Census," *Municipal Yearbook 1975,* p. 22.

48. For a discussion of federation in Toronto see, CED, *Reshaping Government;* Frank Smallwood, *Metro Toronto: A Decade Later* (Toronto: Bureau of Municipal Research, 1963).

49. CED, *Reshaping Government,* p. 80.

50. John J. Harrigan, *Political Change in the Metropolis* (Boston: Little, Brown and Co., 1976), p. 237.

51. Gail Cook, "The Effect of Metropolitan Government on Resource Allocation: The Case of Education in Toronto," *National Tax Journal,* 26 (December, 1973), pp. 585-590.

52. Harrigan considers Miami/Dade the closest thing in the United States to a federated system (*Political Change,* pp. 232-238). In the Miami system, the county government operates as the upper tier areawide government while existing municipal governments operate as the lower tier governments. See e.g., Aileen

Lotz, "Metropolitan Dade County," in ACIR, *Regional Governance*, pp. 6-16; Edward Sofen, *The Miami Metropolitan Experiment* (Bloomington: Indiana University Press, 1963).

53. For a discussion of the Twin Cities area see, e.g., Ted Kolderie, "Governance in the Twin Cities Area of Minnesota," in ACIR, *Regional Governance*, pp. 112-140; Stanley Baldinger, *Planning and Governing the Metropolis: The Twin Cities Experience* (New York: Praeger Publishers, 1971).

54. See Daniel Elazar, *Federalism: A View From the States* (New York: Thomas Y. Crowell, 1966), chapter 4.

55. Kolderie, "Twin Cities," p. 115.

56. Recall that under the Fiscal Disparities Act, 40 percent of tax increments accruing to a local government from commercial development go into a metropolitan wide fund for distribution to all local governments.

57. Kolderie, "Twin Cities," p. 131.

58. Robert E. McArthur, "The Atlanta Regional Commission," in ACIR, *Regional Governance*, pp. 37-42.

59. This is the strategy developed by the ACIR in its study of *Regional Decision Making* (Washington, D.C.: Government Printing Office, 1973), chapter XI.

60. CED, *Reshaping Government*.

61. Gail Cook, "The Effect of Metropolitan Government"; Daniel Grant, "A Comparison of Predictions with Experience"; Harold Kaplan, *Urban Political Systems* (New York: Columbia University Press, 1967); Richard C. Gusteley, "The Allocational and Distributional Impacts of Government Consolidation: The Dade County Experience," *Urban Affairs Quarterly*, 12 (March 1977), pp. 349-364.

62. Douglas Yates, "Service Delivery and the Urban Political Order," in Hawley and Rogers, *Improving the Quality of Urban Management*.

63. Frances Frisken, "The Metropolis and the Central City: Can One Government Unite Them?" *Urban Affairs Quarterly*, 8 (June 1973), pp. 395-422.

64. Carver, "Responsiveness," pp. 223-225.

Index